# Get in there & Cook

Also by Richard Sax

Cooking Great Meals Every Day (with David Ricketts)

The Cookie Lover's Cookie Book

From the Farmer's Market (with Sandra Gluck)

New York's Master Chefs

Old-Fashioned Desserts

Eat at Joe's (with Jo Ann Bass)

Classic Home Desserts

Lighter Quicker Better (with Marie Simmons)

# Get in there & Cook

A master class for the starter chef

# Richard Sax

### with David Ricketts

Clarkson Potter/Publishers
New York

Grateful acknowledgment is given to reprint the following:

"Creamy Polenta with Mascarpone" from *The Union Square Cookbook* by Danny Meyer and Michael Romano. Copyright © 1994 by Danny Meyer and Michael Romano. Reprinted by permission of HarperCollins Publishers. "Beef and Black Bean Chili" adapted from *The Greens Cookbook* by Deborah Madison and Edward Espe Brown. Copyright © 1987 by Edward Espe Brown and Deborah Madison. Used by permission of Bantam Books, a division of Bantam Doubleday Dell Publishing Group, Inc. Dried bean pressure cooker information from

Published by Clarkson N. Potter/Publishers, 201 East 50th Street, New York, New York 10022.
Member of the Crown Publishing Group.

Random House, Inc.  New York, Toronto, London, Sydney, Auckland
http://www.randomhouse.com/

CLARKSON N. POTTER, POTTER, and colophon are trademarks of Clarkson N. Potter, Inc.

Printed in the United States of America

Design by Richard Ferretti

Library of Congress Cataloging-in-Publication Data
is available upon request.

ISBN 0-517-70358-0

10  9  8  7  6  5  4  3  2  1

First Edition

For

my mother, Fran,

my brother, Ken,

my sister, Diana,

my nephew, Jeremy, and

my niece, Erica

And for all those

who work to feed

the homebound

# ACKNOWLEDGMENTS

Obviously, all my students from my cooking classes over the years are my coauthors for this book. Their questions frequently made me look for a better and simpler answer. And then there are some specific colleagues and friends who helped me clarify my thinking for this book, both recently and in the distant past.

**Roy Finamore,** my editor and friend, who had the idea for this book, and then tasted much of the food as I worked on the recipes, offering his suggestions as I cooked and wrote.

**Arlene Feltman,** director of Macy's De Gustibus cooking series in New York City, gave me literally a platform from which to teach for over a decade.

**Bill Leiderman,** the director of the original New School's culinary program in New York City back in the late seventies, let me put together some of my first cooking classes.

**Michael and Arianne Batterberry,** the creators and first editors of the groundbreaking Food & Wine magazine, asked me as test kitchen director for the magazine to develop a monthly cooking school feature.

**Marie Simmons,** with whom I've coauthored a monthly column for Bon Appétit magazine for several years, was always at the quick and ready to answer one of my endless telephone calls about cooking dilemmas.

**Nick Malgieri,** a dear friend, outstanding pastry chef, and master baking teacher, with a vast amount of cooking knowledge, was always willing to share that information with me, as well as gossip.

**Zanne Stewart,** food editor of Gourmet magazine, a fellow lover of books and food, told me many stories about cooking experiences, drawn from her lifetime of exploring food.

**Judith Weber,** my agent, always thought this book was a good idea.

**Barbara Kafka,** food columnist, cookbook author, television commentator, and friend of Richard Sax, provided several recipes for Richard's unfinished manuscript.

# CONTENTS

# FOREWORD

In 1975 I was introduced to Richard Sax in Providence, Rhode Island, by our mutual friend John Leo, a professor at the University of Rhode Island, and fellow eater and cook. He suspected that Richard and I might share the same love of French fries—we did. We gabbed for hours about mayonnaise, the perfect hamburger, and restaurants. A year later, I left a law career to help Richard run a restaurant on Martha's Vineyard, a happy time for both of us.

Richard was always the teacher—that was one of his best skills. His first job after graduating from Northwestern University, in fact, was teaching high school English in New Jersey. There he also coached drama and staged elaborate theater productions—his flair for the theatrical was to surface later in his cooking classes.

As food editor and test kitchen director for the *International Review of Food & Wine* magazine in the late seventies—his first food editorial position—Richard developed a monthly cooking school feature. Again, it was Richard at his best: teaching.

Throughout the almost twenty years of his food career, Richard continued to share his intimate love of food: in cooking classes around the country, on TV, in videos, and even when casually pulling together a simple dinner for friends. This book, his final one, is the natural accumulation of all those years of cooking, eating, and teaching.

As Richard and I both pursued food careers in New York City, we remained friends over the years—traveling and eating together and sharing in the travails of each other's lives. I assisted him in some of his first cooking classes and collaborated with him on his first cookbook, *Cooking Great Meals Every Day* (Random House, 1982). When I began to split my time between a house in upstate New York and the city, Richard would often visit—current book manuscript in hand and ready for some quiet work time.

Richard died on September 1, 1995, at the age of forty-six. He had practically finished the manuscript for this book. His aim was to write a teaching book for the beginning cook, much in the style of how he ran his cooking classes. We had talked about the direction of the book, and I had tasted some of the food he was developing. When Roy Finamore, his editor at Clarkson Potter, and Judith Weber, his agent, approached me about completing Richard's book, I said I would have to think about it. The more I considered it, the more it made sense to me. Richard and I had known each other in the "early years," and we had worked together on the first book. My finishing his last book now seemed to be the appropriate conclusion. So I said yes.

My hope now, Richard, is that you like what I've added to your words.

**David Ricketts**
**Provincetown, Massachusetts**
**August 1996**

# INTRODUCTION

My aim is to take the fear out of cooking. Take the time to learn a handful of basic cooking techniques through my recipes and you'll soon discover, if you haven't already, that working in the kitchen is fun. And the results—the food itself—are one of the best pleasures of life. I don't mean to imply that cooking is a breeze, requiring no work at all or thinking or planning. But once you get the hang of it, you'll be surprised how easily things will go. And besides, any pleasure requires a little effort.

In this book, I offer a basic repertoire of doable recipes that you or anyone, no matter how inexperienced, can produce in not much time. More importantly, the book offers you much more than just formulas: Each recipe is accompanied by questions and answers, explanations, variations, and digressions. This "back-and-forth dialogue" is similar to the way I teach my cooking classes and encourages you to understand how cooking works: Why is a hot skillet necessary for sautéing? Why is braising a good cooking technique for a shoulder of beef? Think of me as a "benevolent friend," not only helping you to get over the fear of cooking, but opening your eyes to see the kitchen as a room in your house where you can be creative and relaxed. If you're a seasoned cook, don't close the book now—read on. You also will find much of interest here: recipes to add to your own collection of favorites, as well as a refresher course in basic kitchen skills.

Even with all this helpful information, the food and how it tastes is what's really important. The 150 recipes and variations are those I would give to any friend who wanted to know how to cook. These dishes form a basic collection of good, honest cooking; they are manageable to prepare and don't require arcane ingredients or exotic equipment. Collectively, they offer a sound introduction to the basic principles and techniques that underlie all cooking.

More to the point, this is delicious food—hearty soups and luscious pastas, Pasta e Fagiole, soy-glazed broiled salmon with cool, crisp marinated cucumbers, and lamb shanks with white beans and gremolata—the kind of dishes that easily become household favorites. This is food that is equally at home at a dinner party with family and friends or as a quiet dinner for one or two. Basics such as how to cook perfect rice and fresh vegetables, tips for green salads, notes on serving cheese and so-called incidentals like coffee, plus a handful of reputation-building home-baked desserts round out the collection.

Cooking is not just recipes, but an ongoing process. So many of these recipes recycle leftovers into interesting new dishes—no reason now to have fuzzy bundles multiplying in the back of your refrigerator. Leftover cooked potatoes are transformed into a Golden Potato Cake; steak with mushroom sauce becomes a steak sandwich; leftover tomato salad is the start of a Grilled

Tomato, Mozzarella, and Basil Sandwich; risotto becomes irresistibly creamy pancakes with Parmesan. And by purposely cooking extra rice or pasta, a stir-fry with fresh vegetables takes just moments the next day.

[...] sections on how to read an ingredient list and recipe, how to get everything on the table at the same time, the basic cooking equipment that every kitchen needs, plus extras that are nice to have, the well-stocked larder,

and other helpful information.

With this book in hand, you will not only be able to turn out a delicious dinner without fuss, but you'll also have fun in the process, entering the realm of cooking [...] provide immediate pleasure.

**Richard Sax**
**New York City**
**May 1995**

# HOW TO USE THIS BOOK

**Here we'll go over all those things that every home cook does instinctively but that are rarely explained to beginners.**

## HOW TO READ AN INGREDIENT LIST, AS WELL AS THE RECIPE

First, before anything—before taking out a pot or pan, or reaching into the cupboard for an ingredient—read the entire recipe, more than once if you have to, in order to have a clear picture of what's going to happen. This should eliminate any mistakes, disasters, or unexpected surprises. Visualize the steps and techniques: "First I drizzle olive oil into a medium skillet and then I place the skillet over medium-high heat. . . ."

Now, go over the ingredient list. Pay attention not just to what the ingredient is, but take note of what's done with it. Is it chopped, diced, smashed? How is it measured? You'll find that "½ cup drained canned tomatoes, chopped" is not the same as "½ cup drained chopped canned tomatoes." The latter is a little more dry than the first, making it more suitable for a sauté, where you don't want a lot of excess moisture in the pan. "One-half cup toasted walnuts, chopped" is different from "½ cup chopped toasted walnuts"; the first measurement is a smaller quantity than the second, which could make a difference when baking a cake or bread. "One cup flour, sifted" is not "1 cup sifted flour"; the second measurement contains less flour than the first quantity, and that will make a difference in baking. "Prepared mustard" is the variety from a jar,

while "dry mustard" is just that, a powder sprinkled from a jar or small can into a dish for a little piquancy. A recipe sometimes will not only specify quantity, but type, as with apples: 8 Cortland apples (about 3 pounds), peeled, cored, and sliced ¼ inch thick. Not only do you know what kind of apple to buy, but you know how much and what to do with them. So even before you get to the recipe directions, you have a good idea what to expect. Remember, too, to play close attention to tablespoon and teaspoon. If you glance quickly at the ingredient list, it's very easy to confuse these two measurements, especially if they are abbreviated—tbsp. and tsp.

Are there ingredient substitutions listed? Can you substitute fresh parsley for fresh cilantro? Can you use white domestic mushrooms rather than chanterelles? A recipe may give you the choice: ½ cup white wine or chicken broth; 1 teaspoon chopped fresh oregano or ¼ teaspoon dried. Some ingredients may even be optional, such as ¼ teaspoon cayenne (optional) or 1 teaspoon grated lemon zest (optional). Whether you use these ingredients will make a difference in taste. See how important it is to carefully read the ingredient list? It's like reading a short story or novel—if you don't know the names of the characters or don't follow the plot development, you won't know what the story is about.

One more thing. Very often I call for salt and pepper to taste, but how do you tell when enough is enough? The proper amount of salt in a dish should bring up or reveal the flavors of the ingredients without the whole dish tasting salty. If you've undersalted, the dish will taste flat or bland. Start out with a small amount, a pinch or two of salt and a grind of black pepper from a pepper mill. Then taste. You can always add more seasoning, but it's hard to take it out once it's in.

Now that you understand the ingredient list, take a look at the directions. Can you visualize the sequence of what's happening? Are there some things you can do ahead, such as chopping and dicing vegetables? Are some things required to be done ahead, such as marinating a flank steak overnight? Do you need to chill something for a few hours, such as a pie dough? Will you be doing more than one task at a time—making a quick pasta sauce while the pasta cooks? How do you tell when the dish is done? The sauce simmers for 20 minutes, or until it is thick enough to coat the back of a spoon. This may seem like a lot to pay attention to, but it really isn't.

After reading the recipe, step back and take the overview. How long should the whole recipe take from start to finish? Do you have the proper pots and pans for the recipe plus any other utensils or equipment called for in the recipe—an 8-quart pot, a food processor or blender, a colander? Once you get in the habit of first reading a recipe carefully, and the more often you do it, you'll find that you'll automatically take mental note of all these things.

## GETTING ORGANIZED AND ACTUALLY COOKING

Once you've read the recipe, it's time to begin the cooking action. Check to make sure you have on hand all the ingredients you'll need and all the necessary cooking equipment. Make a shopping list of ingredients to pick up at the store. Decide whether you can improvise with what cooking equipment you have if you seem to be missing something. A metal colander placed in a saucepan is a perfectly acceptable steamer basket if you don't have the collapsible variety.

Gather and assemble all of the ingredients. Organize them on the counter. Once you start cooking, you don't want to be hunting around for a spice or a bag of flour. It also helps to arrange them in order of use, remembering that ingredients are listed in that order in the recipe. Measure and prepare ingredients as indicated in the ingredient list before moving on to the directions. If you need to preheat the oven, allow 15 minutes for the oven to get up to the required temperature. (It's not a bad idea to keep an oven thermometer in the oven to check your oven's accuracy.) And now you're on the way—to high adventure!

## A FEW BASICS

### BELL PEPPER BASICS

**To core and seed:** My favorite way of cleaning bell peppers (it wastes a little flesh, but it's quick) is to cut the four "sides" away from the pepper, leaving the seeds attached to the stem. If there are any white ribs attached to the inside of the flesh, shave them away with a knife and discard them. Then go ahead and cut up the peppers as directed in the recipe. If cutting into slivers, cut each quarter in half crosswise, then thinly slice each piece, forming short, thin slivers.

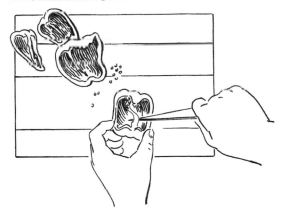

**To roast and peel:** Roasting bell peppers heightens their sweet flavor and loosens the skins for easy peeling—no chewy little bits of skin. Preheat a broiler and place the peppers on a broiler pan rack or baking sheet lined with foil. Broil 4 to 6 inches from the heat, turning the peppers occasionally with tongs, until the skin is blackened and blistered on all sides. Place in a closed paper bag or loosely cover with aluminum foil. The hot peppers will continue to steam, loosening the skin even more. When cool enough to handle, cut the peppers in half through the stem ends. With your fingers or a paring knife, remove the stem and then scrape away the seeds with

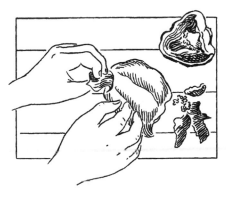

your fingers or the tip of the knife; cut away the ribs. Peel off the skin with your fingers or the tip of the knife. Now you're ready to proceed with the recipe.

### HOT CHILI PEPPER BASICS

Since chili peppers get their heat from the ribs and seeds, you may want to remove them to temper the fire. Remember one important rule: After you handle hot chili peppers, wash your hands thoroughly and never touch your eyes or other sensitive areas; the volatile oils can sharply sting. For that matter, make sure you wash all work surfaces and utensils. For extra protection, wear rubber kitchen gloves.

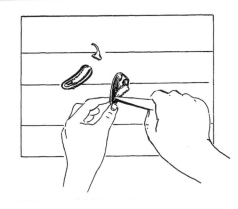

**To seed and derib:** With a small, sharp paring knife, halve each chili lengthwise. With the tip of the knife or your fingers (make sure you have no cuts or scratches if you're not wearing gloves), remove the stem. With the knife tip, scrape out the seeds and then cut out the ribs.

### DRIED BEAN BASICS

While most dried beans need to be soaked before cooking, there are some exceptions: lentils and split peas are never soaked, as well as most heirloom beans (often called "new crop"). Before soaking dried beans, place them in a strainer or colander and rinse with cold water. Sort through them and pick out any discolored or broken beans. Now you have the option of using an overnight soak or a quick soak.

**Overnight soak:** Place the rinsed beans in a large bowl and add enough cold water to cover the beans by 2 inches. Let stand overnight—if your kitchen is very warm, refrigerate to avoid souring. The next day, drain the beans, discarding the soaking liquid. Rinse the beans and cook according to the recipe directions.

**Quick soak:** Place the rinsed beans in a large saucepan and add enough cold water to cover by 2 inches. Heat to boiling. Turn the heat to medium and simmer, uncovered, for 2 minutes. Remove the saucepan from the heat, cover, and let stand for 1 hour. Drain the beans, discarding the liquid. Rinse the beans and cook according to the recipe.

**Pressure cooker:** For the complete rundown on how to cook dried beans in a pressure cooker, see Lorna Sass's excellent book, *Cooking Under Pressure* (William Morrow & Company, Inc., 1989).

Unless I'm really rushed, I prefer to soak beans overnight, since this helps them to retain their shape better and not split or crumble.

One more tip: When cooking beans, don't add salt until the end—any earlier and the beans will toughen.

## MAKING FRESH BREAD CRUMBS

Whenever you have leftover bread, use it to make fresh bread crumbs. With a long, serrated knife, cut off all the crusts. Now cut the bread slices about an inch thick; then cut across, forming 1-inch cubes. Place the bread cubes on a tray and let them dry out, standing at room temperature, for an hour or so. Then place them in a food processor and process steadily until reduced to crumbs—but not to a powder. One slice of bread makes about ½ cup of fine crumbs.

Store bread crumbs in the freezer in a covered container. Let the crumbs come to room temperature in their covered container before using to avoid any excess moisture.

## CELERY STRINGING

To make celery a little easier to chew, especially if there is a fair amount of it in a dish, you may want to remove the strings. Slip the tip of a small paring knife under the ends of the strings at the stem end and pull back the strings along the length of the rib. Repeat this all around the rib.

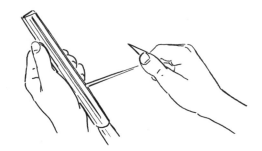

## WHERE TO GET CITRUS ZEST

Zest is the outermost colored part of the rind of a lemon, lime, orange, or other citrus fruit. When the zest is removed, none of the bitter white pith underneath should be attached. The citrus oil in the zest is what infuses a dish with an intense citrus flavor. You can use a zester to remove the zest in thin strips for garnishing; chop the strips if you want to add the zest during cooking. A swivel-bladed vegetable peeler removes the zest in long, wide strips. Cut the strips into julienne or chop fine and add to the dish, or toss whole strips into soups or other cooking broths and remove before serving.

## A WORD ABOUT COFFEE

I hated the taste of coffee until I was well into my twenties; only as I began to eat in good restaurants did I realize what I'd been missing. Gradually coffee has become one of the major pleasures of my life.

I'm always amazed, though, at how few Americans insist on drinking really good coffee (although that certainly has changed in many cities with the spread of coffee bars dispensing everything from a cup of the simple brew to double decaffeinated caffe latte with skim milk). There's really nothing difficult about making good coffee at home: Just insist on beans that are freshly roasted and ground (many of us do this at home ourselves). When you're having your beans ground, specify whether you're using a drip, percolator, or other type of pot. The standard for measuring ground coffee is 2 level tablespoons to one 8 ounce cup. Never let coffee boil and once made drink as soon as possible. A good thermos will keep it warm for a bit, but don't let it sit around too long or it will develop a bitter taste. And don't reheat it. Whether using an electric coffeemaker or a simple drip, be sure your coffee-making equipment is always sparkling clean.

## CUCUMBER BASICS

Trim off the ends of the cucumber. With a vegetable peeler, peel off the skin. Cut the cucumber in half lengthwise, and with a melon baller or spoon, remove the seeds.

## GARLIC BASICS

To quickly peel a clove of garlic, lay the flat side of a chef's knife on top of the clove, press on the blade with your hand (keeping fingers and other tender parts away from the sharp edge), and smash the clove. Cut off the hard end and slip off the skin. Many people prefer to use a garlic press; however, this can add a metallic taste and it's another tool to clean. Roasting garlic results in a wonderfully pungent, sweet puree that can be stirred into soups and stews, sauces, and salad dressings. To roast, separate the cloves of garlic from the head. Discard the loose papery skins, but do not peel. Place in a small, shallow baking dish, drizzle with a little olive oil, and toss to coat. Bake in a preheated 300° F. oven until the garlic is softened, about 45 minutes. Let cool. Cut off the hard end of each clove and squeeze the garlic pulp into a small bowl. Now you're ready to use the roasted garlic puree wherever you would like a deep flavor accent. Keep refrigerated in a glass jar or other easily cleaned covered container—plastic will absorb the flavor of the garlic—and use within a few days.

## GREENS CLEANING

You can rinse most greens in a colander under cold running water to remove any grit or dirt; just be sure to separate the leaves for thorough cleaning. For greens that tend to be very sandy, such as farmstand spinach (not the stuff in the plastic bags), whole heads of leafy lettuce, and arugula, first plunge them into a sink or dish pan of warm water; this relaxes the leaves, loosening the dirt for easier rinsing. Then lift the leaves to a colander and rinse under cold water. If the leaves are limp after the warm water treatment, crisp them in several changes of cold water. Dry in a salad spinner or blot with paper towels and then wrap in paper towels and place in the refrigerator to crisp further.

To de-string sugar snap peas or green beans, grasp the thin string at one end and slowly pull away from the flat side of the bean.

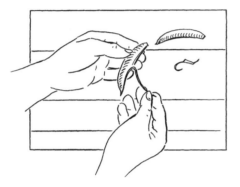

## HERBS AND SPICES

Herbs and spices add fragrance as well as flavor to even the simplest of foods. This is the chance to be really creative. Herbs come from the plant's leaves and stems and are used either fresh or dried, while spices are derived from the plant's seeds, roots, bark, and berries or flower buds.

If using fresh herbs, wash them gently and shake off the excess moisture. Wrap them in paper towels and refrigerate them up to a week. The exceptions to this, however, are basil and mint, which turn black when refrigerated wet. Store bunches of these herbs, unwashed and upright with their stems in a jar of water in the refrigerator, covered loosely with a plastic bag.

For most fresh herbs, use just the leaves, avoiding the tougher stems, although with parsley, you can include the stems. Chop fresh herbs just before using and add to hot dishes toward the end of the cooking time since the heat will dissipate the flavor.

Dried herbs and spices should be stored in a dark, cool place. To test herbs and spices, crush a bit between your fingers and sniff. If the spice lacks its characteristic aroma or smells dry and dusty, discard. Most dried herbs and spices should be discarded after six months, so buy in small quantities. The general rule of thumb is to substitute 1 teaspoon of dried herb for each tablespoon of fresh.

Following is a list of basic herbs and spices, but as you cook more and discover your tastes, feel free to add your favorites:

| | |
|---|---|
| **basil** | **oregano** |
| **bay leaf** | **paprika** |
| **chili powder** | **ground red pepper** |
| **ground cinnamon** | (cayenne) |
| **ground cloves** | **black and white pepper-** |
| **curry powder** | **corns** (freshly ground in a |
| **dill** | pepper mill adds much |
| **ground ginger** | more spirited flavor than |
| **whole nutmeg** (freshly | the bottled dried) |
| grated in a grater adds | **rosemary** |
| much more pungent | **salt** |
| flavor) | **thyme** |

## GRATING GINGER

If you're unfamiliar with fresh ginger, it has a peppery, slightly sweet flavor. A thin-skinned root, it can be peeled with a paring knife and then sliced or chopped, or you can grate it, unpeeled, on the small holes in a hand grater (don't use the smallest holes since all they do is turn everything into mush). I like to use the ginger in marinades, toss it into stir-fries, whisk it into salad dressings, and add it wherever else I want a surprising flavor. Tightly wrapped, the unpeeled ginger can be refrigerated for up to 1 week or frozen for up to 2 months.

## LEEK CLEANING

Cut off the hairy part of the root end. To clean whole leeks, start about 1 inch above the root end and slice the leek lengthwise to the end. If the leek is large, slice lengthwise into quarters. Swish in a sink or bowl of warm water to release the grit. If you're going to slice the leek crosswise into rounds, go ahead and do that, and then place the rounds in a strainer and swish under warm tap water. Blot dry with paper towels.

## MUSHROOM BASICS

**To clean fresh mushrooms:** Trim the mushroom stems if they're tough; either gently twist them off or cut with a small, sharp paring knife. To remove any dirt or grit from the surface of the mushrooms, gently swipe with a small, soft bristled brush (there are special mushroom cleaning brushes if you want to go that route) or lightly brush with dry paper towels (for more stubborn particles, use a dampened paper towel). Avoid soaking in water, since mushrooms can become soggy; rinsing is okay. Blot dry with paper towels before using.

**To store:** Always refrigerate fresh mushrooms and never wash them until ready to use. If packaged when you purchase, unwrap, leave in their tray or container, and wrap with paper towels. If bought in bulk, store in a brown paper bag.

**Dried mushrooms:** These are available all year round and can be substituted for fresh; figure 2 ounces of dried will replace 8 ounces of fresh. To reconstitute dried, rinse and then soak in hot water to cover for 15 to 30 minutes, or until softened. Lift the mushrooms out of the water, letting the excess drain back in. Rinse to remove any remaining grit and then handle them as called for in a recipe. Don't throw out the flavorful soaking liquid, even if the recipe mentions nothing about it. The grit from the mushrooms remains here, so strain it through a sieve lined with dampened paper towels or a paper coffee filter. If called for in the recipe, fine; otherwise, refrigerate or freeze and use as a flavor enhancer for soups, sauces, or whatever.

## SHELLFISH BASICS

First of all, be absolutely sure that your fish purveyor is reputable and takes very good care of his stock. Buy only clams that are tightly closed. Mussels may be slightly open but should close up tightly when tapped. Anything else means the shellfish is not alive and should not be purchased. Plan your buying trip so it's the last stop and you'll be arriving home soon after. Rinse the shellfish with very cold water and drain well. Arrange in a shallow pan, cover lightly with a dampened cloth or paper towel, and store in the coldest part of the refrigerator. Don't refrigerate in a plastic bag. Use the shellfish as soon as possible and definitely within 48 hours.

**To clean shellfish:** Scrub with a stiff brush and rinse several times in clean, cold tap water. Avoid letting them sit in water. The beard in a mussel, a strawlike thread sticking out of the shell, should be grasped with the fingers and pulled out.

## SHRIMP BASICS

In rinse and devein shrimp with kitchen shears, cut through the shell along the outer curve and into the shrimp about 1/16 inch to expose the thin, dark vein. Peel back the shell from the cut and gently separate the shell, including the tail, from the shrimp. With the tip of a small paring knife, pull out the thin vein and discard. Rinse the shrimp.

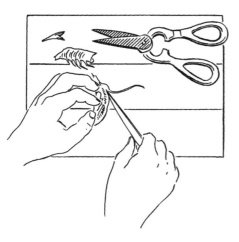

## TOMATO BASICS

The best of the season's tomatoes, grown locally in your own area, are usually available only for a few weeks in late summer. With a little planning, you may freeze or can some thick, fresh tomato sauce made from these ripe beauties to enjoy fresh tomato flavor throughout the autumn and winter. As a winter alternative, canned imported plum tomatoes and some domestic brands (do your own taste comparisons) are usually a better choice than anything fresh; except, very often, you may be able to find decent fresh plum tomatoes year-round, especially if you happen to live close to an Italian neighborhood.

**To ripen:** For best flavor, ripen tomatoes at room temperature and never refrigerate them raw. If you must, tolerate them only for a day or two. To reduce any refrigeration by buying tomatoes and planning their use judiciously so you're not caught with an abundance of overripe tomatoes. To encourage the ripening process, place the tomatoes in a closed brown paper bag.

**To peel:** Often a recipe calls for peeling tomatoes to avoid those unsightly loose, curled skins infiltrating a dish; they can be chewy, too. (If your recipe calls for straining the tomato mixture at some point, then there is really no sense in peeling the tomatoes beforehand.) There really is nothing difficult about peeling. The trick is to loosen the tomato skins without cooking any of the flesh directly underneath. Cut out the core from the stem end with a small paring knife. At the opposite end or base of the tomato, cut a very shallow X in the skin. With a slotted spoon or a perforated or wire skimmer, gently lower the tomatoes into a pot of boiling water for about 20 seconds. Quickly remove the tomatoes and place under cold running water or plunge into a large bowl of cold water to stop any cooking. Starting at the X, peel off the skin with your fingers or, if particularly stubborn, with the tip of a paring knife. And there you have it—a peeled tomato.

**To seed:** Some people have a visual thing about seeing tomato seeds speckling a dish; they can also add a bitter flavor and some claim they cause indigestion. In addition, if the watery chambers that contain the seeds are not drained, they can dilute the consistency as well as the flavor of a dish. If the tomatoes haven't already been cored for peeling, do it now. Cut across the equator of the tomato with a very sharp knife—you don't want to crush a very ripe tomato with a dull knife.

Holding the tomato half over a bowl, gently squeeze out the watery pulp along with the seeds; you may even want to poke your index finger into the chambers to scrape out any reluctant seeds, or you can use a spoon. (And after all the unpleasant things we've said about seeds, you still may want to save this seedy liquid for broths and soups.)

## SOME COOKING TERMS

**Blanch:** to cook an ingredient very quickly in a large quantity of boiling liquid—to set the color, as with green beans; to remove a strong flavor, as with garlic or onion; or to make removing a skin easier, as when peeling a tomato.

**Boil:** to heat liquid to a point where bubbles break the surface and steam rises; ranges from a gentle but steady eruption to a violent rolling boil.

**Braise:** to first brown meat or vegetables in a little fat in a pot and then cook, tightly covered, in a small amount of liquid for a long period of time either on top of the stove or in the oven.

**Deglaze:** to release the flavorful browned bits from the bottom of the skillet, after sautéing and removing excess fat, by adding a small amount of liquid—broth, wine, even water—to the pan and stirring.

**Parboil:** to cook food partially by boiling it briefly in water.

**Poach:** to cook food immersed in a simmering liquid in a covered pan, usually on the stovetop.

**Roast:** to oven-cook meat, fish, or vegetables in an uncovered pan, usually resulting in a browned outside and moist inside.

**Sauté:** to cook food quickly in a small amount of fat in a skillet or fry pan over medium heat, stirring it frequently to preventing sticking or scorching.

**Sear:** similar to sautéing, but at a higher temperature. The object is to seal in juices and do it as soon as the food hits the pan; the high heat of a broiler will also sear food.

**Simmer:** to cook just below the boiling point on a very low heat; tiny, steady bubbles just barely break the surface.

**Steam:** to cook food in a basket placed over a boiling or simmering liquid in a covered container so the food is surrounded by the steam.

**Stir-fry:** to cook cut-up ingredients by tossing continually in a minimum of fat over a large surface area, such as a wok or large skillet, over high heat.

**Sweat:** to cook ingredients in a small amount of fat over low heat in a covered pan. If you're keeping an eye on your diet, this can also be done in a small amount of water or other flavorful liquid, such as broth. Sweating releases natural juices.

## SAUTÉ BASICS

I begin with sautéing, because once you've mastered the elements of this cooking technique, you're well on your way to making yourself at home in the kitchen. Other methods such as braising and roasting, often begin with sautéing for searing, a variation of sautéing which seals in juices and develops color by caramelizing the natural sugar in the food. The process is easy. Food is first cooked in a small amount of fat. The flavorful crusty bits left in the pan are dissolved by deglazing, adding a small amount of liquid to the pan. Other liquids can be added and reduced, or boiled down, to evaporate moisture and concentrate flavor. And this is your sauce. For a successful sauté, keep the following in mind:

• Ingredients should be cut in a uniform size for even cooking.

• Be sure all ingredients are dry. Otherwise they won't brown but just steam and stew in their own juices.

• Use a heavy skillet that permits good browning over medium heat for sautéing or high heat for searing.

• The fat medium can be butter, oil, or a combination. The oil mixed with the butter allows for a higher sautéing heat without burning the butter. Use only enough fat to coat the bottom of the skillet. Or, if you're using nonstick cookware, you can use even less fat. In this age of concern about fat, recipes often call for "sautéing" with a little water in a nonstick pan.

• Be sure the fat is hot before you add the food. Oil should be lightly rippling without smoking and butter foam should have subsided. The dry pieces of food should sizzle as they hit the pan.

• The larger the piece of food being sautéed, the lower

the heat; otherwise the outside of the food can burn before the heat penetrates to the center.

• Don't crowd food in the pan. The surface of the pan should be covered with a single layer of food, with a little space between each piece. Too many pieces and the food will steam much and the fat will burn.

• Once the food is in the pan, leave it in the hot fat for about 30 seconds before tossing and stirring. This promotes browning.

• Regulate the heat carefully so that the fat sizzles steadily but not so furiously that the food burns.

• Add ingredients in the order of their cooking time.

## DEGLAZING BASICS

• First, pour off excess fat from the hot skillet. Add a small amount of liquid such as water, wine, liquor, beer, stock or broth, vinegar, or tomato and other juices. Return to the heat and quickly scrape up any browned bits from the bottom and sides of the pan with a wooden spoon. To burn off the harsh alcohol taste, flame any alcoholic liquid by tipping the pan carefully toward the flame until the liquid ignites, or just simmer the liquid for a minute or two. These deglazing juices, slightly thickened, can now be used as a sauce.

• Once the pan is deglazed, you can now add another liquid, usually stock, broth, or cream, which is then reduced for a subtler and slightly more abundant sauce. Several liquids can be added in this manner, reducing after each addition. This is called stratification.

• Pour a small amount of the sauce from a spoon as it reduces to recognize the perfect napping consistency: A properly cooked sauce will coat the food lightly and evenly.

## ROASTING BASICS

Usually large pieces of meat are roasted, so you'll need a big enough pan and one with low enough sides to allow the hot air to circulate around the food. If there is a layer of fat, place the roast, fat side up in the pan, so the meat will self-baste. Placing the roast on a rack in the pan will let heat circulate around the food and keep it out of any fat that drains into the pan. Here are a few more tips to keep in mind for roasting:

• Preheat the oven. Sometimes it's good to start at a high temperature briefly to seal in the juices and brown the outside, and then reduce the oven temperature to moderate for most of the roasting.

• Don't cover a roast with an aluminum foil tent—this will steam the meat—unless the roast is browning too quickly.

• Let the roast stand for 15 minutes before carving. This allows the meat to reabsorb the juices, keeping the meat moist.

## BRAISING BASICS

Braising—long, slow simmering, covered, in a small amount of liquid—is best suited to the tougher, less expensive cuts of meat, such as chuck, shoulder, rump, and brisket, and "tougher" vegetables, such as Belgian endive or celery. The process involves a few simple steps:

• The meat is first browned in fat to seal in the juices (sautéing).

• Seasoning vegetables and aromatics such as spices and herbs are cooked briefly in fat, and the meat or other food is then arranged on top of this aromatic bed in another pot.

• The pot should be just large enough to hold the meat and liquid without crowding.

• The added liquid is first used to deglaze (page 24) any pans used for sautéing, and is then added to the pot with a little wine, broth, water, leftover meat gravy, tomatoes, or other flavorful liquid.

• Simmering, covered, may be done either on top of the stove or in the oven for a more even, all-around heat (less chance of scorching the bottom of the pot).

• The sauce or juices are thoroughly degreased—using a large metal spoon or skimmer, removing all the fat and foam from the surface of the liquid. If time permits, refrigerate the pot overnight and then easily remove the solidified grease from the top the next day.

• Always taste and correct the seasonings before serving, adding salt and pepper and whatever other seasoning is needed.

## STEAMING BASICS

With steaming, a much lower percentage of nutrients are leeched out of the food than with blanching or boiling. Be sure the lid fits tightly when you steam; you may want to first cover the pot tightly with aluminum foil and then cover with the lid. Avoid opening during cooking—you don't want to lower the cooking temperature and you could get a nasty steam burn. Pour enough liquid into the pan to a depth of about 1 inch—in any event, the liquid should come no closer than 1 inch to the bottom of the steamer basket. Foods can be steamed over a flavored liquid such as a broth or over water with a few thin slices of aromatics such as ginger, garlic, lemon, or lime in it. Be sure the water doesn't boil away during the steaming. If necessary, carefully pour in more boiling water without wetting the food.

## FISH BASICS

~~You can too pick nice is to do fish at the market and you'll be rewarded. Fish is too easy to spoil~~ — ... and choose your fish source as carefully as you would your doctor. Purchase fish displayed on ice in a refrigerated case. The flesh of fillets, steaks, and other cuts should be translucent, firm but springy to the touch, unblemished, without discoloration around the edges, and with no tears. The smell should be reminiscent of the sea or briny. If the odor is fishy or ammonia-like, it's a sure sign that it's over the hill. And don't hesitate to ask to take a sniff—if the fish merchant is reputable, he certainly shouldn't mind.

Nowhere is timing more important than in cooking fish, yet nothing could be simpler. The easiest and the most reliable method of timing was developed by the Fisheries Council of Canada. Simply lay the whole fish (fillet or steak) flat and measure at its greatest thickness (or height). Then just calculate about 10 minutes cooking time (regardless of the method) per inch of thickness. When the fish is properly cooked, it should be opaque in the center and the top should be firm, not springy to the touch. If you cook fish to the point where it flakes when prodded with a fork, you've gone too far; it should just *begin* to flake.

## A FEW BASIC CUTS: EVEN AND PRECISE

Cutting ingredients evenly is important so that they cook at the same rate. Equally important are aesthetic choices: Identical ingredients cut in hair-fine julienne versus large fat chunks will be perceived differently by the eyes and mouth. As you begin preparing a dish, try to have a conception, however hazy, of your final result.

**Mince:** to chop very finely, in pieces no larger than 1/8 inch. Minced garlic is often called for.

**Fine chop:** to cut in even 1/4- to 1/2-inch pieces, usually square shaped.

**Medium chop:** to cut in even pieces about 1/2 inch square.

**Coarse chop:** to cut in even pieces about 3/4 to 1 inch square.

**Slice:** to cut parallel pieces ranging in thickness from 1/16 to 1/2 inch.

**Dice:** to cut in cube shapes, ranging from very small, 1/8 inch, to large, 1/2 to 1 inch.

**Julienne:** to cut in long, even stick shapes, usually $1 \times 1/8 \times 1/8$ inch. These can range from tiny matchsticks, $1 \times 1/16 \times 1/16$, to large "batons," $2 \times 1/4 \times 1/4$ inch.

**Sliver:** to cut food into thin strips, thinner than julienne.

**Shred:** to cut in long, thin, even strands, often done with greens. Chiffonade is a fine shred.

## HOW TO "CHOP" AN ONION

Use this method for chopping and dicing an onion; once you've mastered the technique, you should be able to fly through the task before the tears begin to fall. First cut the onion in half through the root end and remove the papery skin. Place an onion half flat side down on the cutting board. Steady the onion with the curled-under fingertips of one hand. Hold the knife blade (an 8- to 10-inch chef's knife with a *sharp* blade is good for

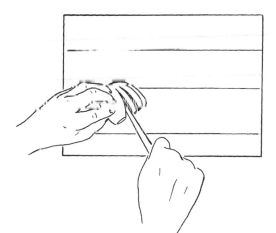

half of the onion. Now you can cut off the root end. For smaller pieces, continue chopping. This method of dicing will also work with other vegetables.

### HOW TO JULIENNE

To cut a vegetable into julienne (long thin sticks), cut the vegetable lengthwise into slices, the thickness depending on the size of the julienne. When you cut, curl under your fingertips on the hand holding the vegetable and use the knuckles as a cutting guide; place the side of the knife against the knuckles (careful of the blade) and use your knuckles to direct the movement. Stack the slices and cut into thin strips, then cut to the desired length.

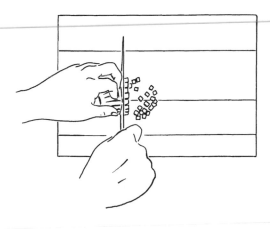

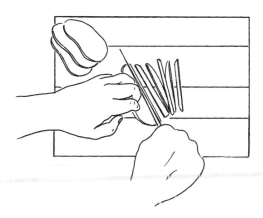

this) horizontal to the board. Beginning at the stem end, cut three or four parallel horizontal slices, the number depending on whether you want to dice or chop it and how large or small the pieces are to be. Cut up to the root end but not through it—the root end will hold the pieces of onion together. Now, cut parallel vertical slices across the onion at right angles to the horizontal cuts, beginning at the stem end and going up to the root end. Then cut parallel vertical slices across the onion at right angles to the first vertical cuts. Repeat with the other

### MEASURING BASICS

For a recipe to work correctly, you need to measure ingredients accurately.

• Measure flour, sugar, and other dry ingredients or solid ingredients in graduated metal or plastic measuring cups that can be filled right up to the top, then leveled with the dull straight edge of a table knife.

• To measure flour, spoon lightly into a measuring cup for dry ingredients, piling slightly above the rim. With the blunt edge of a table knife, a chopstick, or other straight flat edge, lightly sweep the excess flour away so the top is level. You want to decompact the flour, so work with a light hand. If you dip the measuring cup into the flour canister, you can increase the amount of flour by almost 50 percent. Work over wax paper and you'll be able to return any spills to the canister easily. If a recipe calls for a sifted measurement, first sift the flour onto a sheet of wax paper and then lightly spoon into the measuring cup.

• To measure granulated white and brown sugars, spoon into the measuring cup and level with a straight edge. Usually brown sugar is firmly packed into the measuring cup.

• Measure liquid ingredients in a spouted clear glass or plastic measuring cup that allows extra room on top to prevent spillage. Place the measuring cup on the counter so it's level and pour in the liquid to the desired level, reading the measure at eye level.

• For small amounts of liquid and dry ingredients, use graduated measuring spoons, making sure the measured amount is level. A precaution: Measure away from the bowl to avoid spilling in extra ingredients.

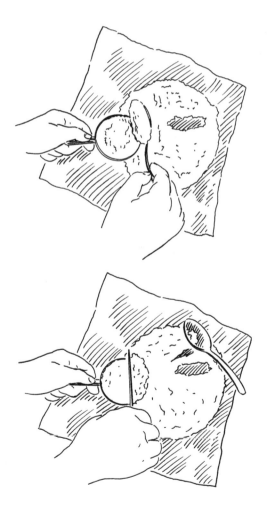

## A FEW FOOD SAFETY TIPS

• Wash your hands before preparing food.

• Before and after handling raw meat and poultry, wash hands, cutting surfaces, utensils, knives, and anything else that comes in contact with the raw ingredients, rubbing rigorously for at least 20 seconds. This prevents bacteria transfer.

• Keep a separate board for raw meat and poultry.

• Sanitize all your cutting boards with a solution of 1 teaspoon chlorine bleach and 1 quart very hot water.

• Be very careful with raw chicken. Thoroughly cook—the meat should reach an internal temperature of 180° F. (160° F. for boneless poultry).

• Thaw meat, poultry, and fish overnight in the refrigerator, not at room temperature. Prepare thawed food right away.

- Keep hot foods hot and cold foods cold; bacteria thrive when foods are held at warm or lukewarm temperatures.
- Let hot foods cool before storing in sealed containers.
- Make sure your knives are sharp—dull requires more pressure and the blade can slip off the food rather than cutting.

## COMPOSING A MENU

Don't be daunted by meal planning, whether it be for yourself, one other, or five others. Remember to keep things simple and don't feel obligated to put out huge amounts of food. A few well-prepared dishes, balanced in flavor, texture, color, and appearance, will be pleasing for both you and your guests. Here are a few principles to keep in mind.

- Decide on your "main course" first, but don't get caught in the traditional trap of thinking you need a slab of meat, a quarter of a chicken, or two pork chops. There is no reason why the "main" can't be a steaming bowl of Farmers' Market Vegetable Soup (page 47), Risotto with Mushrooms (page 83), or Panzanella, a bread salad (page 202). The meal doesn't always have to be something substantial. Then whatever your choice, balance it with side dishes, which could be nothing more than Tri-Color Roasted Peppers (page 170) or a simple Tossed Green Salad with Balsamic Vinaigrette (page 193) and a slice of good-quality crusty bread from a nearby bakery.
- Many of us were raised to think that the dinner plate needs three things on it: a protein, a starch, and a vegetable—three separate islands. Rethink this. Pasta e Fagioli, a hearty bean and pasta soup-stew (page 72), combines all these elements in one dish without any

meat, while Chicken and Vegetable Curry (page 114) is a similar one-dish meal but with meat.

- Think about textures, playing them against each other—chewy versus melt-in-your mouth, crisp against smooth: Creamy Mashed Potatoes without Cream (page 176) is a nice pairing with crispy Broiled Mustard-Crumbed Cornish Hens (page 120), and Open-Faced Dijon Steak Sandwich (page 135) is perfect with lightly steamed crunchy sugar snap peas (page 164) dressed with a balsamic vinaigrette (page 193).
- Blend flavors, making sure they complement rather than compete. Strongly flavored Soy-and-Ginger-Glazed Salmon (page 94) is appropriately offset with a tamer rice pilaf (page 182).
- Beginning as well as more experienced cooks often forget that a diner first feasts with the eyes. Mix together colors as well as shapes and sizes. Here's a good combination: brown Seared Double Lamb Chops (page 148) with smaller pieces of steamed green broccoli florets (page 164). Or how about lively red Bruschetta with Basil-Marinated Tomatoes (page 38) as an accompaniment to golden yellow Summer's Best Corn Chowder (page 52)?

## HOW DO I GET EVERYTHING ON THE TABLE AT THE SAME TIME?

One of the main hurdles this book can ease for you are the perennial questions: What do I do first? How do I get all the dishes on the table at the same time?

The solution is not in listing game plans that guide you through in order. That's fine for one menu, but the trick is to *get yourself thinking* so that you instinctively grasp which items can be gotten out of the way first.

Let's look at a sample menu:

## A SIMPLE DINNER FOR FRIENDS

- Soy and Ginger Glazed Salmon (page 91)
- Rice pilaf (page 102)
- Green salad (page 193)
- **Bread and butter**
- **Brown Butter Pear Cake (page 225)**

Actually, this is *more* than I would normally prepare for a simple dinner at home. I'd probably not make a dessert, ending up with a piece of cheese and/or fruit or ice cream after dinner or later in the evening. But this would be a manageable menu for having guests for a friendly, not overly elaborate dinner. Note that this meal has no separate first course; if you like, put out a few olives, such as kalamatas, with a predinner glass of white wine. Or you could make The Best Cheese Wafers (page 37) the day before.

The first and key question to ask—for any meal— is, what can be (or needs to be) done first and gotten out of the way? Marinating the salmon comes to mind, because you want the flavors of the marinade—ginger and soy—to soak in or meld with the fish. Another one that jumps out is baking the cake. First of all, you want to get the cake in the oven as soon as possible, so that once it's out, it has time to cool before serving. Also, once you've popped the cake in the oven, you'll have 45 minutes as it bakes to get the rest of the meal done.

Another do-ahead is cleaning and drying the lettuce, plus, if you like, making a salad dressing. (All of this assumes, by the way, that you are preparing everything in the hour or two before serving time. If you can do a couple of things, like cleaning lettuce, a day ahead, it will ease your way still further.)

So let's work out a *game plan,* an order of attack, that uses time most efficiently:

### GAME PLAN

1. **Preheat the oven.** Chill the white wine. If possible, set the table ahead of time.

2. Quickly **marinate the salmon;** cover with plastic wrap and set aside at room temperature.

3. **Make the browned butter for the cake,** put the cake together, and place in the oven. You now have 45 minutes, while the cake bakes, to get everything else done.

4. **Make the salad:** Wash and dry the lettuce; refrigerate. Make the dressing (or just take out the oil and vinegar, which you can drizzle on as you toss the salad greens).

5. **Cook the rice:** Rice takes longer than the salmon, so you want to start it first. If necessary, the finished rice can be kept warm. (If you were adding a green vegetable to this menu, you could start the rice, put on steaming water for the vegetable, then start the salmon, then put on the green vegetable.)

   Now, we're getting close to countdown, cooking the foods that will be served as the guests sit down.

6. Take the cake out of the oven and place on a rack to cool. Raise the oven temperature to broil. **Broil the salmon.**

7. **Toss the salad;** place on serving plates. Set out bread and butter.

8. Transfer the salmon to warm serving plates. Spoon on some of the rice pilaf; garnish with a fresh herb or watercress sprig if you like. Pour more wine and **dig in.**

9. After dinner, dessert is ready and waiting, with nothing to do but **serve the cake.**

Now that you see how to think about putting a meal together and do it a few times *(start simple),* planning the best use of your time, for any given group of dishes, will start to become automatic. This kind of thinking will, in effect, become a part of your life.

## WHAT EVERY KITCHEN SHOULD HAVE

Remember, *it pays to buy the best.* You'll have it forever.

### KNIVES
These should be all high-carbon stainless steel.
**Must-haves:**
- Chef's knife, 8 or 10 inches (all-purpose)
- Paring knife, 3 or 4 inches (for trimming vegetables and other small cutting jobs such as julienning a carrot)
- Serrated knife (for bread, tomatoes, and other soft foods)

**Nice to have:**
- Utility knife, 6 inches (like a small chef's knife)
- Slicing knife, 12 inches (for carving roasts)
- Flexible boning knife, for chicken, or a rigid one for large cuts of meat (only if you cook a lot and plan to bone your own meat)
- Cleaver, for cutting up poultry or chopping

### POTS AND PANS
- 1-, 2-, and 4-quart saucepans. Nonstick is good for one size you'll use a lot.
- 8- and 12-inch skillets. I recommend heavyweight nonstick.
- Lightweight stockpot (not aluminum)
- Roasting pan
- Dutch oven with tight-fitting lid or Le Creuset stew pan
- Ridged grill pan

### BAKEWARE
- Two 8- or 9-inch round cake pans
- Two 8- or 9-inch square cake pans
- Pie pan (9½ inches is a good all-purpose size)
- 2 baking sheets (I recommend nonstick)
- 1 muffin pan (ditto)
- Loaf pan (9 × 5 inches)
- Wire cooling racks

### MISCELLANEOUS
- Colander
- Four-sided hand grater
- Steaming rack
- Tongs
- Kitchen timer
- Measuring cups (dry and liquid measure)
- Measuring spoons
- Whisks
- Large and small sieves
- Cutting boards
- Rubber and metal spatulas
- Wooden spoons

- Large metal spoons (plain and slotted)
- Rolling pin

## APPLIANCES

- Food processor (not essential, but very useful)
- KitchenAid electric mixer (if you bake a lot)
- Blender
- Spice/coffee grinder or mini-food processor

## A FEW NICE-TO-HAVE EXTRAS

- Cast-iron skillet
- Wok
- Springform pan
- Jelly-roll pan
- Pizza pan
- Instant-read thermometer
- Candy/deep-fat thermometer
- Kitchen shears

# A FEW GADGETS I COULDN'T DO WITHOUT

- **A good pepper mill**—for use in the kitchen as well as at the table. There is no substitute for freshly ground pepper—it adds a wonderfully pungent flavor. Some cooks like two mills, one for black and one for white peppercorns.
- **A swivel peeler**—or better, several. I buy several inexpensive peelers and toss them as soon as they are no longer sharp.
- **Mouli rotary grater**—As useful at the table, for grating cheese over pasta, soups, and the like, as in the kitchen. Unsurpassed for fluffy ground nuts.

- **Restaurant-size flexible rubber spatula**—scrapes a whole mixing bowl clean in a few quick strokes. Buy a couple.
- **Zester**—small hand gadget for grating citrus zests in thin, neat strands.
- **A small electric grinder**—or preferably two, one for coffee beans, one for spices.
- **Several wooden spoons**—in various sizes
- **A tomato knife**—just a small, inexpensive version of a bread knife, but useful for all sorts of kitchen jobs
- **Flame Tamer**—for slow cooking with no danger of scorching
- **Salad spinner**—for perfectly dried salad greens. How did we ever get along without this?

# STOCKING THE LARDER

First, take a look at what you already have. That means looking in the back of the pantry, checking out the bottom shelf of the refrigerator, and thoroughly cleaning out cupboards. Make sure nothing has outlived its expiration date. Now you're ready. Make a shopping list of those staples you need to replace or fill in with for the first time. Once you've stocked these items, that's it for a while. But be sure to check your supplies from time to time, and when you notice you're close to running out of something, add it to your next shopping list. Use the following categories as a guide.

**Herbs and Spices** (page 20)

**Oils, Vinegars, and Condiments**
**oils** (pure olive and extra-virgin; vegetable, including canola; dark Asian sesame); **vinegars** (red wine, cider,

distilled white, balsamic, rice); **Dijon mustard; hot pepper sauce; Worcestershire sauce; soy sauce; ketchup; mayonnaise; honey; maple syrup**

**Pantry Items**
**canned tomato products** (whole, crushed, sauce, paste); **canned chicken and beef broths; canned soups; canned beans** (kidney, cannellini, black, pinto, and the like); **canned corn; canned tuna; pasta; rice** (white, brown, basmati, wild, and the like); **peanut butter; jellies and jams; raisins; oatmeal and other cereals; sun-dried tomatoes; red and white wines**

**Refrigerated and Frozen**
**milk; eggs; butter or margarine; cheeses; yogurt; lemons; parsley; frozen vegetables**

**Pantry or Refrigerator**
**onions; garlic; potatoes**

**Baking** (even if you're only an occasional baker, these are good items to have on hand since many of them are called for in nonbaking cooking):
**baking powder; baking soda; sugars** (granulated, light and dark brown, confectioners'), **cornstarch; flour** (all-purpose); **unsweetened cocoa powder; vanilla extract** (pure)

## WEEKLY SHOPPING

Try to plan your menus in advance—even a few days ahead will help to organize your kitchen duties. Gather together the recipes and make a list of what you need

to buy according to how items are arranged in your supermarket, aisle by aisle. Follow this plan and you'll avoid doubling back for forgotten items, plus you won't become the victim of impulse buying.

## GENERAL SUGGESTIONS

• Never shop on an empty stomach.
• Avoid taking a crowd with you—too many distractions.
• Brand names are often more expensive than store or house labels. But sometimes it pays to buy the brand labels: For paper towels and canned tuna you may want to stick with the brand labels.
• Economy sizes can in fact be more expensive and you wind up with more than you can possibly use.
• Fresh is usually better than frozen, but some frozen vegetables are extremely convenient and the quality is quite good: corn kernels, peas, tiny onions.

## CLEANING UP AS YOU GO

This is self-explanatory. Clean as you go and when you're ready to serve dinner, you won't have a teetering stack of dirty pots and pans. Wash and place in the drain board, or if a dishwasher is nearby, load it as you go. When dinner is done, you'll only have to deal with the dishes. And if you're lucky, others may help.

One

# APPETIZERS AND NIBBLES WITH DRINKS

**Technique:** | The Best Cheese Wafers
covering sticky dough with wax paper
for rolling

**Techniques:** | Bruschetta with Basil-Marinated Tomatoes
salting tomatoes to draw out juices and
concentrate flavor/roasting garlic

**Techniques:** | Fresh Salsa with Avocado
salting tomatoes to draw out juices and
concentrate flavor/tossing avocado with citrus
juice to prevent discoloration

**Techniques:** | Beer-Steamed Shrimp with Romescu Sauce
steaming/toasting nuts

**Appetizers should be just that—appetizing and irresistible, honing the appetite to a sharp edge in anticipation of what's to follow.** The flavors need to be bold and clean, carrying their own weight, especially if paired with wine or a selection of more serious cocktails. The advantage of the beginning of a dinner party is that appetizers are pques so the first tastes always seem to be the most delicious. The danger: too much of a good thing—the trick is to perk up the appetite without dead ening it. Idiup potato chips and crackers are indeed an easy beginning, but are apt to fill you up prematurely, dulling the senses to anything that follows.

The trap often waiting for beginner cooks is the desire to dazzle with over-wrought (often contrived and very labor-intensive) appetizers and too many of them. Keep it simple—that's always some of the best kitchen advice I can give.

The selection of recipes in this chapter is clearly not exhaustive, but it offers nib-bles with clean, distinctive flavors that awaken the appetite, getting the juices flowing—they should be a tease. And these recipes fulfill what I consider perhaps the most important criterion for food served before a meal: They can be prepared ahead, with no last-minute fussing, so you can enjoy your own party along with the guests.

# THE BEST CHEESE WAFERS

These are from Martha Nesbit of Savannah, Georgia. This has become one of my favorite recipes for entertaining. **Freeze the dough in portions** and you can bake a few of these whenever you need to serve something to nibble with drinks.

MAKES 48 TO 72 TWO-INCH WAFERS OR 100 TO 120 ONE-INCH WAFERS

1/4   **pound (1 stick) unsalted butter, softened**

2   **cups sifted all-purpose flour**

1   **teaspoon salt**

1/2   **teaspoon cayenne**

1   **pound sharp Cheddar cheese, shredded (4 cups)**

**1.** Beat the butter with an electric mixer at medium-high speed until fluffy and light colored. Meanwhile, resift the flour with the salt and cayenne onto a sheet of wax paper. Reduce the mixer speed to low and beat in the flour mixture, then the grated cheese just until blended. Do not overmix; the mixture will be quite crumbly. Gather together with your hands; the dough should just hold together. If it's too dry and crumbly, sprinkle with a few drops of cold water and then toss together with a fork until it does hold together. Divide the dough into thirds. Wrap each portion in plastic wrap and refrigerate for at least 30 minutes—this will make the dough easier to roll out.

**2.** Preheat the oven to 400°F. Working with a third of the dough at a time, place a portion on a lightly floured work surface. Flatten the dough with your hand and **cover with a sheet of wax paper.** Roll out as thinly as possible.

**3.** With a 2¼-inch fluted or plain biscuit cutter (or the rim of a glass), cut out rounds of dough and place them 1 inch apart on an ungreased nonstick baking sheet. If you'd like smaller, bite-size wafers, cut them about 1¼ inches in diameter. (If your sheet is not nonstick, coat lightly with nonstick cooking spray.) Repeat with the remaining dough. Gather all of the scraps together, reroll, and cut.

**4.** Bake the wafers until golden, 10 to 12 minutes (or 7 to 10 minutes for smaller ones). Do not overbake. Transfer with a metal spatula to a wire rack and cool slightly. Serve warm. Or cool completely and then store in a tightly covered tin (these wafers keep well for several days).

As guests arrive, I like to serve these with a glass of wine or, for a very special occasion, a flute of Champagne. They're also delicious as an accompaniment to a simple green salad.

With a sticky dough such as this one, the rolling out is easier if you first **cover the dough with a sheet of wax paper**—no crumbly bits to keep removing from the rolling pin.

The dough, wrapped in plastic wrap, **can be kept for 3 or 4 days in the refrigerator or 6 months in the freezer.**

**To defrost the dough, let stand in the refrigerator overnight or at room temperature until workable.**

I like to serve this as a first course, before a simple plate of pasta, or pair it with a green salad for a light supper or lunch. If planning on a larger crowd, double or even triple this recipe.

When you salt tomatoes this way, their flavor **concentrates** almost into a marmalade. So even if your tomatoes are less than perfect, you'll capture some of the flavor reminiscent of the best August crop.

**Roasting garlic,** whether it be the whole head or individual cloves, tames and mellows its flavor.

# BRUSCHETTA WITH BASIL-MARINATED TOMATOES

This Southern Italian specialty is really just an open-faced sandwich—slices of toast, usually in thicker slabs than the currently popular bite-size crostini, are covered with a rustic topping. This recipe here is based on *bruschetta rosa* (red bruschetta) from Michael Romano, the splendid chef at Union Square Cafe, one of my favorite New York restaurants. Put the tomato mixture together in the afternoon, then serve with a knife and fork as the late summer sun begins to set.

MAKES 6 SERVINGS

2½ to 3 pounds ripe, best-quality tomatoes, peeled, seeded, and cut into
    ½-inch dice (Tomato Basics, page 22)
    Coarse (kosher) salt or sea salt
½ cup shredded fresh basil leaves, plus 6 small basil sprigs, for garnish
4 to 6 large garlic cloves
    Olive oil
    Freshly ground black pepper, to taste
6 large slices sourdough or coarse country bread

**1.** Place the diced tomatoes in a nonreactive colander in the sink or over a large plate with a rim. **Sprinkle the tomatoes with** a light coating of **salt** (usually about 1½ teaspoons), plus ¼ cup of the basil; toss to combine. Let the tomatoes stand for 45 to 60 minutes to allow the excess juices to drain, tossing once or twice. Discard the juices.

**2.** Meanwhile, preheat the oven to 375°F. Remove any loose skin from the garlic cloves, but leave a thin layer of skin on each one. Place in a pie plate or other shallow baking dish and drizzle with a light coating of olive oil. **Roast the garlic** until soft when pierced with a small knife blade but not yet browned, usually 12 to 15 minutes. Set the garlic aside to cool.

**3.** When cool enough to handle, peel the garlic. To mince, cut each clove lengthwise into 4 or 6 sections; then very thinly slice crosswise. Place it in a medium bowl with ½ cup olive oil and the remaining ¼ cup basil. Add the drained tomatoes to the bowl with a few generous grinds of pepper. Gently mix with a rubber spatula. Taste and add a little more salt if needed to bring out the tomato flavor.

This is not meant to be a neat-looking plate. Be generous in spooning the extra juices over the bread—it will soak up all that delicious flavor.

**4.** At serving time, toast the bread in a toaster or on a baking sheet under a preheated broiler (or grill the bread over medium hot coals), until lightly golden on both sides. To serve, place a slice of toast on each serving plate. Spoon the tomato mixture over each slice, spooning on some of the oil and juices so they run over the edges. Garnish each bruschetta with a small basil sprig and serve with a knife and fork.

## VARIATION: BRUSCHETTA WITH BASIL-MARINATED TOMATOES AND LEMON

Prepare the tomato-oil mixture as in Bruschetta with Basil-Marinated Tomatoes. Add the grated zest and juice of 1 lemon to the tomato-oil mixture.

## VARIATION: BRUSCHETTA WITH BASIL-MARINATED TOMATOES AND SPINACH

Prepare the tomato-oil mixture as in Bruschetta with Basil-Marinated Tomatoes. Remove the tough stems from ½ pound fresh spinach. Wash in several changes of clean water. Place the spinach with water clinging to leaves in a large saucepan and cover. Steam, uncovering and tossing occasionally, until slightly wilted, about 2 minutes. Remove the spinach to a cutting board and let cool. Coarsely chop and add to the tomato-oil mixture.

**BONUS RECIPE**

## TOMATO-BASIL SAUCE FOR PASTA

MAKES 4 SERVINGS

Prepare the tomato-oil mixture as in Bruschetta with Basil-Marinated Tomatoes. Cook 12 ounces of pasta according to package directions; drain well. Toss with room temperature tomato mixture. Serve, topped with shavings of Parmesan cheese.

Serve with tortilla chips or over grilled or broiled fish or chicken.

For this kind of recipe, I like using plum tomatoes since good-quality ones are available year-round and their mealy texture is perfectly suited to this type of sauce.

Here again, as in the bruschetta on the previous pages, we're salting the tomatoes, and draining off the excess juices in order to concentrate the flavor.

Tossing the avocado with citrus juice prevents its flesh from darkening. The same trick works with bananas, apples, and pears.

# FRESH SALSA WITH AVOCADO

This fresh, chunky mixture beats the jarred versions hands down. The avocado is a special rich touch, although if you prefer, it can be omitted—the salsa is still delicious.

6 to 8 ripe plum tomatoes, cored, seeded, and cut into 1/2-inch chunks (Tomato Basics, page 22)

Coarse (kosher) salt or sea salt

1/2  red or yellow bell pepper (or better, some of each), trimmed and diced

2  or 3 jalapeño peppers (fresh or pickled), trimmed, seeded, and minced (Hot Chili Pepper Basics, page 17), or use 2 to 3 tablespoons drained canned chopped jalapeños

1/2  red onion, finely chopped

2  scallions (white and green portions), trimmed and thinly sliced

1  garlic clove, minced

2  tablespoons chopped fresh parsley leaves, or 1 tablespoon *each* chopped fresh parsley and fresh cilantro

Freshly ground black pepper, to taste

Juice of 2 small limes

1  ripe avocado

**1.** Place the diced tomatoes in a nonreactive colander in the sink or over a large plate with a rim. **Sprinkle the tomatoes with** a light coating of **salt** (usually about 1 1/2 teaspoons); toss to combine. Let the tomatoes stand for 45 to 60 minutes to allow the excess juices to drain, tossing once or twice. Discard the juices.

**2.** Meanwhile, combine the bell pepper, jalapeños, onion, scallions, garlic, parsley, black pepper, and half of the lime juice in a medium bowl; toss gently with a wooden spoon. Stir the drained tomatoes into the salsa and let stand at room temperature for 30 to 60 minutes to allow the flavors to blend. If you want, pour off some of the excess liquid, but leave the salsa quite moist.

**3.** Cut the avocado lengthwise in half; remove the pit. Halve the halves lengthwise and remove the skin, keeping the flesh whole. Cut the flesh into 1/2-inch chunks and place in a small bowl. Add the remaining lime juice; **toss avocado** very gently with a rubber spatula to avoid mashing it. Add the avocado and lime juice to the salsa, again tossing very gently. Taste, and correct the seasonings if needed, adding more salt, pepper, or lime juice to balance the flavors. Serve at cool room temperature.

BONUS RECIPE

## QUESADILLA WITH MONTEREY JACK CHEESE AND FRESH SALSA

For each quesadilla, spoon ¼ cup of the Fresh Salsa with Avocado over a 6- to 8-inch flour tortilla. Sprinkle evenly with ½ cup of shredded Monterey Jack cheese and top with a second tortilla. Gently press down with your hand to flatten. Bake on a baking sheet in a 350°F. oven for 3 to 4 minutes or microwave at full power for 1 to 2 minutes or until the cheese melts and the filling is hot. Cut into wedges.

I like this, cut into wedges, for a first course, or when it's just me, for a snack in the afternoon, or even lunch.

This shrimp is also tasty served with the salsa on page 40. And the romescu sauce makes an excellent dip for vegetable crudités, tortilla wedges, and pita triangles.

~~Enclosed almonds and nuts have already had their skins removed.~~

If the hazelnuts still have their skins, you'll want to remove them to avoid any bitterness in the finished dish. After you've toasted the nuts, rub them in a clean cloth kitchen towel or paper towel to remove the skins.

This is one of those instances when good-quality canned tomatoes are better than fresh, since all of the ingredients for the sauce are pureed together.

What can I substitute for the Crab Boil? The commercially prepared seasoning mix is an old standby, but you can make your own: In a mortar with a pestle, crush together 2 garlic cloves, 6 allspice berries, and 1/2 teaspoon dried red pepper flakes.

# BEER-STEAMED SHRIMP WITH ROMESCU SAUCE

Based on the traditional Catalan sauce made with hot chilies and ground almonds, this simple, colorful dip packs a flavorful punch, which the ground nuts help mel-

Romescu Sauce

  2  red bell peppers
  4  large garlic cloves, thin skins left on
     Olive oil
  1/4  cup (about 2 ounces) whole almonds, preferably blanched
  1/4  cup (about 2 ounces) whole hazelnuts, preferably blanched
  3  canned plum tomatoes, drained
  1 1/2  tablespoons red wine vinegar or sherry vinegar, or more to taste
     Fresh lemon juice
     Salt and freshly ground black pepper, to taste
     Pinch of cayenne
  3  tablespoons chopped fresh herbs, such as parsley and chives

Beer-Steamed Shrimp

  1  bottle or can (12 ounces) beer
  1  tablespoon Crab Boil or Old Bay Seasoning
  1 1/2  to 2 pounds shrimp, peeled but with tails left on (Shrimp Basics, page 22)
     Lemon wedges, for serving

1. **To make the Romescu Sauce:** Heat the broiler, with a rack set so the bell peppers can fit under the heat source (Bell Pepper Basics, page 16). Place a large sheet of foil on a baking sheet and arrange the peppers and garlic on it; rub lightly with a little olive oil. Broil, turning frequently with tongs, until the peppers and garlic are evenly charred. The garlic usually takes 8 to 10 minutes; remove when it is done. The peppers usually take 12 to 15 minutes; remove from the broiler with tongs, slip into a paper bag, and close. Let stand until cool enough to handle.

**2.** Meanwhile, **toast the almonds and hazelnuts** in a dry skillet over medium heat, stirring frequently, until fragrant and beginning to become lightly golden, usually about 8 minutes. Remove from the heat and set aside to cool.

**3.** Cut the bell peppers in half. Working over a bowl to catch the juices, remove the charred skins, seeds, and stems from the peppers. Coarsely chop the flesh. Strain the pepper juices and reserve. Trim off the hard stem ends from the roasted garlic and peel off the skins. Place the bell peppers, garlic, almonds, hazelnuts, and tomatoes in a food processor or blender; process until nearly smooth. With the machine running, gradually add ⅓ cup olive oil in a thin stream. Blend in the vinegar, a squeeze of lemon juice, salt and black pepper, and the cayenne. Scrape the sauce into a small bowl; stir in the herbs. Now taste and correct all seasonings if needed, adding more salt, pepper, cayenne, vinegar, and lemon juice; this sauce should be well seasoned, with a slight tang of vinegar. Cover and set aside at room temperature for at least 30 minutes. Taste and correct the seasonings again before serving. (The romescu sauce can be made a few days ahead and refrigerated, tightly covered.)

**4. To make the Beer-Steamed Shrimp** (Steaming Basics, page 25): Bring the beer and Crab Boil (or spices) to a boil in the bottom of a steamer. Arrange the shrimp over a steamer rack, tightly cover, and steam just until the shrimp turn pink, 3 to 4 minutes. Quickly stir the shrimp once about halfway through the cooking time. To serve hot, just arrange the shrimp on a platter as described below in step 5 and dig in. To serve cold, place the shrimp in a single layer in a large bowl or shallow pan of ice. When cold, drain well on paper towels and arrange on the platter.

**5.** To serve, select a narrow serving bowl and scrape the romescu sauce into the bowl. Place the bowl in the center of a large serving platter. Arrange the shrimp around the bowl, scatter with lemon wedges, and serve hot or cold.

**Toasting nuts** enhances their flavor, adding a subtle richness to a dish. Using the top of the stove is the easier method, but a 350°F. oven works well, especially if you already have the oven on for another job. Spread the nuts on a jelly-roll pan and stir them occasionally with a metal spatula while "roasting," until lightly browned and aromatic, about 3 to 5 minutes.

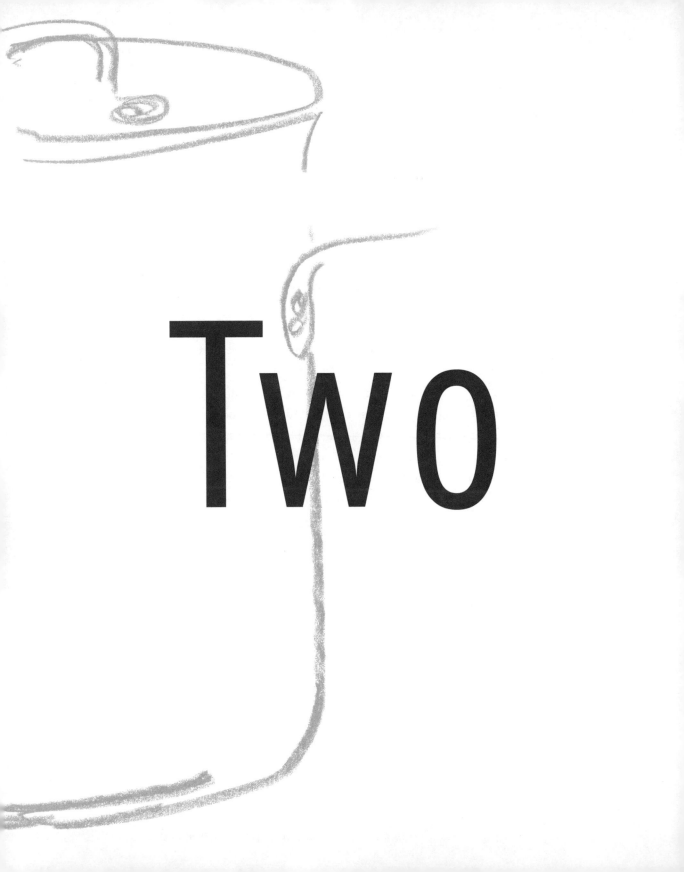

# Two

# SOUPS

**Techniques:** Farmers' Market Vegetable Soup
sweating vegetables/thickening with vegetable
purees/substituting low-fat milk for cream

**Techniques:** Nine-Bean Soup
soaking dried beans/replacing some of oil with
water to reduce fat

**Technique:** Grandma's Mushroom-Barley Soup
soaking dried mushrooms

**Techniques:** Summer's Best Corn Chowder
removing corn kernels from cobs/using cobs to
enhance flavor of broth/thickening soup with
potato and vegetable puree/making soup ahead
so flavor will deepen

**Techniques:** Tuscan-Style Tomato and Bread Soup
thickening soup with bread/seasoning with fresh
herbs/garnishing with thin shavings of Parmesan

**Technique:** Curried Cream of Broccoli Soup
making creamless "cream" soups

**Carmen Miranda, already a big star in Brazil, when asked what she needed to be happy, replied, "A good bowl of soup and the freedom to sing."**

Good homemade soup is one of the cornerstones of home cooking. Make a pot and you'll have meals for several days—and beyond, if you freeze some of it. In all of the world's cuisines, soups have always represented a form of alchemy: The almost magical transformations of a few inexpensive ingredients—including bits or into a rich homemade meal. Even though we're used to thinking that soups require long hours of simmering—hours that many of us cannot afford—they can also be a quick affair to throw together. And when they do require long simmering, most of the cooking need not be closely watched, so you can go about other things.

Soups move effortlessly through the seasons, adapting readily to whatever is best in the market. The recipes in this chapter clearly illustrate this, whether using fall vegetables or summer corn or a winter mix of dried beans.

Exactness is not required for soup making, so this cooking is very forgiving for beginning cooks—there's practically no way to make a mistake, and there is lots of room for variations and improvisations.

Although soups are often served as a first course, my choices here are meant to be dinner for guests or a quiet supper for one or two, without much else on the menu except perhaps a salad and a loaf of bread. Soup is ideal for entertaining—wonderfully complex but easily made the day before (in fact, flavors usually improve). When the doorbell rings, all you need do is gently reheat the soup.

# FARMERS' MARKET VEGETABLE SOUP

This is a basic method for a hearty, peasant-style soup; you can use it with any combination of vegetables in season.

MAKES 6 MAIN-COURSE SERVINGS

- 2 tablespoons olive oil
- 3 medium-large onions, peeled, halved, and sliced
- 2 leeks, trimmed, halved lengthwise, thickly sliced crosswise, and washed well (Leek Cleaning, page 21)
- 3 carrots, trimmed, peeled, and sliced 1/4 inch thick
- 3 large garlic cloves, sliced
- 1 1/2 teaspoons salt
- 1/2 teaspoon fresh thyme leaves or 1/8 teaspoon dried
- 1/8 teaspoon dried red pepper flakes
  Pinch of dried tarragon
- 4 potatoes, peeled, quartered lengthwise, and sliced crosswise 1/4 inch thick
- 2 cans (about 14 ounces each) chicken broth, preferably reduced-sodium
- 3 cups cold water
- 3/4 cup **low-fat** or whole milk, or more as needed
- 1/8 teaspoon freshly grated nutmeg
  Freshly ground black pepper, to taste
- 1 or 2 tablespoons cold unsalted butter (optional)
  Chopped fresh parsley, for serving

**1.** Heat the oil in a large pot or casserole over medium heat. Add the onions, leeks, carrots, garlic, salt, thyme, pepper flakes, and tarragon. Reduce the heat to low; cover and **cook slowly** or **sweat**, stirring occasionally, until the vegetables begin to soften and release some of their moisture, about 10 minutes.

**2.** Stir in the potatoes, broth, and water. Cover and bring to a boil; skim off the foam with a skimmer or large metal spoon. Lower the heat; boil gently, partially covered, until the vegetables are quite tender, about 45 minutes. →

Served with a salad and good bread, this soup is a satisfying supper in itself.

To keep soups light, I often use low-fat milk rather than whole milk or even heavy cream. Since 2% milk is not that significantly lower in fat than whole, I stick with the 1%—do the same, especially if you're keeping an eye on fat.

Slow cooking in a covered pot is called "sweating." What you're doing is coaxing the juices out of the vegetables—you want the flavorful juices drawn into the soup, or sauces, as the case may be. When you sauté, you're doing the opposite: sealing the juices in.

Note that only half of the vegetables are pureed, so the soup retains some chunky texture. For a smoother soup, puree all of the solids.

Most soups freeze well, except those made with cheese, cream, or other dairy products. When thawed and reheated, they may separate and curdle. The solution is easy—just freeze the soup without these ingredients and then stir in when gently reheating. Also keep in mind that some vegetable pieces, such as squash and green beans, and pasta become soft when frozen and reheated. So if you are making the soup ahead and freezing, add these ingredients to the soup after thawing and as you're reheating it.

**3.** Remove half of the vegetables with a slotted spoon to a food processor; **puree.** If using a blender, work in smaller batches. Scrape the puree back into the soup, stirring to combine. Stir in the milk, nutmeg, and pepper; return nearly to a simmer over very low heat. Thin with more milk, if desired. Taste and correct the seasoning, adding more salt, herbs, and spices if needed. If you like, remove the pan from the heat and swirl in the butter to cover the surface of the soup. The butter should remain in a very soft puddle atop. Serve hot, sprinkled with a little chopped parsley.

**BONUS RECIPE**

## VEGETABLE PUREE

It's very easy to transform this soup into a puree to serve as a vegetable course. Just strain all of the vegetables and then puree, adding only as much of the cooking liquid as needed for the desired consistency. Taste and adjust the seasonings accordingly.

## VARIATION: VEGETABLE SOUP WITH FRESH GREENS

Adding shredded greens to this soup adds color, texture, and nutrients, and slipping them into the pot at the last moment keeps them a beautiful bright green.

1  **pound fresh spinach leaves, stems discarded, washed well, and coarsely shredded (Greens Cleaning, page 19; you can also use other greens, such as Swiss chard, arugula, or kale)**

Scatter the shredded spinach over the surface of the finished soup in step 3 before adding and heating the milk through. Cover and boil gently until the spinach is wilted but still bright green, usually about 2 minutes. Stir the spinach into the soup and then serve immediately.

# NINE-BEAN SOUP

Packaged mixes of dried beans can be found in specialty and health food stores. Or just combine a number of types of dried beans yourself—the actual number of different kinds is not all that important.

MAKES 6 MAIN-COURSE SERVINGS

- 2 medium-large red or yellow onions, chopped
- 1 tablespoon olive oil
- 4 carrots, trimmed, peeled, and sliced
- 4 garlic cloves, thinly sliced
- 4 teaspoons paprika, preferably **Hungarian**
- 1 teaspoon dried marjoram
- 1 small dried hot chili or a pinch of dried red pepper flakes
- 1½ tablespoons tomato paste
- ½ pound dried mixed beans, **soaked** overnight in enough cold water to cover by 2 inches and drained (or use quick-soak method, Dried Bean Basics, page 17)
- 3 cups reduced-sodium chicken broth or vegetable broth
- 2 tablespoons chopped fresh parsley
- 1 tablespoon balsamic vinegar or red wine vinegar, or to taste
  Salt and freshly ground black pepper, to taste
- 4 scallions (white and green portions), trimmed and thinly sliced on a sharp diagonal

**1.** Combine the onions, oil, and about 1 tablespoon of **water** in a nonreactive large, wide nonstick saucepan; cook over low heat until the onions are softened, about 5 minutes. Add the carrots and garlic; cook, stirring, until the carrots soften, about 5 minutes. Stir in the paprika, marjoram, and hot chili pepper; cook, stirring, for 1 minute longer. Add the tomato paste, drained soaked beans, chicken broth, and 6 cups of water. Bring to a boil. Skim the foam off the top with a skimmer or large metal spoon. Partially cover the pan, lower the heat, and simmer the soup until the beans are quite tender, about 1½ hours.

**2.** Stir in the parsley, vinegar, and salt and pepper. Taste and correct the seasonings, adding more vinegar, spices, and herbs, if desired. Remove the hot chili. Serve, sprinkled with scallions.

Served with a salad and thick slices of toasted bread, this hearty soup makes a satisfying, wholesome meal.

Hungarian paprika is a spice ground from a variety of dried red peppers and is more flavorful than the regular store-bought variety. Its flavor can range from sweet to spicy-hot. My preference for this soup is the slightly hot.

Since you're already soaking and cooking dried beans, plan for other meals by preparing a big batch, 1½ pounds of beans or more. You can freeze the cooked beans in 2-cup containers and have them on hand for other soups and main-course dishes, such as salads and rice and bean dishes.

To use a little less fat when cooking the vegetables for a soup, I use the water trick. I replace some of the oil with water and this, along with a nonstick pan and cooking over low heat, coaxes the natural juices out of the vegetables and into the soup.

It's always a good idea to get to know the food purveyors you frequent on a regular basis—butcher, fishmonger, produce manager, owner of a local farm-stand, and even the supermarket deli per-son. They're usually great sources of infor-mation about foods and how to prepare them, plus they can often pro-vide special services, as in this recipe where you need the short ribs cut and trimmed.

Any time you soak dried mushrooms, be sure to use the flavorful strained liquid in the recipe—even if the recipe doesn't tell you to. It adds lots of earthy flavor.

Since I'm always pour-ing excess fat out of pots and skillets, I'm used to eyeballing these amounts. If you're not, measure out 1, 2, and 3 tablespoons of water and take a look at how much that is. Then you'll know.

# GRANDMA'S MUSHROOM-BARLEY SOUP

This recipe is adapted from one my mother has been feeding our family for years. A small amount of dried mushrooms provides lots of flavor. This recipe looks long, but it couldn't be easier.

1 to 1½ ounces dried mushrooms, such as porcini, shiitake, or a combination

2½ to 3 pounds short ribs of beef (or meaty soup bones), cut by your butcher into 2- to 3-inch pieces, excess fat trimmed
Salt and freshly ground black pepper, to taste

2 tablespoons vegetable oil, or as needed

2 medium-large onions, coarsely chopped

2 garlic cloves, minced

3 or 4 carrots, trimmed, peeled, and sliced ¼ inch thick

2 or 3 celery ribs, trimmed (leafy tops chopped and reserved), strings removed (Celery Stringing, page 18)

10 ounces fresh mushrooms, white or wild, such as shiitake, chanterelles, portobellos, or a combination (Mushroom Basics, page 21), stems trimmed flush with the caps, caps sliced ¼ inch thick, and the stems coarsely chopped

⅔ cup barley

⅓ cup dried lima beans
Fresh parsley stems, tied in a bundle (optional)

½ cup chopped fresh parsley

**1. Soak the dried mushrooms** in enough warm water to cover until softened, usu-ally 20 to 30 minutes.

**2.** Meanwhile, pat the beef ribs dry with paper towels. Salt and pepper them lightly. Heat the oil in a large heavy pot or casserole over medium heat. Add the ribs, work-ing in batches if necessary to avoid crowding the pot; sauté, turning several times with tongs, until nicely browned on all sides, 10 to 15 minutes. Transfer the ribs to a plate and set aside. If there are more than about 2 tablespoons of fat in the pot, **discard the excess.**

**3.** While the ribs cook, drain the dried mushrooms over a small bowl, allowing the liquid to go through a sieve lined with a paper coffee filter or dampened paper towel. Rinse the soaked mushrooms under cold running water to remove any grit; trim and discard any tough stems. Coarsely chop the mushrooms.

**4.** After the ribs are browned, make sure the fat in the pot is still hot. Add the onions, garlic, about one-third of the carrots, and half of the celery to the pan; stir. Add the chopped fresh mushroom stems and the dried mushrooms along with the soaking liquid. Cook, stirring frequently, until the vegetables soften and begin to turn lightly golden, about 8 minutes.

**5.** Return the ribs to the pot, along with any juices they have given off. Add the barley, limas, and 9 cups of water; the solid ingredients should be covered. Bring to a boil, scraping up any browned bits from the bottom of the pan with a wooden spoon (Deglazing Basics, page 24). With a skimmer or large metal spoon, skim off any froth that rises to the surface as the liquid comes to a boil.

**6.** Lower the heat to maintain a steady, gentle simmer. Stir in the reserved leafy celery tops and parsley stem bundle. Partially cover and simmer until the beef is nearly tender, about 2 hours. Watch the heat and adjust if necessary; the liquid should not boil. Skim occasionally and add a little more cold water from time to time if needed to keep the solid ingredients covered.

**7.** Add the remaining carrots and celery. Stir the sliced fresh mushroom caps into the soup. Again, add a little more water if needed to cover. Simmer, partially covered, until the carrots are tender, about 35 minutes longer.

**8.** Remove the ribs from the soup with a slotted spoon and transfer to a plate. Remove and discard the parsley stem bundle, if using. With a skimmer or large metal spoon, remove any fat from the surface of the soup. With a paring or boning knife, cut the meat away from the bones, discarding the bones. Cut the meat into bite-size pieces and return them to the soup. Add salt and pepper to taste, if needed. Stir most of the chopped parsley into the soup. Serve in soup bowls, sprinkling each portion with a little more chopped parsley.

**When reheating this soup, you may need to thin it with a little water since the barley will absorb liquid as it stands.**

**For a quick microwavable lunch or snack, freeze soups in individual microwave-safe containers.**

Try serving this chowder for a summer supper, either as a first course before barbecued meats, fish, or poultry or as a main course with a green salad and a loaf of your favorite ~~...~~ ~~bread~~

To remove corn kernels, hold the ~~husked~~ ~~corn~~ cob vertically by the stem end, with the narrow end in a bowl. Using a special corn kernel scraper or a paring knife and starting at the top of the cob, slice down the length of the cob, cutting off the kernels by scraping the knife under the kernels and into the cob itself to release some of the milky corn pulp. Repeat, turning the cob, until all of the kernels and a lot of the pulp are in the bowl.

If time allows, place the diced tomatoes in a colander, sprinkle with coarse (kosher) salt or sea salt, and let drain for 45 to 60 minutes.

# SUMMER'S BEST CORN CHOWDER

Here's a creamy chowder with full corn flavor; note that it's made without flour or cream. With shrimp added (see the variation opposite), the chowder becomes a great height-of-summer supper. And the recipe makes enough to feed a crowd or ~~provide ample leftovers.~~

~~...~~

2   teaspoons vegetable oil

4   thick slices bacon, cut into $1/2$-inch lengths

3   medium-large onions, coarsely chopped

5   slender carrots, trimmed, peeled, and sliced $1/4$ inch thick on a sharp diagonal

3   slender celery ribs, trimmed, strings removed (Celery Stringing, page 18), and sliced on a sharp diagonal $1/4$ inch thick

1   pound (4 or 5 small-medium) new or boiling potatoes, peeled, quartered lengthwise, and cut crosswise $1/2$ inch thick

2   cans (about 14 ounces each) chicken broth, preferably reduced-sodium

3   fresh thyme sprigs or $1/2$ teaspoon dried

7   cups **corn kernels** with milky pulp (cut and scraped from 11 to 15 ears), 4 or 5 cobs reserved

$2^{1/2}$   cups whole milk, or more as needed

Salt and freshly ground black pepper, to taste

3   large ripe tomatoes, peeled, cored, seeded (Tomato Basics, page 22), and cut into large dice

3   tablespoons $1/2$-inch lengths snipped fresh chives

Pilot, oyster, or other plain crackers, for serving

**1.** Combine the oil and bacon in a nonreactive large, heavy saucepan or casserole over medium heat. Cook the bacon fairly slowly, stirring frequently with a wooden spoon and pouring off the excess fat once or twice, until the bacon pieces are lightly golden but only partially crisp, 10 to 15 minutes. With a skimmer or slotted spoon, transfer the bacon to a paper towel–lined plate to drain; set aside. Pour off all but 2 tablespoons of the bacon fat from the pan.

**2.** Add the onions, carrots, and celery to the pan, tossing with a wooden spoon to coat. Sauté over medium heat, tossing frequently, until the vegetables have softened slightly but are not browned, about 5 minutes. Add the potatoes, chicken broth, 1½ cups of water (which should only partially cover the solids), and thyme. Break or cut the reserved **corncobs** in half; tuck them into the liquid. Cover and simmer the soup gently until the potatoes are tender but not mushy, about 15 minutes.

**3.** If you have time, uncover the soup and set aside to cool at room temperature for about an hour, to allow the flavor to develop even more and the fat to rise to the top of the soup for easy skimming. Remove and discard the thyme sprigs and corncobs, using a small knife to scrape all possible pulp and liquid from each cob back into the soup. Skim the fat and froth from the surface with a skimmer or large metal spoon.

**4.** Stir the corn kernels with their liquid into the soup. Bring to a simmer over medium heat and then simmer, adjusting the heat as needed, until the kernels are tender, about 3 minutes. With a skimmer or slotted spoon, transfer about 3½ cups of the solids to a food processor; process until coarsely pureed. Stir the puree back into the soup along with the milk; return nearly to a simmer (do not boil or the milk may curdle). Adjust the consistency so the soup is lightly **thickened** (if necessary, puree slightly more solids and return the puree to the soup, or thin as needed with a little more milk). Season to taste with salt and a few generous grinds of pepper. (The recipe can be made **in advance** to this point, cooled, and then refrigerated. The flavor of the chowder will deepen on standing, so do so if possible.)

**5.** Return the chowder to a simmer, if necessary. Stir in the reserved bacon, the tomatoes, and half of the chives; cook gently for few moments to heat the tomatoes through. Correct the seasonings again; add a little more milk, if needed, to thin the soup slightly. Serve hot in wide soup bowls, scattering the remaining chives on the surface of each portion. Pass pilot, oyster, or other plain crackers alongside.

## VARIATION: CORN AND SHRIMP CHOWDER

¾ **pound small-medium shrimp, peeled and deveined (Shrimp Basics, page 22)**

Scatter the shrimp over the surface after adding the bacon and tomatoes in step 5. Cover and simmer (do not boil) just until the shrimp turn pink and are opaque, about 3 minutes. Then proceed as directed in the recipe.

Simmering the corncobs in the soup adds plenty of real corn flavor. Try not to waste anything when you're cooking.

I like to add texture and body to a soup by thickening it with a vegetable puree rather than with the more traditional butter and flour combination, or roux. This adds more flavor as well as nutrients and without the fat you would use for the roux. Pureed starchy vegetables, like potatoes and beans, add the most body. Pureed cooked carrots, onions, mushrooms, broccoli, or peas are also excellent thickeners, but with a lighter touch. I use this same thickening method for stews, such as Chicken and Vegetable Curry and Chicken Paprika (see pages 114 and 117).

**Save this** for a fine mid-summer night's supper or simple light lunch, with a salad.

**How do I store leftover tomato paste?** Tomato paste is available in ~~tubes, which is, if you can use the exact amount called for in a recipe without worrying~~ about leftovers—the tube goes right back in the refrigerator. But when I do have to open a can, I use the amount I need and then scoop out level measuring tablespoons of the remainder, place them on a wax paper–lined baking sheet, and freeze them. When frozen, I scoop the measured amounts into a sealable freezer bag and store in the freezer for up to 6 months for easy access.

# TUSCAN-STYLE TOMATO AND BREAD SOUP

From Tuscany, this dish is a "pap" of dead-ripe tomatoes and coarse country bread. As the Italians put it, this soup is "comforting like the mother." Notice in the ingredient list that in some instances dried herbs should *not* be substituted for the fresh—the special flavor of fresh makes a noticeable difference.

MAKES 4 TO 6 FIRST-COURSE SERVINGS

2   tablespoons olive oil

1   large or 2 medium-size yellow onions, coarsely chopped

4   scallions (white and green portions), trimmed and thinly sliced

⅓   cup chopped fresh basil leaves, plus several small sprigs for garnish (do not substitute dried)

8   or 10 fresh sage leaves, chopped (if available; do not substitute dried)

4   fresh oregano sprigs, leaves stripped from stems and chopped (if available, or substitute a small pinch of dried oregano)
Salt, to taste
Pinch of dried red pepper flakes

4   garlic cloves, thinly sliced

2   to 2½ pounds ripe tomatoes, peeled and seeded (Tomato Basics, page 22)

1   teaspoon **tomato paste**

8   ounces coarse Italian, peasant, or sourdough bread with crust, preferably 1 or 2 days old, cut into 1-inch cubes (4 to 6 cups)

3   cups chicken broth, preferably reduced-sodium homemade
Freshly ground black pepper, to taste
Fruity extra-virgin olive oil, for serving
Parmesan cheese shavings or freshly grated Parmesan cheese, for serving

**1.** Heat the olive oil in a nonreactive large saucepan or casserole over medium heat. Add the onions, scallions, half of the basil, the sage, oregano, a sprinkling of salt, and the dried pepper flakes. Cook, stirring occasionally, until the onions soften, about 10 minutes. Add the garlic and cook, stirring, until the onions are very soft and lightly golden, about 5 minutes longer.

**2.** Add the tomatoes, either breaking them into rough chunks with your fingers as you add them to the pot or breaking them up with a wooden spoon as they cook. Stir in the tomato paste and a sprinkling of salt. Cover the pan and stew the tomatoes gently for about 20 minutes, stirring them with a wooden spoon from time to time and breaking them up even more as they cook.

3. Meanwhile, if the bread is not day old, dry out the cubes of bread slightly on a baking sheet in a 300°F. oven. Add the **bread cubes** to the tomato mixture and cook, stirring, for about 5 minutes, so that the bread cubes absorb the tomato juices. Stir in the broth and bring the mixture to a boil. Partially cover the pan, remove from the heat, and set aside for at least 1 hour so the bread can thicken the soup.

4. Reheat the mixture over medium heat until it is warmed through. Stir in the remaining basil, plus more salt and pepper to taste, if desired. Serve warm, topping each bowlful with a basil sprig and drizzling some extra-virgin olive oil over each portion. **Form thin shavings of Parmesan** with a vegetable peeler, letting a few shavings fall over the surface of each portion of the soup. (Or simply pass a bowl of grated Parmesan at the table.) Make sure there's a pepper mill on the table.

Thickening the soup with cubes of bread adds a satisfying richness that cannot be duplicated by other thickeners such as flour.

To form thin shavings of Parmesan, have the cheese at room temperature. Hold the cheese over each portion of soup and use a vegetable peeler to peel off thin shavings, letting them drop onto the soup.

In the summer serve this soup chilled. You can substitute fresh lime juice for the lemon juice.

Follow this basic technique for any pureed vegetable soup. And then experiment with different seasonings to complement the ingredients you're using. This technique will work for any of your favorite cream soup recipes— just replace the heavy cream with potato.

For a thicker soup, increase the amount of potato—doubling the amount makes for a soup with a substantial texture.

For a slightly sweet taste, use half all-purpose potatoes and half sweet potatoes.

The fresh ginger adds a touch of sweetness plus a pleasant spicy heat.

# CURRIED CREAM OF BROCCOLI SOUP

Despite what I've called this recipe, you won't find any heavy cream in the ingredient list. Pureed cooked **potato thickens** the soup and adds a creamy texture.

MAKES 4 SOUP-COURSE SERVINGS

1½ pounds broccoli, trimmed, stalks and florets separated, and each cut into ½-inch dice

2   medium all-purpose **potatoes** (about 8 ounces), peeled and cut into ½-inch dice

1   medium onion, chopped

3   cups chicken broth

1   tablespoon curry powder

2   teaspoons grated **fresh ginger**

1   teaspoon ground coriander
    Coarse (kosher) salt, to taste

1   teaspoon fresh lemon juice

4   teaspoons plain yogurt

1   tablespoon very thinly sliced scallion greens

**1.** Combine the broccoli stalks, potatoes, onion, broth, curry powder, ginger, and coriander in a large saucepan. Bring to a simmer over medium heat. Cover and cook until the broccoli stalks and potatoes are crisp-tender, about 10 minutes. Add the broccoli florets and cook another 10 minutes until all are very tender. Set the saucepan aside, covered, to cool slightly, about 10 minutes.

**2.** With a slotted spoon, transfer the solids to a food processor. Puree until smooth. With the motor running, gradually add the hot broth from the saucepan.

**3.** Return the soup to the saucepan. Bring to a simmer. Season to taste with salt. Stir in the lemon juice. Ladle the soup into bowls. Garnish with yogurt and a sprinkle of scallion tops.

## VARIATION: CURRIED CREAM OF CAULIFLOWER SOUP

For the broccoli, substitute 1¼ pounds of cauliflower (1 small head), trimmed and cut into small dice. Add all at once in step 1 and proceed with the recipe.

## VARIATION: CURRIED CREAM OF CARROT SOUP

For the broccoli, substitute 1¼ pounds of carrots, trimmed, peeled, and thinly sliced. Add all at once in step 1 and proceed with the recipe.

## VARIATION: CURRIED CREAM OF JERUSALEM ARTICHOKE SOUP

For the broccoli, substitute 1½ pounds of Jerusalem artichokes, peeled and cut into small dice. Add all at once in step 1 and proceed with the recipe.

## VARIATION: CURRIED CREAM OF CELERY ROOT SOUP

For the broccoli, substitute 1½ pounds of celery root, peeled and cut into small dice. Add all at once in step 1 and proceed with the recipe.

# Three

# PASTA AND RISOTTO

**Techniques:** | Basic Chunky Tomato Sauce
adding fresh herbs at end of cooking/using oil and
butter for sautéing/sautéing garlic/reducing a
liquid to thicken

**Technique:** | Pasta with Tomato Sauce and Ricotta
cooking fresh pasta

**Techniques:** | Spaghetti and Meatballs
making meatballs/flavoring oil with garlic/testing
pasta for doneness/how to serve pasta

**Techniques:** | Linguine with Red Clam Sauce
steaming shellfish in a sauce/flavoring with fresh
parsley/cooking pasta in a sauce

**Techniques:** | Orecchiette with Mushrooms, Ham, and Peas
quick sauté for sauce/which pasta shape goes with
which sauce/adding pasta cooking liquid for sauce

| Winter Pasta with Fresh Greens, Cherry Tomatoes,
and Roasted Garlic
**Techniques:** | roasting garlic/low-fat method for pasta sauces

**Techniques:** | Pasta e Fagioli (Pasta and Bean Soup-Stew)
sautéing vegetables in oil/mashing beans to thicken/adding fresh herbs at end of cooking

Techniques: | Rigatoni with Summer Vegetables and Italian Fontina
adding pasta cooking liquid for sauce/adding cubes of cheese

**Techniques:** | Pasta with Marinated Tomatoes and Four Cheeses
salting tomatoes to concentrate flavor/adding cubes of cheese for sauce

**Technique:** | Old-Fashioned Macaroni and Cheese
making white sauce

**Techniques:** | Luscious Baked Pasta Gratin
making a gratin/sweating vegetables with water

**Technique:** | Pasta Frittata
using leftover pasta

**Technique:** | Basic Method for Risotto
cooking risotto

**Technique:** | Risotto Primavera
adding vegetables to risotto

**Technique:** | Creamy Polenta with Mascarpone
cooking polenta

**We all grew up with pasta, in some form or another, regardless of our ethnic backgrounds.** Pasta has always been the mainstay of the efficient home cook, lending itself to satisfying and endless variations. And because pasta dishes can usually be tossed together in a matter of minutes, they're ideal for after work or for improvised suppers with friends.

Perfect pasta is as easy as bringing a pot of water to the boil. The trick is not to overcook—you're aiming for al dente, firm but tender to the bite, with no hard, white center core.

A great source of complex carbohydrates, the pasta noodle itself contains very little fat and no cholesterol (except if it's an egg noodle) as long as you don't drench it with a fat-laden cream sauce. This chapter includes some light pasta and sauce combinations as well as versions of a few baked casserole favorites where I've reduced or eliminated the amount of the usual heavy cream and cheese.

If you're not acquainted with the wonders of risotto, then this is a good place to start. When a food stylist friend of mine goes to a potluck dinner, she brings all the ingredients for risotto and then makes it on the spot while everyone watches, chatting away and offering cooking tips. If you can manage it and are not intimidated by a crowd in the kitchen, cooking with others can be a satisfying social occasion. Although risotto is actually a rice dish, its ease of preparation, despite the aura of mystery—or difficulty—that surrounds its making, and its practically endless versatility are traits that make it a logical partner with pasta as part of a cooking repertoire.

As for polenta, one of my favorite foods, this simple dish has become more and more a staple side dish. Its simplicity is a perfect foil for stews and sauces, and it is well worth the time and attention it requires.

**Why do I use a combination of butter and oil for sautéing?** The oil allows for sautéing at a higher heat without burning the butter.

**When you sauté garlic, do not overbrown it over too high a heat—this can produce a bitter flavor. Use your nose—when you smell the aroma of garlic in the air, it's probably done. If, however, you sauté garlic very slowly over very, very low heat, it will caramelize to a golden brown, acquiring a delicious sweet flavor.**

# PASTA

## BASIC CHUNKY TOMATO SAUCE

For quick pasta dinners, tomato sauces are among the best bets. Tomato sauces can be made with fresh tomatoes or canned tomatoes, or with a combination of the two.

This basic sauce, chunky and flavorful, is cooked briefly, tossed with pasta a minute or so, a carbohydrate-rich, satisfying meal in minutes. I often prepare a big batch in late summer, buying a bushel of overripe tomatoes at the farmers' market at a give-away price. The sauce can then be canned or frozen in small containers and I can enjoy the fresh taste of summer throughout the fall and winter. Last fall, Roy Finamore (editor and originator of this book) and I simmered up 75 pounds of tomatoes—hot, tiring work, but we've each reaped the rewards all year long.

If fresh basil is available, add a few leaves, finely shredded, as you remove the sauce from the heat.

MAKES 2 1/2 TO 3 CUPS

- 1 tablespoon unsalted butter
- 1 tablespoon olive oil
- 1 onion, coarsely chopped
- 2 or 3 garlic cloves, minced
- 3 pounds fresh tomatoes, peeled, seeded (Tomato Basics, page 22), and coarsely chopped, or use a combination of fresh and canned tomatoes
- 1 teaspoon salt, or to taste
- 1 bay leaf
  Pinch of dried thyme or oregano (optional)
  Freshly ground black pepper, to taste
- 2 tablespoons chopped fresh parsley
- 2 tablespoons finely shredded fresh basil (optional)

**1.** Heat the **butter and oil** in a nonreactive heavy saucepan over medium heat. Add the onion and sauté, stirring occasionally, until wilted, 4 to 5 minutes. Add the garlic and **sauté** until the onion is very soft, about 2 minutes longer.

**2.** Add the tomatoes, salt to taste, the bay leaf, and thyme or oregano. **Boil,** uncovered, over medium-high heat until the liquid reduces to a thick puree and binds the chunks of tomato, 15 to 20 minutes. Stir often to prevent scorching. Remove the bay leaf.

**3. Just before serving, add** pepper to taste, salt if needed, the parsley, and the **fresh basil,** if using.

## VARIATION: CHUNKY TOMATO SAUCE WITH MUSHROOMS

Sauté 1 to 1½ cups (2 to 4 ounces) sliced white mushrooms in 1 tablespoon olive oil in a nonstick skillet over medium-high heat until softened, about 4 minutes. Add to the tomato sauce as it is finished.

## VARIATION: CHUNKY TOMATO SAUCE WITH OLIVES AND CAPERS

Add 2 tablespoons slivered black olives—kalamata are a good choice—and 2 tablespoons rinsed and drained capers to the sauce when it is done.

Boiling down or reducing a liquid is an excellent way to thicken and concentrate its flavor without using flour, cornstarch, or other thickener that often produces a heavier texture with a muddy flavor.

Cooking fresh herbs too long will cause them to lose their fresh, bright green color. For best results, add at the end of the cooking.

Served with a crisp green salad and a freshly baked loaf of crusty whole wheat bread, this makes a festive supper for four, or three if the appetites are truly ravished.

If you can get freshly made ricotta at an Italian dairy store or cheese shop, by all means use it since it does make a real difference.

Fresh pasta is incomparably tender and full of flavor—a pasta machine for rolling can be a worthwhile investment if you use it often. If you have a nearby source for homemade pasta, take advantage of it. However, the quality of domestic and imported dried pasta is such that it is excellent in any dish. Fresh pasta cooks very quickly—in fact, you should begin to test for doneness about a minute after adding the pasta to the boiling water. The obvious advantage of dried pasta is that it keeps longer than fresh. The fresh is best used as quickly as possible, although it can be refrigerated for a day or two; it can also be dried.

# PASTA WITH TOMATO SAUCE AND RICOTTA

This is one of the simplest pasta dishes, based on a dish I ate at Trattoria da Alfredo in Greenwich Village in the 1970s. The sautéed sliced mushrooms are optional, but they add nice texture and flavor notes.

Makes 4 servings

2½ cups basic Chunky Tomato Sauce (page 62)

Salt, to taste

1 pound **ricotta** cheese, preferably **freshly made**

¼ teaspoon freshly grated nutmeg, or more to taste

Freshly ground black pepper, to taste

1 tablespoon unsalted butter (optional)

1 tablespoon olive oil (optional)

1½ to 2 cups (2 to 4 ounces) thickly sliced mushrooms (optional, Mushroom Basics, page 21)

1 pound wide **pasta**, such as green tagliatelle or fettuccine, preferably **fresh**

2 tablespoons chopped fresh basil or parsley

Freshly grated Parmesan cheese, for serving

**1.** Prepare the tomato sauce. Keep warm in a nonreactive medium saucepan. Bring a large pot of water to a boil for the pasta. Add a little salt.

**2.** Meanwhile, in a large serving bowl, use a wooden spoon to beat the ricotta with salt and pepper to taste and nutmeg until fluffy. Set aside at room temperature.

**3.** If you'd like to include sautéed mushrooms in this dish, heat the butter and olive oil in a large nonstick skillet over medium-high heat. Add the mushrooms; sprinkle with salt and pepper to taste, and let them sit for a few moments until sizzling. Sauté, tossing frequently with a wooden spoon, until lightly golden, about 4 minutes longer. Remove from the heat and cover to keep warm.

**4.** Add the pasta to the boiling water and boil until just tender, usually 2 to 3 minutes for **fresh pasta,** longer for dried. Drain well.

**5.** Divide the pasta among 4 warmed serving bowls (or arrange in a large serving bowl). Ladle the hot tomato sauce over the pasta, dividing equally. Gently spoon the ricotta mixture over the center of each portion. Scatter the mushrooms over, if using, then sprinkle with the basil or parsley. Serve immediately, passing grated Parmesan cheese and a pepper mill at the table.

## VARIATION: PASTA WITH TOMATO SAUCE, RICOTTA, AND GRILLED EGGPLANT

Substitute grilled eggplant slices for the mushrooms.

Peel a small eggplant and cut lengthwise into ¼-inch-thick slices. Brush both sides of the slices with olive oil and season with salt and pepper. Place on a grill rack or broiler-pan rack coated with nonstick cooking spray. Grill eggplant 4 to 6 inches above medium-hot coals or from preheated broiler until lightly browned on both sides, about 10 minutes. Cut into small pieces.

The best pasta is made from hard durum wheat, which gives the pasta a firm texture.

Flavored pastas, whether fresh or dried, add a whole other dimension to the usual pasta dish. Spinach and whole wheat types are readily available, but look for carrot, beet, wild mushroom, and herb varieties. Flavored fresh pasta generally has a more pronounced flavor than dried and can range from tomato or basil to blue corn or cilantro. For flavored dried pasta, choose a lighter sauce, while for fresh pasta, you can pair it with a stronger sauce.

For a leaner meatball, substitute ground turkey for some or all of the ground meats.

Don't buy already grated Romano, Parmesan, or other hard cheeses, which lose their flavor as they sit (and are more expensive per pound than a whole piece). Purchase chunks of the cheese and grate as needed for the best flavor. Refrigerate or freeze the chunks, well wrapped, for up to 6 months.

Soaking soft bread crumbs in milk makes for meatballs with a softer, richer texture.

Be sure to handle the meat lightly. Mashing or squeezing the mixture will result in tough meatballs.

Sizzling a whole garlic clove in oil to flavor it, then discarding it, is traditional in Sicily and Southern Italy. It's a good way to flavor with garlic without overwhelming.

# SPAGHETTI AND MEATBALLS

Self-important gourmands will sneer that "there's no such dish in Italy." True, but admit it—don't you love spaghetti and meatballs? These are tasty, and this is a heartier dish than most of the pastas in this collection.

**Meatballs**

| | |
|---|---|
| ½ | pound ground beef chuck, well chilled |
| ½ | pound ground pork, well chilled (or use a total of 1 pound chuck) |
| ½ | cup soft fresh bread crumbs |
| ⅓ | cup milk |
| ¼ | cup well-beaten egg (about 1½ large eggs) |
| ¼ | cup **freshly grated** Romano or Parmesan cheese |
| ¼ | cup chopped fresh parsley |
| 1½ | teaspoons salt |
| | Freshly ground black pepper, to taste (be generous) |
| 2 | tablespoons olive oil |
| 2 | large garlic cloves, smashed and peeled |

| | |
|---|---|
| 2½ | to 3 cups Basic Chunky Tomato Sauce (page 62) or any tomato sauce |
| 1 | pound dried spaghetti |
| ¼ | cup chopped fresh parsley (optional) |
| | Freshly grated Parmesan cheese, for serving |

1. **To make the meatballs:** Mix together the ground meats until thoroughly blended. Stir together the bread crumbs and milk in a small bowl; let stand a few minutes for the **crumbs to soften.** Combine the beaten egg, cheese, parsley, salt, and pepper to taste in a medium bowl. Turn the bread crumbs into a strainer in the sink; press gently with your fingertips to squeeze out as much milk as possible. Stir the moistened crumbs into the egg mixture; then add the mixed meats. With your fingers, combine the meat with the bread crumb mixture without **mashing or squeezing.**

**2.** Place a sheet of wax paper on a dinner plate. Form meatballs with the meat mixture, using your palms to roll them evenly to slightly less than 1 inch in diameter. Place the meatballs on the wax paper as you form them (you should finish with a total of 30).

**3.** Heat 1 tablespoon of the olive oil in a large nonstick skillet over medium heat. Add half of the garlic to the skillet and **let it sizzle** gently until golden, about 3 minutes. Discard the garlic. Place half of the meatballs in the hot skillet without crowding; cook without stirring until golden brown on the bottom, about 3 minutes. Adjust the heat if necessary; the meat should sizzle, but gently. Turn the meatballs over with tongs and cook until brown on that side, about 2 minutes longer. Now cook the meatballs for 2 or 3 minutes longer, rolling them around in the skillet with a wooden spoon or turning them with the tongs, so they are browned all over. As the meatballs are done, remove them with a slotted spoon to a plate. Repeat with the remaining oil, garlic, and meatballs.

**4.** With a paper towel, blot the fat from the skillet. Add the tomato sauce to the skillet and bring to a simmer, using a wooden spoon to scrape up the browned bits in the bottom of the pan into the sauce. Return the meatballs to the sauce. Cover the skillet and simmer for 5 minutes. Turn the meatballs over with tongs; simmer for 5 minutes longer. Cut into one meatball; they're done when the center of the meat is no longer pink.

**5.** Shortly before serving time, bring a large pot of water to a full rolling boil for the pasta. Add salt, then slip the spaghetti into the water. Boil until just **al dente,** firm but tender, usually 10 to 12 minutes. Meanwhile, if necessary, reheat the meatballs and sauce in the skillet. Drain the spaghetti well, then divide among 4 warmed pasta bowls. Stir the parsley and some freshly ground pepper into the sauce. Spoon the meatballs and sauce over the spaghetti, dividing evenly. Serve immediately, passing freshly grated Parmesan and a pepper mill at the table.

Al dente, which literally means "to the tooth" in Italian, is the proper stage to which to cook pasta. It means the pasta is tender but still has a bite of firmness (but not rawness) at its center. To test, run a strand under cold water first, then bite. You should not see any white, uncooked portion in the center of the pasta. Don't overcook; mushy pasta is not one of life's pleasures.

How do I serve pasta? Heated serving bowls and plates are a must; I have a set of inexpensive wide, shallow bowls from Italy that I use especially for pasta, rice, and hearty soups. I use flat plates for more elegant arrangements.

Where to dish? Pasta with a hearty sauce can be tossed in a large bowl or shallow serving dish, then ritually dished up at the table. For more studied presentations or where guests can mix their own ingredients, I arrange individual plates in the kitchen and then serve.

For a main course, count four portions for a pound of pasta with sauce, or for large appetites, three. As a first course, serve small plates of pasta, remembering less is more; a pound of pasta will be enough for six to eight first-course portions.

Steaming the clams right in the sauce keeps them moist and also infuses the sauce with their flavor.

We're so used to seeing parsley as a sprig garnishing a plate that we think it's good for nothing more. Not so. Chopped and added to a dish in sufficient quantity, it can add lots of fresh, almost minty flavor. Also keep in mind there are two types: the familiar frilly curly sprig, which is quite mild, and the "greener"-flavored flat-leaf parsley, often called Italian.

For this dish, I like to toss the drained, very slightly undercooked pasta in the sauce to finish cooking for a moment or two. The sauce infuses the pasta with even more flavor and the starch from the pasta helps to thicken the sauce slightly.

# LINGUINE WITH RED CLAM SAUCE

If you can find Manila clams or the tiny clams called cockles (with meat the size of your smallest fingernail), use them here. They steam to tender perfection very quickly in the tomato sauce. As per Italian tradition, no grated cheese is used with seafood pasta sauce. With a salad, good bread, and a glass of red or white wine (you prefer either), this is a wonderful meal—relaxed, gregarious, and utterly satisfying.

MAKES 2 MAIN-COURSE SERVINGS

Salt, to taste
1½ cups Basic Chunky Tomato Sauce (page 62)
½ pound dried linguine
2 to 2½ dozen small clams, such as Manila, littlenecks, or cockles, rinsed well under cold running water (Shellfish Basics, page 21)
2 tablespoons chopped fresh flat-leaf parsley
Freshly ground black pepper

**1.** Bring a large pot of water to a boil for the pasta. Add a little salt.

**2.** Meanwhile, place the tomato sauce in a nonreactive wide deep skillet or casserole. Cover and bring to a boil over medium heat.

**3.** When the water is boiling, add the linguine.

**4.** After a couple of minutes, scatter the clams in an even layer over the boiling tomato sauce. Adjust the heat to maintain a steady but not violent boil; cover tightly. **Steam** the clams just until their shells open, no longer, about 5 minutes. (Tiny cockles can take as little as 3½ minutes, littlenecks usually 7 or 8 minutes. Timing can vary; don't overcook.) As soon as the clams open (discard any that don't), turn off the heat and **sprinkle with the parsley** and pepper to taste (you shouldn't need any salt). Leave the lid ajar.

**5.** When the linguine is slightly undercooked, drain well. Add the pasta to the sauce in the pan over low heat and **toss** with 2 large spoons, turning the pasta over to coat it with the sauce. Then transfer to serving bowls. Serve at once, bringing an extra bowl to the table for the empty shells.

## VARIATION: LINGUINE WITH MUSSEL SAUCE

Substitute an equal amount of mussels for the clams and steam the same way.

# ORECCHIETTE WITH MUSHROOMS, HAM, AND PEAS

This is a comforting dish, put together in minutes. It is also good made with fusilli.

MAKES 2 MAIN-COURSE SERVINGS

|  | Salt, to taste |
| --- | --- |
| 2½ | tablespoons olive oil |
| 1 | garlic clove, smashed and peeled but left whole |
| 2½ | to 3 cups (6 to 8 ounces) white mushrooms (Mushroom Basics, page 21), halved and thickly sliced |
|  | Freshly ground black pepper, to taste |
| ¾ | cup frozen peas (right from the freezer) |
| ½ | cup slivered good-quality country ham (or use prosciutto) |
| ½ | pound dried orecchiette, fusilli, or cavatelli (or other short pasta) |
| ⅓ | cup freshly grated Parmesan cheese, plus more for serving |

1. Bring a large pot of water to a boil for the pasta. Add a little salt.

2. Meanwhile, heat 2 tablespoons of the olive oil with the garlic in a large skillet over medium heat. Let the garlic sizzle until golden, 1 to 2 minutes. Then, discard it. Raise the heat to medium-high.

3. Add the mushrooms to the skillet; sprinkle with salt and pepper to taste. Let them sit and sizzle for 1 to 2 minutes as they begin to release their liquid. Then begin to toss the mushrooms frequently with a wooden spoon until they wilt and begin to brown, 3 or 4 minutes. Break up the frozen peas and scatter them in with the mushrooms. **Sauté,** tossing constantly, until the peas are heated through, about 3 minutes. Add the ham and toss for 1 minute longer.

4. Add the pasta to the boiling water and boil until al dente, firm but tender. With a mug, carefully remove about 1 cup of the pasta cooking liquid (page 71) and set it aside. Drain the pasta well; return it to its pot and place over medium-low heat. Add the mushroom mixture, the remaining ½ tablespoon olive oil, the Parmesan cheese, and ⅓ cup of the reserved pasta cooking water. Sprinkle with pepper and toss gently with 2 large spoons until the ingredients are well combined. Add a little more liquid if the mixture doesn't seem nicely moist.

5. Serve immediately, passing more Parmesan and a pepper mill at the table.

This is one of the easiest strategies for pasta—you quickly sauté a mixture of ingredients, which is then combined with the cooked pasta, becoming its "sauce." Often the topping is ready in the time it takes to cook the pasta.

Which shape for which sauce? Regular strands, such as spaghetti and vermicelli, go well with tomato sauces, olive oil and garlic, pesto, and clam and seafood sauces; narrow strands—angel hair and spaghettini—marry better with delicate, not-too-chunky sauces. Fettuccine and linguine (long, flat noodles) take well to butter and grated hard cheeses, cream-based sauces, and clam and seafood sauces. Chunky sauces with bits that get caught in nooks and crannies are meant for short pasta shapes, such as rotelle, ziti, penne, rigatoni, fusilli, radiatore—you get the idea. If you want to use tiny shapes—orzo, ditalini, conchigliette—cut the ingredients in the sauce to the same size as the pasta. Added to soups and stews, these shapes add body.

How do I serve this? Here again (as with hearty soups), pasta is an example of a dish classically served as a first course, though I find it filling enough to serve as a meal. With nothing more than a green salad, bread, and a glass of red wine, you've got a comforting midweek supper.

Roasting garlic tames its flavor, leaving it sweet and mellow. When you do roast the cloves, roast extra ones; they will keep for about a week in the refrigerator and can be tossed into soups, pastas, stews, and salad dressings. Longer roasting (Garlic Basics, page 19) results in a deliciously pungent taste.

# WINTER PASTA WITH FRESH GREENS, CHERRY TOMATOES, AND ROASTED GARLIC

This is a good example of a pasta dish that's thrown together in about the time it takes to bring the water to a boil. Note the variation with slivers of leftover roasted chicken.

**Roasted Garlic**

6 to 8 large garlic cloves, thin skins left on

1 teaspoon olive oil

**Pasta**

Salt, to taste

1 tablespoon olive oil

1 red onion, thinly sliced

1 yellow bell pepper, cored, seeded (Bell Pepper Basics, page 16), and cut into long, thin slivers

2 scallions (white and green portions), trimmed and thinly sliced on a sharp diagonal

¼ teaspoon dried red pepper flakes

1 pound dried rigatoni, penne, ziti, or other short pasta

2 bunches escarole or broccoli rabe, trimmed and cut into 1-inch-wide ribbons

12 ripe cherry tomatoes, halved

Pinch of freshly grated nutmeg

Shredded fresh basil leaves (optional)

¼ cup freshly grated Parmesan cheese, or more to taste, for serving

Freshly ground black pepper, for serving

**1. To roast the garlic:** Preheat the oven to 375°F. Toss the garlic with the oil in a small baking pan. Roast in the oven until tender when poked with a small knife, 12 to 15 minutes. Cool, peel, and halve the garlic cloves lengthwise.

**2. To prepare the pasta:** Bring a large pot of water to a boil. Add a little salt.

**3.** Meanwhile, heat the olive oil in a large nonstick skillet over medium-high heat. Add the red onion, bell pepper, scallions, pepper flakes, and a sprinkling of salt;

cook, tossing with a wooden spoon, until the onion is crisp-tender, 2 to 3 minutes. Add the roasted garlic and cook for 1 minute longer. Remove from the heat.

**4.** Add the pasta to the boiling water and cook until partially done, 6 to 8 minutes. Add the escarole or broccoli rabe to the pot and cook until the pasta and greens are just tender, about 5 minutes longer. With a mug, scoop out and set aside about 1 cup of the **pasta cooking liquid.** Drain the pasta and greens well.

**5.** Return the pasta and greens to the pasta pot and set over low heat. Add the bell pepper mixture, tomatoes, nutmeg, and basil. Heat through, tossing and adding enough of the reserved pasta cooking liquid to moisten the mixture as well as a sprinkling of the grated cheese. Taste and correct the seasonings, adding salt, pepper flakes, and/or nutmeg, if needed. Serve immediately, sprinkled with more cheese and fresh pepper.

Here's an old trick long used in Italian kitchens: Add a little pasta cooking liquid to the drained pasta to moisten it and a sprinkling of grated Parmesan to make a "sauce" that's low in fat.

## VARIATION: PASTA WITH GREENS, CHERRY TOMATOES, AND ROASTED CHICKEN

Add 1 to 2 cups roasted chicken strips when you heat the ingredients through in step 5. This is great when you have some leftover chicken but not enough to make an entire meal.

This variation is also delicious with leftover cooked ham, whether it be baked or a country ham. Substitute for the 1 to 2 cups roasted chicken.

How do I serve this? While it can be a first course, I think of this hearty soup-stew as a meal in itself. Serve with a green salad, good bread, and a soft red wine, such as a Merlot, Chianti, or Rioja. Then try fruit, an ice, or ice cream for dessert.

I usually use canned broth for soups like this, since it will get a flavor boost from all of the fresh vegetables as it simmers.

Sautéing vegetables first in olive oil is the basis for almost all soups. It provides a subtle background of flavors against which the main ingredients can play. When you sauté vegetables (or virtually anything), it's important that the pan and the fat be hot before adding the food. It helps prevent sticking, loss of juices, and the food from steaming and becoming soggy. Don't crowd the pan or the food will steam. Get in the habit.

# PASTA E FAGIOLI (PASTA AND BEAN SOUP-STEW)

A personal version of the soul-satisfying Italian peasant dish, this has become a favorite supper at my house. The pasta and beans, when combined, form a com-

MAKES 6 MAIN-COURSE SERVINGS

- 1 to 2 tablespoons fruity olive oil, plus more for serving, if desired
- 2 red or yellow onions, halved and thickly sliced
- 2 small carrots, trimmed, peeled, and sliced 1/2 inch thick
- 1/2 red or yellow bell pepper, cored, seeded (Bell Pepper Basics, page 16), and cut into thin strips about 1 inch long
- 4 garlic cloves, minced
- 1/3 cup shredded fresh basil leaves or 1/2 teaspoon dried
  Pinch *each* of dried oregano and dried red pepper flakes
- 1 bay leaf
- 3 or 4 ounces smoked ham, cut into 1/4-inch dice (optional)
- 1 cup drained canned whole tomatoes
- 7 cups **chicken broth**, or 3 1/2 cups *each* of chicken broth and water
- 4 cups cooked white beans (Dried Bean Basics, page 17), or 2 cans (19 ounces each) cannellini beans, drained and rinsed
- 2 1/2 cups (5 ounces) dried rotelle (wheel) pasta (or use shells, rigatoni, penne, or other short pasta)
  Salt and freshly ground black pepper, to taste
- 2 scallions (white and green portions), trimmed and thinly sliced on a sharp diagonal
  Freshly grated Parmesan cheese, for serving

**1.** Place a nonreactive deep saucepan over medium-high heat. Add the olive oil and heat for a few moments. Add the onions, carrots, and bell pepper; **sauté,** tossing occasionally, until softened slightly, about 8 minutes. Add the garlic, 3 tablespoons of the fresh basil (or 1/2 teaspoon dried), oregano, pepper flakes, bay leaf, and ham; cook, tossing, until the vegetables are softened, about 2 minutes longer.

**2.** Add the tomatoes and cook, crushing the tomatoes against the bottom of the pot with the side of a wooden spoon, until they are reduced to the consistency of a thick tomato sauce, about 6 minutes. Add the chicken broth and beans and bring to a boil. As the mixture comes to a boil, use the wooden spoon to **mash** about one-quarter of the beans against the side of the pot to thicken the soup slightly (the broth should be quite thin at this point; it will thicken more later). With a skimmer or a large metal spoon, skim off any froth from the surface as necessary. Lower the heat, cover, and simmer for 20 minutes. (You can prepare the soup **in advance** to this point. Cool, and then refrigerate for a day or two.)

**3.** Ten to 15 minutes before serving, return the soup to a boil. With a skimmer or large metal spoon, spoon off all possible fat and foam from the surface. Add the pasta and stir immediately. Boil gently, uncovered, until the pasta is nearly al dente, firm but tender, 6 or 7 minutes.

**4.** If you have time, turn off the heat, cover the soup, and set aside for 5 to 10 minutes to allow the flavors to combine.

**5.** Return the soup to a simmer, gently stirring often from the bottom of the pan. Degrease again, if needed. Thin with a little water if the soup is too solid. Add a few generous grinds of pepper to taste, salt, if needed, and the **remaining fresh basil.** Remove the bay leaf.

**6.** Serve immediately, sprinkling each serving with scallion greens and drizzling with a little more olive oil, if you like. Pass freshly grated Parmesan cheese and a pepper mill at the table.

## VARIATION: PASTA AND BEAN SOUP WITH SHREDDED SPINACH

Wash 12 to 16 ounces of spinach well (Greens Cleaning, page 19); discard the stems. Gather up the spinach leaves in a bunch, and with a large chef's knife, shred the spinach leaves crosswise in ribbons about 1/2 inch wide. After removing the fat from the soup in step 5, stir in the spinach and cook, stirring once or twice, until the spinach wilts but is still bright green, about 3 minutes. Omit the scallions and serve.

Mashing some of the beans against the side of the pot helps thicken the soup flavorfully and without fat; you can use this technique with any bean or lentil soup or stew.

Leftovers of this dish are even better the next day or 2 or 3 days later. However, since both the beans and pasta will absorb liquid after standing, you may need to thin the soup with a little water or broth to the desired consistency.

Adding fresh basil and scallions at the last minute keeps them bright green.

Crunchy bread sticks—
that's what I would
serve with this—and a
lemon ice for dessert.

Italian fontina d'Aosta
is a rich cheese with a
mild nutty flavor and
excellent melting prop
erties, making it a per
fect toss together with
hot pasta.

# RIGATONI WITH SUMMER VEGETABLES AND ITALIAN FONTINA

If you have fresh herbs on hand, add a sprinkling of thyme, oregano, and/or chervil along with the basil.

Salt, to taste

1 tablespoon olive oil

1 red onion, cut into slivers

1 medium red bell pepper, cored, seeded (Bell Pepper Basics, page 16), and cut into slivers

1 small yellow bell pepper, cored, seeded, and cut into slivers
Pinch of dried red pepper flakes

2 scallions (white and green portions), trimmed and sliced

2 garlic cloves, thinly sliced

3 large (or 4 medium) ripe tomatoes, peeled, cored, seeded (Tomato Basics, page 22), and cut into ¾-inch dice

3 tablespoons chopped fresh basil or parsley

1 pound dried rigatoni or penne

⅔ cup ¼-inch diced **Italian fontina** or mozzarella cheese
Freshly ground black pepper, to taste

⅓ cup freshly grated Parmesan cheese

**1.** Bring a large pot of water to a boil for the pasta. Add a little salt.

**2.** Meanwhile, heat the oil in a nonreactive large nonstick skillet over medium-high heat. Add the onion, red and yellow bell peppers, pepper flakes, and a sprinkling of salt. Cover and sweat (or cook) for 3 minutes. Uncover and cook, tossing with a wooden spoon, until the vegetables are crisp-tender, about 2 minutes longer. Add the scallions and garlic; cook, stirring, until the scallions soften, 1 or 2 minutes longer. Transfer the vegetables to a plate.

**3.** Add the tomatoes and about half of the basil to the skillet. Sprinkle with salt and cook, tossing, until the tomatoes break down slightly and soften, usually 4 or 5 minutes.

**4.** Meanwhile, add the pasta to the boiling water; cook until al dente (page 67), firm but tender, usually 8 to 10 minutes. With a mug, carefully scoop out about ½ cup of the pasta cooking liquid (page 71). Drain the pasta. Return it to its pot along with the vegetables, tomatoes, and enough of the reserved liquid to moisten the pasta and sauce slightly. **Add the fontina or mozzarella** and black pepper and toss just until the cheese begins to melt but is still in cubes. Serve immediately, sprinkled with the remaining basil, Parmesan cheese, and a few grinds of black pepper.

Both fontina and mozzarella are delicious added to pasta this way —they melt slightly but still retain their shape, so you get their flavor in small bursts.

I like to serve this with a small plate of marinated roasted red and yellow bell peppers (Bell Pepper Basics, page 16).

If you can get freshly made ricotta (usually made with whole milk, available in cheese shops and Italian markets, it will add an especially sweet, rich flavor to this dish.

The heat of the pasta combines with the diced mozzarella and fontina cheeses to melt and form a creamy no-cook "sauce" that has much less fat than butter-and-cream "Alfredo" pasta sauces.

Parmigiano Reggiano is the true name of the highest-quality, genuine Parmesan cheese produced in the Emilia-Romagna region of Italy. Its rich, nutty flavor with a touch of sweetness is welcome in all kinds of pasta preparations.

# PASTA WITH MARINATED TOMATOES AND FOUR CHEESES

This is a favorite summer dish. Don't even think of making it unless you have the reddest, ripest, juiciest summer tomatoes.

2½ pounds best-quality ripe tomatoes, cored, seeded (Tomato Basics, page 22), and cut into ¾-inch cubes

½ cup shredded fresh basil leaves

1 garlic clove, minced

Salt, to taste

1 cup part-skim or **fresh** whole-milk **ricotta** cheese

2 tablespoons milk

Freshly ground black pepper, to taste

Pinch of freshly grated nutmeg

2 ounces fresh **mozzarella** cheese, cut into ½-inch dice (about ½ cup)

2 ounces Italian **fontina** cheese, cut into ½-inch dice (about ½ cup)

1 pound dried rigatoni or other short pasta

Freshly grated **Parmesan** cheese

**1.** Combine the tomatoes, basil, garlic, and a sprinkling of salt in a colander. Place in the sink or over a plate with a rim. Let stand at room temperature for about 1 hour.

**2.** In a large serving bowl, mix the ricotta, milk, pepper, and nutmeg with a wooden spoon until fluffy. Stir in the mozzarella and fontina. If not serving right away, cover with plastic wrap; leave the cheese mixture at room temperature.

**3.** Bring a large pot of water to a boil for the pasta. Add a little salt. Add the pasta; cook until al dente (page 67), or firm-tender, usually 8 to 10 minutes. Drain well and add to the ricotta mixture; toss with 2 wooden spoons until the **cheeses begin to melt.**

**4.** Spoon the tomato mixture over the top of the pasta and serve immediately, passing some grated Parmesan and a pepper mill at the table.

# OLD-FASHIONED MACARONI AND CHEESE

This is from Kempie Miles Minifie, a fine cook who comes up with many of those mouthwatering meals in *Gourmet* magazine.

There are many ways to make macaroni and cheese, many of them good. But the best is starting with a white sauce base. And I like the crumbs on top—it reminds me of my junior high school cafeteria lunches, which collectively were among the most horrifying experiences of my growing up. So why now do I want to re-create the food from that time?

MAKES 6 SERVINGS

Salt, to taste

3 tablespoons unsalted butter

3½ tablespoons all-purpose flour

½ teaspoon paprika

3 cups cold milk

1 tablespoon Worcestershire sauce

Freshly ground black pepper, to taste

¾ pound dried short pasta, such as short rigatoni, shells, elbows, rotelle (wheels), or farfalle (butterflies)

10 ounces extra-sharp Cheddar cheese, coarsely grated (about 2¾ cups)

1 cup soft fresh bread crumbs (Making Fresh Bread Crumbs, page 18)

**1.** Preheat the oven to 375°F. with a rack in the middle. Butter a 2-quart shallow baking dish, such as an 8-inch square baking dish or an 8-inch oval gratin dish.

**2.** Bring a large pot of water to a boil, then add salt.

**3.** Meanwhile, prepare the **white sauce:** In a heavy saucepan, melt the butter over medium heat. Add the flour and paprika and cook, stirring constantly with a wooden spoon, for 3 minutes. Add the cold milk all at once. Bring the sauce to a boil, whisking frequently. Lower the heat as needed and simmer, whisking, for 5 minutes. Remove the pan from the heat and stir in the Worcestershire sauce and pepper.

**4.** Add the pasta to the boiling salted water and boil, stirring now and then, until just tender, with a slight firmness in the center. (The pasta will be cooked again in the oven, so don't overdo it now.) Drain the pasta in a colander. ➝

A white sauce carries flavor and adds richness to a dish without the danger of breaking down or separating when subjected to heat.

**5.** Return the pasta to its cooking pot; add the white sauce and 2 cups of the grated Cheddar cheese. Transfer the mixture to the prepared dish. (You can prepare this in advance to this point. Lay a sheet of wax paper on the surface; cool and chill, if necessary. I prefer to bake the macaroni and cheese shortly after putting it together, so it doesn't ~~become overcooked.~~) In a small bowl, combine the bread crumbs with the remaining ~~...~~ cup Cheddar. ~~... over the ...~~

**6.** Bake until golden and bubbling, ~~... only 15 to 30 minutes.~~ If you'd like to brown the surface further (I usually do), turn on the broiler, with the rack positioned about 6 inches from the heat. Run the baking dish under the hot broiler until the topping is golden brown, 1 to 2 minutes (watch carefully to prevent burning). Let the macaroni and cheese stand for about 10 minutes before serving. Serve hot.

## LUSCIOUS BAKED PASTA GRATIN

Baked pasta dishes are among my favorites. In the old days (Before Cholesterol), I used to moisten pasta and vegetables with tomato sauce combined with heavy cream. Yum. This gives similar results with much less fat. This is very loosely based on a recipe called "Bully's Pasta" from my friend, cookbook author Anna Teresa Callen.

MAKES 4 MAIN-COURSE SERVINGS

Salt, to taste

4 tablespoons olive oil, or as needed

8 fresh or wild mushrooms, cleaned, halved, and thickly sliced (Mushroom Basics, page 21)

Freshly ground black pepper, to taste

2 onions, halved through the root end and sliced crosswise

3 garlic cloves, minced

1 can (16 ounces) whole tomatoes in thick puree

3 tablespoons chopped fresh basil leaves, or a pinch of mixed dried herbs, such as basil, oregano, and/or thyme

Pinch of dried red pepper flakes

2/3 cup frozen peas

This is very good served with just a plate of sliced ripe tomatoes, drizzled with a little balsamic vinegar and sprinkled with chopped parsley. Or try a few spears of Belgian endive, thinly sliced, tossed with sliced red onion, and drizzled with balsamic vinegar.

½    pound dried rigatoni or rotelle (wheels)

⅓    cup ¼-inch diced Italian fontina cheese

¾    cup freshly grated Parmesan cheese (about 2 ounces)

1½   tablespoons cold unsalted butter, cut into bits

**1.** Preheat the oven to 400°F. Butter a 2-quart gratin dish or shallow baking dish and set aside. Bring a large pot of water to a boil for the pasta. Add a little salt.

**2.** Heat 2 tablespoons of the olive oil in a nonreactive skillet over medium-high heat. Add the mushrooms; sprinkle with salt and pepper and let sit for 1 to 2 minutes, until they sizzle and begin to release their liquid. Sauté, tossing with a wooden spoon, until lightly golden, 4 or 5 minutes. Transfer with a slotted spoon to a plate and set aside.

**3.** Add the remaining 2 tablespoons oil to the skillet. Add the onions, 1 tablespoon water, and a sprinkling of salt. Cover the pan and **sweat** or cook for 3 minutes. Uncover the pan; continue to sauté until the onions are soft but not limp, 2 to 3 minutes longer. Add the garlic; cook until the garlic is lightly golden, 1 to 2 minutes. Add the tomatoes, basil, pepper flakes, and a few grinds of black pepper. Bring to a boil, breaking up the tomatoes with a wooden spoon. Reduce the heat and simmer until lightly thickened but still liquid, about 15 minutes. Then stir in the reserved mushrooms and the peas.

**4.** Meanwhile, add the pasta to the boiling water; boil until al dente, firm but tender. Drain and rinse quickly under cold water.

**5.** Now layer the ingredients in the gratin dish as follows: Drizzle a little of the tomato sauce into the baking dish. Add about one-third of the pasta and then half of the remaining sauce. Sprinkle on half of the fontina and a little of the Parmesan. Repeat as follows: half of the remaining pasta, half of the remaining sauce, all of the remaining fontina, and a sprinkling of the Parmesan. Top with the remaining pasta and then with the remaining sauce. Sprinkle the remaining Parmesan generously over the top. Dot with the butter.

**6.** Bake until the pasta mixture is bubbly and the top is crusty, 25 to 30 minutes. If you'd like to brown the surface further (I usually do), turn on the broiler and position a rack about 6 inches from the heat. Run the baking dish under the hot broiler until the topping is golden brown, 1 to 2 minutes (watch carefully to prevent burning). Let the pasta stand for a few minutes before serving hot.

What's a gratin? Gratin is a French word referring to the delicious crusty top, usually of bread crumbs and/or cheese, that covers a baked casserole. A hot oven or a final run under the broiler is what creates the crispness. Remember an old-fashioned crusty-topped macaroni and cheese? That's a good example of a gratin.

Sweating the onions with a little water means you can use less oil (hence less fat) and still coax the flavorful juices from the onion without scorching the pan.

This makes a hearty lunch (or breakfast) when you have some leftover pasta on hand.

Serve warm or at room temperature, cut into wedges directly from the pan. A fresh salad and a glass of white wine would be nice companions.

# PASTA FRITTATA

MAKES 4 SERVINGS

1 tablespoon olive oil or butter

1 red onion, cut into slivers

1 red bell pepper, cut into short slivers (Bell Pepper Roaster, page 116)

1 yellow bell pepper, cut into short slivers (optional)

1 garlic clove, minced

3 ripe tomatoes, halved, cored, seeded (Tomato Basics, page 22), and cut into ¾-inch dice

Salt, to taste

3 tablespoons chopped fresh basil, or a mixture of basil and parsley

Freshly ground black pepper, to taste

8 eggs

3 tablespoons milk

1 tablespoon unsalted butter

6 ounces (about) cooked angel hair or spaghetti (about 3 cups)

1 to 1½ cups coarsely shredded fresh mozzarella and/or Italian fontina cheese

2 or 3 tablespoons freshly grated Parmesan cheese

**1.** Heat the olive oil or butter in a nonreactive 10- or 9-inch skillet, preferably non-stick, over medium-high heat. Add the onion, bell peppers, and garlic and sauté, tossing with a wooden spoon, until the vegetables are crisp-tender, about 6 minutes. Add the tomatoes, sprinkle with salt, and cook, stirring and tossing, until the liquid evaporates somewhat, 4 or 5 minutes. Add the basil and a few grinds of black pepper. Transfer the vegetable mixture to a plate, leaving a few spoonfuls in the skillet.

**2.** While the vegetables and tomatoes cook, whisk the eggs, milk, and a sprinkling of salt and pepper in a medium bowl until very well blended. Set the egg mixture aside.

**3.** Melt the butter in the skillet; lower the heat to medium. Add half of the cooked pasta, pressing it into an even layer. Top with half of the vegetables. Sprinkle with half of the mozzarella cheese; repeat, layering the pasta, vegetables, and cheese. Evenly pour the egg mixture over the ingredients.

**4.** Cook over medium heat, giving the skillet a quick shake occasionally after the edges begin to set. Lower the heat slightly if the mixture is sizzling too loudly; the eggs should set rather slowly. Preheat the broiler.

**5.** When the frittata has set but most of the center of the top layer is still liquid, turn off the heat. This usually takes about 15 minutes, but check earlier. Sprinkle the surface with Parmesan cheese and brown the cheese under the broiler for 1 or 2 minutes. Watch carefully; you want the eggs to set but not brown too much. Set skillet aside to cool to warm or room temperature. Then cut into wedges and serve.

A risotto doesn't really need much for an accompaniment—a simple green salad, a little crusty bread, and a glass of wine.

Spooned out in smaller portions, risotto is a ~~~~~~~~~~~~ first course.

I find making risotto contemplative, perfectly suited for when I'm eating alone. And when I make it for friends, it seems to lend a certain intimacy to the table.

What kind of rice do I use for risotto? A medium-grain rice, since it has the requisite amount of starch and remains firm-textured yet wonderfully creamy at the end of the cooking. Arborio is the most commonly available Italian medium-grain rice (often mistakenly described as short-grain), although Carnaroli and Vialone Nano work equally well.

Cooking the rice first in hot fat helps keep the grains separate. I do the same thing when making pilafs (page 182).

# RISOTTO

## BASIC METHOD FOR RISOTTO

Risotto is actually rice—Arborio, Carnaroli, or Vialone Nano, to be precise, ~~important grains that cannot million~~ ~~this is cooked slowly in a pot until~~ ~~each kernel comes independently on season. The result is a rice risotto; the~~ rice retains its firmness but is bathed in a thick "sauce." Risotto with no additions can be a side dish, but toss in pieces of chicken, vegetables, seafood, mushrooms, or whatever and it easily becomes a meal. Despite warnings of most traditional recipes to stir constantly, you can walk away from risotto as it cooks. Just be sure to stir at least every few minutes or so.

MAKES 4 MAIN-COURSE SERVINGS

 2 cans (about 14 ounces each) reduced-sodium chicken broth, fat removed
 1 cup cold water, or more if needed
 1 tablespoon olive oil, or as needed
 1 medium onion, coarsely chopped
 1 cup medium-grain white rice (**Arborio, Carnaroli, or Vialone Nano**)
 1/3 cup freshly grated Parmesan cheese, plus more for serving
   Salt and freshly ground black pepper, to taste
 1/4 cup chopped fresh chives and/or fresh parsley (optional)

**1.** Bring the broth and water to a simmer in a medium saucepan. Adjust the heat so the broth is just below a simmer; the surface will sort of shimmer. Put a ladle into the pan.

**2.** Meanwhile, place a fairly deep saucepan on the burner next to (or in front of) the broth. This pan should be on the burner you're most comfortable at. Add the olive oil and turn heat to medium-high. Add the onion; cook, stirring once or twice with a large wooden fork (if you have one) or a wooden spoon, until slightly softened, about 3 minutes. Add the rice and stir to coat with the oil (drizzle with a little more oil if needed to coat the rice). **Cook,** stirring occasionally, until the rice begins to turn translucent, 2 or 3 minutes. Add a couple of ladlefuls of the hot broth, enough to cover the rice. Start timing now. Adjust the heat to maintain a steady, gentle boil.

**3.** Cook, stirring frequently with the wooden fork or spoon, until the broth has been absorbed and the rice is not quite dry, usually 4 to 5 minutes. Moisten with another ladleful or two of broth, or just enough to cover the rice. Adjust the heat as needed to maintain a gentle boil. Now continue to add the broth each time it has been absorbed, usually about every 5 minutes or so.

**4.** Continue this process, adding broth and stirring, until the rice is just tender with a slight firmness at its core, usually about 25 minutes total. Stir in the 1/3 cup Parmesan cheese, salt and pepper to taste, and another ladleful of broth. (You may not need all of the broth; if you've used it all, add a splash of water.) The finished risotto should now be quite moist, with a little starchy broth between the grains of rice — but not soupy. If it's too wet, continue to stir over medium heat for a couple of minutes; otherwise, turn off the heat. Stir in the herb(s). Taste and correct the seasonings, adding more salt, pepper, and/or herbs, if needed. Serve immediately, passing grated Parmesan at the table for sprinkling.

## VARIATION: RISOTTO WITH MUSHROOMS

Add 6 or 8 mushrooms (white or wild, or a combination), halved, sliced, and sautéed, as in step 2 of Risotto Primavera (page 84), then stirred in as in step 5.

## VARIATION: RISOTTO WITH SEAFOOD

Omit the grated Parmesan cheese for this seafood risotto, and instead of the chopped fresh chives or parsley, use an herb such as fresh tarragon or dill and add in step 4. You have choices for this risotto, depending on the kinds of seafood you like. You can use 3/4 pound medium shrimp, peeled, deveined, and cut crosswise in half (or if mixing with other seafood, about 1/3 pound); 1 pound well-scrubbed mussels (or 1/2 pound if mixed with one or two other choices); and/or 1 1/2 pounds well-scrubbed small clams (or 1/2 pound if mixed with other choices). Add the seafood in step 4, allowing 10 minutes cooking time for the clams and 5 minutes cooking time for the shrimp and mussels. Be sure to stir the seafood well down into the rice. (See Shellfish Basics, page 21, and Shrimp Basics, page 22.)

When I think about making a risotto, I first check my refrigerator for **leftovers**. A little bit of cooked chicken, broccoli, or other vegetables can easily be added. The trick is to stir these in at the right time, to avoid overcooking—leftovers are probably best added toward the end of the cooking, since they just need to be reheated.

# RISOTTO PRIMAVERA

This is a colorful risotto, brightly flecked with spring vegetables. The ingredient list makes this look complicated, but it's actually a quick supper. I love to make it when I'm eating alone (I usually use only about ¾ cup rice and 2 cans of broth, leaving out the water. And there are still leftovers, which I either reheat for lunch the next day or make into pancakes—page 88.)

I've given instructions for cooking asparagus right in the risotto, but another way that works as well is to use previously cooked asparagus spears. In fact, if you have a few **leftovers** of most anything in the refrigerator, that can be a great reason to decide to make risotto in the first place.

MAKES 4 MAIN-COURSE SERVINGS

- 2 cans (about 14 ounces each) reduced-sodium chicken broth
- 1 cup cold water, or more if needed
- 3 tablespoons olive oil, or as needed
- 6 mushrooms (white or wild, or a combination), cleaned (Mushroom Basics, page 21), halved, and thickly sliced
  Salt and freshly ground black pepper, to taste
- 1 onion, coarsely chopped
- 1 carrot, trimmed, peeled, and sliced diagonally ¼ inch thick (optional)
- 1 cup Arborio, Carnaroli, or Vialone Nano rice (page 82)
- 8 asparagus spears, bottoms trimmed, bottom halves peeled, and spears cut diagonally in 2-inch lengths (keep tender tips separate)
- ½ cup frozen or shelled fresh peas
- ⅓ cup freshly grated Parmesan cheese, plus more for serving
- ¼ cup chopped fresh chives and/or fresh parsley

**1.** Bring the broth and water to a simmer in a medium saucepan. Adjust the heat so the broth is just below a simmer; the surface will sort of shimmer. Put a ladle into the pan.

**2.** Meanwhile, place a fairly deep saucepan on the burner next to (or in front of) the broth. The pan should be on the burner you're most comfortable at. Add 1½ tablespoons of the olive oil and heat over medium-high heat. Add the mushrooms; sprinkle with salt and pepper to taste, and let sit until they begin to sizzle, 1 to 2 minutes. Toss with a large wooden fork, if you have one, or a wooden spoon until the mushrooms are just softened, about 4 minutes longer. Transfer the mushrooms to a plate and set aside.

**3.** Heat the remaining 1½ tablespoons oil in the pan. Add the onion and carrot and cook, stirring now and then, until slightly softened, about 3 minutes. Add the rice and stir to coat with the oil (drizzle with a little more oil if needed to coat the rice). Cook, stirring occasionally, until the rice begins to turn translucent, 2 to 3 minutes. Add a couple of ladlefuls of the hot broth, enough to cover the rice. Start timing now. Adjust the heat to maintain a steady, gentle boil.

**4.** Cook, stirring frequently with the wooden fork or spoon, until the broth has been absorbed and the rice is not quite dry, usually 4 to 5 minutes. Moisten with another ladleful or two of broth, just enough to cover the rice. Adjust the heat as needed to maintain a gentle boil. Continue to add broth each time it has been absorbed, usually about every 5 minutes or so. Set the tips of the asparagus aside; add the spear pieces to the rice 12 or 13 minutes from the moment you started timing.

**5.** When the rice is almost but not quite tender, usually after about 18 minutes, stir in the reserved asparagus tips, peas (breaking them up if frozen), and more broth. Continue to cook, stirring, until the rice is just tender, with a slight firmness at its core, about 5 minutes longer. Stir in the ⅓ cup Parmesan cheese, the reserved mushrooms with their juices, freshly ground pepper, and another ladleful of broth. (You may not need all the broth; if you've used it all, add a splash of water.) The finished risotto should now be quite moist, with a little starchy broth between the grains of rice—but not soupy. If it's too wet, continue to stir over medium heat for a couple of minutes. Otherwise, turn off the heat. Stir in the chives. Taste and correct the seasonings, adding more pepper and/or herbs, if needed. Serve immediately, passing grated Parmesan at the table for sprinkling.

**In Venice, a properly cooked risotto is called** *all'onda*—**which means "in the waves." It still should be somewhat liquid as it arrives at the table. In fact, Venetians say that by the time the last person at the table is served, the texture of risotto should be only slightly firmer than when it first arrived at the table.**

I especially like this for a **light supper,** with a salad of strongly flavored greens such as escarole, romaine, and radicchio, or for a weekend lunch.

## PARMESAN RISOTTO PANCAKES

This way of using leftover risotto is so delicious that it's almost worth making a big batch of risotto just so you can enjoy these pancakes. By adjusting the amounts proportionally, you can transform any amount of leftover risotto.

MAKES 2 SERVINGS

1½  cups (about) leftover risotto (of any type)

1  egg, beaten, as needed

2  tablespoons freshly grated Parmesan cheese
    Salt and freshly ground black pepper, to taste, if needed

½  cup diced Italian fontina (page 74) or mozzarella cheese (optional)

1  tablespoon olive oil, or a mixture of oil and butter

**1.** In a medium bowl, stir the risotto gently with a fork. Stir in enough of the beaten egg to hold the mixture together without making it too wet. It should take a little less than 1 egg. (Toss any extra egg into a hot nonstick skillet for an almost instant scrambled egg—cook's treat.) Add the Parmesan cheese and salt and pepper, if needed. Then gently fold in the fontina cheese, if using.

**2.** Heat the oil in a large nonstick skillet over medium heat. Spoon the risotto mixture into the pan, forming 4 small pancakes and flattening them gently with the back of the spoon. Cook until golden brown on the bottoms, about 5 minutes. Gently turn the pancakes over with a spatula and brown the other sides, about 5 minutes longer. Shake the pan from time to time to prevent sticking. Serve hot.

# POLENTA

## CREAMY POLENTA WITH MASCARPONE

Polenta is one of my favorite foods—it's Italy's version of cornmeal mush. Like risotto, it requires some attention during its slow cooking, but these are moments I enjoy for quiet contemplation. As I've mentioned elsewhere in these pages, the Union Square Cafe in New York City, with its gifted chef/co-owner Michael Romano and innovative co-owner Danny Meyer, is one of my favorite spots for a leisurely, chatty lunch. When this dish first appeared on their menu, I couldn't get enough of it. I borrow this recipe from their excellent cookbook, *The Union Square Cookbook*.

MAKES 4 MAIN-COURSE SERVINGS

5 cups milk

1 cup **polenta** (medium-grain yellow cornmeal, not instant)

5 tablespoons **mascarpone** cheese (2½ ounces)

1 teaspoon coarse (kosher) salt

⅛ teaspoon freshly ground white pepper

3 tablespoons **Gorgonzola** cheese (2 ounces), crumbled (optional)

¼ cup walnuts, lightly toasted (optional)

**1.** Slowly bring the milk to a boil in a 2-quart nonreactive saucepan, stirring occasionally with a wooden spoon to prevent scorching. To avoid lumpy polenta, follow this method carefully: Hold the cup of polenta in one hand and a firm whisk in the other. Slowly pour the polenta into the milk with a sprinkling motion and whisk constantly until all the polenta is absorbed.

**2.** Turn the heat down to very low. Using the wooden spoon again, thoroughly stir the polenta every 10 minutes for 1 hour. At the end of the cooking, the polenta should have the consistency of firm mashed potatoes, and it will have lost its raw corn taste and gritty texture. Stir in the mascarpone and season with the salt and white pepper. Spoon onto plates and serve as is, or take it one step further by moving on to the next step.

**3.** Heat the broiler. Spoon the polenta into a heat-resistant dish, dot the top with the crumbled Gorgonzola, and slide the dish under the broiler to melt the cheese. Sprinkle with the toasted walnuts and serve.

You can serve this as a first course, or as a side dish with poultry, in which case it's probably best to omit the Gorgonzola and walnuts. But my favorite way to have this is as a main course, with a simple green salad on the side, dressed with a balsamic vinaigrette, and a glass of chenin blanc.

Polenta is actually a mush made from cornmeal. You can serve it hot and creamy, or you can let it cool to a firm texture, cut it into squares, and then fry it in a skillet in a little fat.

A cow's-milk cheese from Italy, mascarpone is very rich, ranging in consistency from double cream to triple cream. For an easy dessert, spoon a little of this over fresh fruit.

Gorgonzola is an Italian cow's-milk cheese with bluish-green veins. As it ages, its already pungent flavor becomes even more so. Delicious with fruit such as apples and pears.

Four

# MAIN DISHES:
# FISH AND SEAFOOD

|  | Seared Scallops |
| **Technique:** | searing |
|  | |
|  | Basic Method for Oven-Poached Fish |
| **Technique:** | oven-poaching fish |

|  | Soy-and-Ginger-Glazed Salmon |
| **Techniques:** | marinating/broiling/fish-cooking rule |
|  | |
|  | Roast Fish with Herbed Crumb Crust |
| **Techniques:** | shopping for fresh fish/roasting fish |
|  | |
|  | Vegetable- and Wine-Braised Fish Fillets |
| **Techniques:** | cooking with wine/braising fish/enriching sauce |

|  | Shrimp Sauté with Garlic and Lemon |
| **Techniques:** | sautéing/deglazing/finishing a sauce with final enrichment |
|  | |
|  | Arroz con Seafood |
| **Technique:** | cooking fish in a casserole or paella pan |

**Technique:**

Main-Dish Seafood Stew

using firm-fleshed fish for stew

Steamed Lobster with Butter Sauce Two Ways

Techniques: steaming a lobster, cutting up a lobster

**For the novice cook, the simplicity of preparing fish may be its best recommendation.** Fish cooks quickly, is lower in fat than meat, and is an excellent source of protein. And the variety of fish now available throughout the country is remarkable, thanks to air freight, refrigerated trucks, flash-freezing on shipboard, and the emergence of aquaculture or fish farming. Many supermarkets, even in the landlocked center of the country, have their own separate fish markets with a splendid array of fish artfully arranged on beds of ice, rivaling what you encounter in seaside towns.

The generally mild and subtle flavor of fish lends itself to a wide range of flavorful preparations, as simple as a squeeze of lemon juice and as complex as a rich seafood stew. Plus it takes well to all types of cooking, as the recipes in this chapter illustrate: broiling, oven poaching, roasting, steaming, sautéing, and simmering. Whatever cooking method you choose, keep in mind two words: Don't overcook. The key is to cook fish just until the center is opaque or milky and no longer translucent. To be absolutely sure, poke a small knife into the thickest part and take a peek.

Treat fish carefully, prepare it simply, and you'll be rewarded with fine results.

# SEARED SCALLOPS

Scallops are my favorite of all seafood. This recipe illustrates the quick method of searing the scallops so they are burnished with gold—a popular restaurant technique you can do at home in no time.

MAKES 2 SERVINGS

¾  **pound sea scallops**
1  **tablespoon olive oil**
   **Salt and freshly ground black pepper, to taste**
   **Fresh lemon juice**
   **Lemon quarters, for serving**

**1.** Remove and discard the small adductor muscle that's found on the side of each scallop. (If you can't find it, don't worry about it.) Pat the scallops dry with paper towels (this is important—if they are too wet, they won't brown).

**2.** Heat the olive oil in a large, heavy skillet, preferably nonstick, over medium-high heat. (Add a little more olive oil to lightly coat the bottom of the pan if your skillet is not nonstick.) Season the scallops with salt and pepper to taste. Place them in the skillet, which should now be very hot, without crowding the pan (work in 2 batches, if necessary).

**3. Sear** the scallops until the bottoms are nicely golden brown, usually about 2 minutes, or slightly longer. Lower the heat to medium if they are sizzling intensely and shake the pan once or twice to be sure they're not sticking. Gently turn the scallops over with tongs and brown the second sides, about 1 minute. Don't overcook—the scallops are **done** when they are just gently set when pressed with a fingertip, but not hard or rubbery.

**4.** Arrange the scallops on serving plates. Sprinkle them with lemon juice, garnish with a quarter of a lemon, and dig in.

## VARIATION: SEAFOOD SAUCE

If you'd like a little more of a sauce, make the recipe as described here; then finish it with the butter/lemon parsley mixture in step 3 of the Shrimp Sauté with Garlic and Lemon (page 97), drizzling the sauce over the scallops.

The flavor is so delicate here that **accompaniments** need be chosen carefully—nothing overwhelming: steamed asparagus (season permitting) or green beans and a little mound of an aromatic rice, such as basmati or texmati.

**Searing** is similar to sautéing, but at a higher temperature. The object is to seal in juices and to do it as soon as the food hits the pan. The high heat of a broiler will also sear food.

A surefire way to test for **doneness** is to cut into the center of one of the scallops—it should be just opaque, or milky.

If **shallots** are not part of your larder, then try them. A member of the onion family that looks rather like large cloves of garlic, shallots add a delicate, subtle onion flavor to dishes—not as pungent as the more familiar yellow onion.

Once you master the method of **oven poaching** (there's nothing to it), try cooking chicken breasts the same way.

# BASIC METHOD FOR OVEN-POACHED FISH

This is the best cooking method I know for guaranteeing moist fish. It's great for a thick fillet (bass, grouper, salmon) as well as for thinner, more delicate fillets like flounder.

> Softened unsalted butter
> 2 tablespoons chopped shallots or scallions (white and green portions)
> Fish fillets (any amount)
> Salt and freshly ground black pepper, to taste
> ¾ to 1 cup dry white wine, as needed
> Cold water
> Watercress sprigs and lemon wedges, for garnish

**1.** Preheat the oven to 400°F., with a rack at the center of the oven. Butter a shallow baking pan or ovenproof skillet that will hold the fish in a single layer. Scatter the chopped shallots in the bottom of the pan. Season the fillets with salt and pepper to taste; carefully arrange them, without crowding, in the pan. Thick fillets can be placed in the pan as is, making sure the fit is not too snug; fold thinner fillets over, with skin (smooth) side inward and the thinner part on top. Pour enough of the wine around the fish to reach about halfway up it; add enough cold water so that the level of the liquids reaches not quite to the top of the fish. Cover with a buttered sheet of parchment or wax paper, buttered side down (this helps keep the fish moist).

**2.** Place the pan on a stove-top burner over medium heat. Bring the liquid just to a boil, watching carefully. The moment it begins to boil, carefully transfer the pan to the oven. **Oven poach** until the fish is just cooked—what you're looking for is the center of the fillet to turn from translucent to opaque. This can take as little as 3 minutes for thin flounder fillets or up to 10 minutes for thicker fillets. Don't overcook.

**3.** With a slotted spatula, lift the fillets from the broth, draining all possible broth back into the pan. (Reserve the poaching liquid for fish soups and stews.) Serve the fish as is, with or without a sauce, garnished with the watercress and lemon. Or cool it in its broth; remove and serve cold with an herbed mayonnaise.

## FISH SALAD

In the event you have leftover poached fish, you have the beginning of a quick salad. Coarsely flake the fish with a fork into a bowl. Then use a rubber spatula to gently fold in enough mayonnaise to bind it without becoming too soupy (the mayonnaise can be reduced-fat and you can enhance it with chopped fresh herbs, such as dill, thyme, rosemary, marjoram, and anything else that strikes your fancy). Other additions can include chopped celery; scallions, shallots, or red onions; and other leftover cooked vegetables. Season with a squeeze or two of fresh lemon juice and a sprinkling of salt and pepper. Garnishes that go well are sliced cucumber, cooked potatoes, green beans, hard-cooked eggs (page 198), olives, and, if the season permits, the ripest tomatoes possible.

For more servings, just double or triple the recipe.

This dish is one of my favorite at-home dinners, along with the marinated cucumbers (page 199) and a crisp Chardonnay, Pinot Grigio, or Gewürztraminer. Serve with baked potatoes or Boiled Golden Potatoes (page 174).

If you are using salmon steaks rather than fillets, turn them with a wide spatula after the first side is nicely golden, about 4 minutes. Spoon the remaining marinade over and broil the second side, basting at least once, until lightly golden, 2 to 4 minutes.

Marinating is an easy way to infuse foods with flavor—the food is soaked or marinated in a seasoned liquid usually containing an acid such as lemon juice or vinegar. Be careful not to marinate fish too long since the acid will begin to "cook" the fish, making for a mushy texture. Also, use a nonreactive container.

Broiling fish results in a golden, slightly crispy exterior and a moist interior.

# SOY-AND-GINGER-GLAZED SALMON

Use salmon fillets (my favorite) or steaks for this quick, tasty main course. Also try this method with fresh tuna steaks and swordfish.

MAKES 2 SERVINGS

2 salmon fillets or steaks (6 to 8 ounces each)
3 tablespoons soy sauce, preferably reduced-sodium
Juice of 1/2 lime or lemon
5 or 6 thin slices peeled fresh ginger
2 garlic cloves, smashed
Small pinch of dried red pepper flakes
Lime wedges, for serving

**1.** To marinate the fish, arrange the fillets or steaks in a shallow ceramic or glass dish just large enough to hold the fillets snugly in 1 layer. Combine the soy sauce, lime juice, ginger, garlic, and pepper flakes in a small bowl; pour over the fish. Turn the fish over to coat with the **marinade.** Cover the dish with plastic wrap and let stand for 15 to 30 minutes at room temperature or 1 hour refrigerated, turning the fish over once or twice. (If you like, the fish can be marinated for up to 3 or 4 hours.)

**2.** Preheat the broiler with the rack about 4 inches from the heat source. Transfer the fish fillets to a broiler pan (disposable ridged foil pans are great for this—no cleanup, although I have started to recycle them), spooning a little of the liquid marinade over the salmon. **Broil** (without turning), basting once or twice with the marinade, until the salmon is glazed a nice golden brown and the fish is just set when pressed gently, but still moist; if you cut into the center, the flesh should be just opaque, not translucent. This should take about 8 minutes, though timing can vary depending on the thickness of the fillets—do not overcook. (Figure approximately 10 minutes cooking time, regardless of cooking method, for each 1 inch of thickness; however, begin checking for doneness a few minutes before the estimated finish.)

**3.** Transfer the fish to heated serving plates. Pour a little of the broiler pan juices over each piece and serve hot, garnished with a lime wedge. Discard any of the remaining marinade, since the raw fish has soaked in it.

# ROAST FISH WITH HERBED CRUMB CRUST

This is good—the mayonnaise-mustard mixture keeps the fish moist, adding a tangy bite that plays nicely against the crunch of the golden bread crumb topping. Herbed crumb crusts have been enjoying something of a vogue in restaurants during the past few years and are actually a throwback to recipes popular in American food magazines back in the fifties and sixties.

This is a variation on a recipe developed by Lori Walther for *Gourmet*.

MAKES 2 SERVINGS

½ cup soft fresh bread crumbs (page 18)

2 tablespoons chopped fresh dill or parsley

1 tablespoon reduced-fat or regular mayonnaise

1 teaspoon fresh lemon juice

½ teaspoon Dijon mustard

2 1-inch-thick halibut fillets (6 to 8 ounces each), or use salmon, scrod, grouper, or striped bass

Salt and freshly ground black pepper, to taste

¼ cup dry white wine

Lemon wedges, for serving

Fresh dill or parsley sprigs, for garnish

**1.** Preheat the oven to 450°F., with a rack in the center. Butter a small baking dish just large enough to hold the fish in a single layer. In a small bowl, toss together the bread crumbs and dill or parsley with a fork; set aside.

**2.** In a cup, stir together the mayonnaise, lemon juice, and mustard until blended. Place the fish fillets in the baking dish. Season the fish with salt and pepper to taste. With a table knife, spread the mayonnaise mixture over the fish. Then sprinkle the bread crumbs over the fish in an even layer; pat them gently so they adhere. Be sure to cover the edges. Drizzle the wine around the fish.

**3. Roast** the fish, uncovered, until it is just cooked through and the crumbs are spotted with gold, usually about 10 minutes. The timing can vary based on your oven and the baking dish you're using. Start checking after about 7 minutes; it may take as long as 13 minutes. With a spatula, transfer each portion to a warm dinner plate. Serve hot with lemon wedges and garnished with a couple of sprigs of dill or parsley.

For more servings, as I do with many other recipes for 2, just double or triple the ingredients.

How much fish to buy? Appetites obviously will vary, but a safe rule of thumb is this: figure on 6 to 8 ounces per serving. For richly flavored fish such as salmon or tuna, smaller portions (6 ounces) will probably do. For lean fish—sole, snapper, cod—up to 8 ounces will be okay.

Once you get fish home, use it within a day. To refrigerate, first pat dry with a damp paper towel. Place in an airtight, nonabsorbent container or on a plate and cover with plastic wrap. Refrigerate at 32° to 35°F.

Try this dish with steamed or sautéed fresh spinach and new potatoes, accompanied by a nice white wine.

Roasting the fish at a high temperature browns the crumbs quickly while keeping the flesh moist.

Don't worry about the alcohol in the **wine**—most of it will cook off.

The cooking technique I use here is really a variation of **braising**: first browning the food in a little fat, and then cooking in a small amount of liquid in a covered skillet or pot. Usually, braising is a long cooking process, but delicate fish requires just a brief cooking time.

For a **rich pan sauce**, swirl 1 to 2 tablespoons of cold unsalted butter into the pan juices after removing the fish from the pan. The skillet sauce should be thick and creamy—the butter should be thoroughly incorporated but not melted completely. Then add the parsley and proceed as directed in step 3.

# VEGETABLE- AND WINE-BRAISED FISH FILLETS

Prepare this simple, low-fat dish with any firm, white fish fillets.

MAKES 4 SERVINGS

1½ teaspoons olive oil

4 red snapper fillets (about 6 ounces each) or any other firm white fish skin on

Salt and freshly ground white pepper, to taste

2 carrots, trimmed, peeled, and cut into thin julienne

2 scallions (white portion with a little of the green), trimmed, halved lengthwise, and thinly sliced lengthwise

½ cup dry white wine

2 tablespoons chopped fresh parsley and/or chives

Lemon wedges, for serving

**1.** Heat the oil in a wide skillet, preferably nonstick, over medium heat. Season the fish fillets with salt and pepper. Place the fish, skin side down, in the skillet. Cook until lightly colored, 1 or 2 minutes.

**2.** Carefully turn the fish over with a spatula. Scatter the carrots and scallions over and around the fish. Pour the **wine** over the fish into the skillet; cover. **Cook gently** or **braise** until the fish is just opaque in the center, usually 8 to 10 minutes. Do not overcook.

**3.** Transfer the fish with a slotted spatula to serving plates and arrange, skin side down. Add the parsley to the pan and swirl the pan to mix. Spoon some of the vegetables and wine over each portion. Serve hot, with lemon wedges.

# SHRIMP SAUTÉ WITH GARLIC AND LEMON

This is actually a version of fish *à la meunière* (which means "Miller's wife's style" in French). This refers to the fact that fish fillets are usually coated with flour (hence "miller") before cooking. Then, in the same pan, a quick sauce is made with butter, lemon, and parsley. This is one of the simplest and tastiest ways to cook any type of seafood. The shrimp don't need to be floured, so the sauce is lighter and "cleaner" tasting.

MAKES 2 SERVINGS

¾ to 1 pound shrimp, preferably large ones, peeled with tails left on and deveined, if you like (Shrimp Basics, page 22)

1 tablespoon olive or vegetable oil
Salt and freshly ground black pepper, to taste

1 garlic clove, minced (you can omit this, if you like)

2 tablespoons unsalted butter, sliced
Juice of 1 large or 2 medium lemons

2 tablespoons chopped fresh parsley
Lemon wedges, for serving

**1.** Rinse the peeled shrimp under cold running water; place on a paper towel–lined plate.

**2.** Heat the oil in a nonreactive large nonstick skillet over medium-high heat. Pat the shrimp dry with paper towels. Add to the skillet, spreading them out in a single layer if possible (if not, sauté in 2 batches). Sprinkle with salt and pepper to taste; scatter the garlic around the shrimp. Let the shrimp sizzle in the hot oil without stirring or turning for about 1 minute. With tongs, turn the shrimp over; sauté, stirring occasionally with a wooden spoon, for 1 minute longer. Toss the shrimp until they just turn pink with no raw traces and are opaque in the center, 1 to 2 minutes more. Transfer the shrimp with a slotted spoon to 2 warm dinner plates.

**3.** Place the butter in the pan and heat, swirling the pan once or twice, until the butter turns nut-brown and fragrant (but not black), usually 2 or 3 minutes. Pour the lemon juice into the pan and let it bubble up for a moment. Turn off the heat and add the parsley, swirling the pan to mix. Drizzle the sauce over the shrimp and serve immediately with lemon wedges.

**How do I serve this?** With orzo, a rice-shaped pasta, or just plain white rice, or brown, or for a slightly nuttier flavor, an aromatic rice such as basmati. And a green vegetable—green beans or broccoli.

**To devein or not to devein?** With smaller shrimp I usually don't devein. In large shrimp, however, the vein, which is actually the intestinal tract, may be gritty and is considered by some to be unattractive—so you may wish to remove it.

The shrimp can be cleaned in advance; chill, covered with plastic wrap.

If I'm juicing 1 or 2 lemon halves directly into a skillet, I'll often do it through a strainer to keep the seeds out.

**Scallops** work very well in this dish. The small, sweet bay scallops are delicious but sometimes hard to find. The more readily available sea scallops are larger, so for quicker cooking, you may want to cut them horizontally in half or even thirds if they are really large. Flour them lightly in the usual *à la meunière* style.

Paella really is a **whole meal in itself.** I would serve a green salad, and I think that would take care of it.

**You can make this with either long-grain rice, or** with Arborio or other medium grain rice. The long-grain rice will result in firmer, more separate grains—a better-looking dish. This is the rice to use if you're serving this to dinner guests. But because of its starch, Arborio rice will stick together slightly, which is more like an authentic paella. It doesn't look as good, but I find the texture and flavor have more character. Either works fine.

An intriguing spice, **saffron** adds a subtle bitterness and a wild, distinctive orange-yellow color to all kinds of dishes. However, it's exorbitantly expensive, since it's derived from the stigma of a nonpoisonous crocus plant. **Turmeric** is frequently used as a much less expensive substitute for its coloring properties rather than its flavor.

# ARROZ CON SEAFOOD

This is a quick version of Spanish paella.

MAKES ABOUT 3 SERVINGS, OR MAYBE EVEN 4

2 tablespoons olive oil

1 red onion, coarsely chopped

1 yellow or red bell pepper, cored, seeded (Bell Pepper Basics, page 16), and cut lengthwise into strips

1 carrot, trimmed, peeled, and sliced on a diagonal ¼ inch thick

4 garlic cloves, minced

1 teaspoon salt

1 cup long-grain white rice or **medium-grain** Arborio rice (page 82)

¼ cup dry white wine

Pinch *each* of **saffron** threads, dried red pepper flakes, and dried thyme

3 canned whole tomatoes, drained and chopped, or 4 oil-packed sun-dried tomatoes, chopped

3 tablespoons chopped fresh parsley

1 can (about 14 ounces) chicken broth or 1 bottle (8 ounces) **clam juice**

½ pound large or medium shrimp (Shrimp Basics, page 22), in the shell

½ pound sea or bay **scallops,** halved crosswise if large

1 cup frozen peas (right from the freezer)

4 to 6 pimiento-stuffed olives, sliced (optional)

Freshly ground black pepper, to taste

**1.** Heat 2 tablespoons of the olive oil in a nonreactive shallow **casserole,** deep sauté pan, or **paella** pan over medium-high heat. Add the onion, bell pepper, carrot, garlic, and salt; sauté, stirring occasionally, just until the vegetables begin to soften, about 5 minutes. Add the remaining 1 tablespoon oil and the rice and stir until the rice is coated with the oil and begins to turn slightly translucent, about 3 minutes. Add the wine, saffron, pepper flakes, and thyme; boil until dry, but don't let the rice brown. (The recipe can be prepared in advance to this point. Cover and let stand at room temperature, then reheat, adding a tablespoon or two of water.)

**2.** Add the tomatoes and 1 tablespoon of the parsley. Pour the chicken broth or clam juice into a 2-cup liquid measuring cup; add enough water to come to 2 cups and add to the pan. Bring to a boil. Stir, lower the heat to a simmer, and cover the pan. Simmer for 15 minutes without stirring. Check every now and then to be sure the mixture isn't boiling.

**3.** Add the shrimp, scallops, peas (breaking them up), and olives; gently stir everything into the rice with a wooden spoon. Add ¼ cup water (this dish should be quite moist) and a few grinds of pepper; cover and simmer until the rice is tender and the seafood is just opaque, 5 or 6 minutes longer. (If you are using Arborio rice, you may need to moisten it with ½ cup water, rather than the ¼ cup. In any case, the rice should be moist but not too soupy.) Be careful not to overcook. To be sure, cut into the center of a scallop and a shrimp. Taste and correct all seasonings, adding salt, pepper, and herbs as needed. Sprinkle with the remaining 2 tablespoons parsley and serve immediately.

Bottled clam juice is one of those convenience foods that makes perfect sense—it's an easy way to intensify the seafood flavor of any dish.

If you can't find scallops, increase the amount of shrimp to 1 pound.

Paella gets its name from the special pan in which it is traditionally cooked and served—a wide, shallow, two-handled affair usually 13 to 14 inches in diameter, which allows for easy absorption of the liquid by the rice and an attractive presentation of all the ingredients.

How do I serve this? Plenty of crusty Italian bread and perhaps a platter of roasted red peppers and artichoke hearts to begin with. For a wine, a Pouilly-Fumé.

Firm-fleshed fish is the choice for fish stews. It holds its shape during the simmering and doesn't disintegrate into a pulpy mess.

# MAIN-DISH SEAFOOD STEW

This zesty seafood stew is lavish but actually easy to make. It's a great dinner party centerpiece. As per Italian tradition, no Parmigiano-Reggiano cheese should be served with seafood sauces.

Stew Base

- 1 tablespoon olive oil
- 1 medium-large red onion, coarsely chopped
- 1 small red bell pepper, cored, seeded (Bell Pepper Basics, page 16), and chopped
- 1 small green bell pepper, cored, seeded, and chopped
- 2 or 3 garlic cloves, thinly sliced
  Good-size pinch *each* of dried oregano and dried red pepper flakes
- 1 bay leaf
- 1 strip orange peel, removed with a vegetable peeler
- 2/3 cup dry white wine
- 1 can (16 ounces) whole tomatoes in puree
- 1 bottle (8 ounces) clam juice or 3/4 cup water

**Seafood**

- 1 dozen littleneck or other small clams (or substitute 1/2 pound sea scallops, cut in 2 or 3 pieces each if large, or use a combination of scallops and clams)
- 10 to 12 ounces thick, **firm-fleshed** fish fillet, such as cod, scrod, or haddock, cut into 1-inch chunks
- 3/4 pound medium shrimp, shelled and deveined (Shrimp Basics, page 22)
- 2 tablespoons *each* chopped fresh parsley and fresh basil (do not substitute dried)
  Few drops of fresh lemon juice
  Freshly ground black pepper, to taste
  Salt, to taste
  Small fresh basil leaves or parsley sprigs, for garnish

You can prepare the tomato base mixture in advance. Then, at serving time, all you have to do is reheat the sauce and drop in the seafood.

1. **To make the stew base:** Heat the oil in a nonreactive large nonstick skillet or deep sauté pan over medium-high heat. Add the onion, red and green bell peppers, garlic, oregano, pepper flakes, bay leaf, orange peel, and 1 tablespoon water; toss with a wooden spoon to coat everything with oil. Cover and sweat or cook, stirring occasionally with a wooden spoon, until the vegetables begin to wilt, 3 or 4 minutes. Uncover and sauté, tossing, until the vegetables are softened, 3 minutes longer.

2. Add the wine; cook, stirring occasionally, until nearly evaporated, about 3 minutes. Add the tomatoes (rinse out the can with a little water and add) and cook, breaking them up with a wooden spoon, for 8 minutes. Add the clam juice and simmer until the sauce thickens lightly, 6 to 8 minutes more. Remove the bay leaf and orange peel. (The recipe can be prepared **in advance** to this point. Refrigerate for a day or two. To continue with this recipe, return the tomato mixture to simmering.)

3. **Adding the seafood:** Place the clams, if using, in the simmering tomato mixture and cover tightly. Simmer gently, adjusting the heat if necessary, until the shells are just beginning to open, about 3 minutes. Gently stir in the chunks of fish and the shrimp, plus the scallops, if you are using them. Cover tightly and simmer until the fish is just opaque and the clams have opened, 4 or 5 minutes longer. Discard any unopened clams. The timing may vary; do not overcook.

4. Turn off the heat. Stir in the parsley and basil, lemon juice, pepper, and a little salt, if needed. Spoon the seafood mixture into 4 wide serving bowls, using tongs to arrange the pieces quickly and attractively. Garnish with basil leaves or parsley sprigs and serve immediately. Pass a pepper mill at the table.

For the beginnings of a delicious **lobster** salad, let the cooked lobster cool, then remove the flesh from the shell.

**Steaming results in a less waterlogged lobster** ~~than if it is boiled.~~

# STEAMED LOBSTER WITH BUTTER SAUCE TWO WAYS

This is certainly one of life's indulgences. As a small boy, I had a book with a picture of a lobster—I was *terrified* of it. It took me quite a few years before I could bring myself to eat one of these creatures. But did I not know what I was missing! Then, when I ran a restaurant on Martha's Vineyard with Prout Robert, I found I wasn't so happy having to kill several dozen lobsters every night, to order.

MAKES 2 SERVINGS

    Coarse (kosher) salt or sea salt

2  live lobsters (1½ pounds each)

**Drawn Butter**

5  tablespoons unsalted butter

    Juice of ½ lemon

    or

**Herb-Butter Sauce**

1  shallot, finely chopped

½  cup dry white wine

2  tablespoons red wine vinegar

2  tablespoons heavy cream (optional)

5  tablespoons cold unsalted butter, cut into pieces

    Fresh lemon juice, to taste

    Pinch of coarse (kosher) salt or sea salt and fresh ground black pepper

2  tablespoons snipped fresh chives

1  lemon, halved

**1.** Bring about 3 inches of water to a rolling boil in a pot large enough to hold the lobsters. Add salt. Plunge the lobsters into the pot and cover tightly. **Steam,** maintaining a steady boil, for 12 or 13 minutes.

**2. To serve with Drawn Butter:** Melt the butter in a small saucepan. Continue to cook over very low heat for another 5 minutes or so. Spoon off any froth from the surface and discard. Spoon the clear butter into 2 ramekins, avoiding any sediment in the bottom of the pan. Squeeze a little lemon juice into each ramekin and serve with the lobster

**3. To serve with Herb-Butter Sauce:** Bring the shallot, wine, and vinegar to a boil in a nonreactive small saucepan or skillet. Boil, uncovered, until the mixture is nearly dry. (If using the cream, add to the saucepan and boil until thickened, usually about 2 minutes. Remove the pan from the heat.) Just before serving the sauce, place the pan over low heat. Heat the mixture for a minute or so. Add the butter, 1 or 2 pieces at a time, swirling it in with a wooden spoon or whisk. The butter should liquefy and become opaque but not melt completely. Continue adding all of the butter; turn off the heat. Add lemon juice, salt and pepper to taste, and the chives. Taste and correct the seasonings, adding lemon juice, vinegar, and salt and pepper, if needed. Serve immediately in a bowl or 2 ramekins.

**4.** With tongs, remove the lobsters from the water, letting all possible water drain back into the pot. Crack the claws with a nutcracker so they can be opened easily. Place the lobster on a work surface, with the tail facing you and top shell down. With a large chef's knife, cut lengthwise through the middle of the tail flesh, cutting the thin shell over the flesh, plus the tail flesh in half, but without cutting through the shell underneath. Serve immediately on large plates (plus an extra plate on the table for shells), flesh side up, with a lemon half for garnish, plus the sauce of your choice. This is real living.

Five

# MAIN DISHES: POULTRY

|  | |
|---|---|
| | Crisp and Juicy Roast Chicken |
| **Techniques:** | trussing/roasting/letting meat rest |
| | |
| | Pan-Sautéed Chicken Breasts |
| **Techniques:** | sautéing and baking/deglazing/creating a pan sauce |
| | |
| | Basic Method for Oven-Poached Chicken |
| **Techniques:** | poaching in simmering liquid/poaching extra chicken for later uses/using a flavored poaching liquid/cooling in the broth/reusing broth for other dishes/other uses for oven-poached chicken |
| | |
| | Chicken and Vegetable Curry |
| **Techniques:** | poaching/thickening with a puree/enriching with yogurt/making curry powder/toasting spices |
| | |
| | Chicken Paprika |
| **Techniques:** | braising/cooking a spice/thickening sauces with vegetable puree/enriching with sour cream |

**Techniques:**

Broiled Mustard-Crumbed Cornish Hens

butterflying/broiling

**Techniques:**

Alsatian Chicken with Beer

braising/enriching with heavy cream

**Techniques:**

Turkey Roasted in a Paper Bag

roasting a turkey/making a giblet gravy

**Technique:**

Brandied Pecan Stuffing

toasting nuts

**Techniques:**

The Four Seasons Cranberry Relish

seasoning bag/caramelizing

**Chicken is prepared in many kitchens, and with good reason—it's economical, easy to prepare, cooks quickly, and is available in all its separate parts.** For the beginning cook and even the more seasoned veteran, chicken presents a good kitchen workout. You can try virtually any cooking technique on the bird with great success: roasting, poaching, broiling, braising, sautéing, casseroling, and even combinations of these. Keep in mind that all these things can be done to turkey parts as well.

The one thing I particularly like about chicken or poultry in general is that its rich, neutral flavor adapts well to just about any flavor scheme you want to create.

I've carefully chosen just a few recipes for this chapter to illustrate basic cooking techniques, beginning with a simple but deliciously moist roasted chicken and moving through some of my favorites borrowed from other cuisines, involving combinations of sautéing and braising and other techniques. Once you've mastered them (or maybe you already have and just need a refresher course), you can improvise and create your own collection of poultry classics.

Also included here is the method for an easily broiled, butterflied Cornish hen, and since every beginning cook should have one, the classic roast turkey.

A final healthful note: You can reduce by almost half the bird's fat if you remove the skin just before serving. Leaving it on during cooking keeps the meat moist and adds flavor without contributing significant amounts of fat to the flesh itself.

If it wasn't apparent before, it should be now—cooking chicken gives you a chance to both learn and further develop a whole range of culinary skills.

**How do I serve this?**
Throw some small red
potatoes, with their
skins on, into the roast-
ing pan and let them
cook right along with
the chicken. A green
vegetable, such as broc-
coli, green beans, sugar
snap peas, or whatever
simply steamed, would
be nice.

Chicken has never
tasted better. Not only
are branded producers
offering more flavorful
birds, but all kinds of
local breeders are
trekking to market their
free-range varieties—
birds that scratch for
their own food. With
such good flavor, a sim-
ple preparation like
roasting is best.

Trussing a bird—tying
up all its loose ends—
holds it together during
roasting so parts don't
dry out and the bird
keeps its neat shape;
the legs and wings hug
the body. Trussing also
prevents any stuffing
from falling out.

If you like, you can
roast the chicken on a
nonstick-coated roasting
rack, placed in a roast-
ing pan in which it fits.
It's not necessary, but it
does help the bird crisp
all the way around and
the fat drains away
from the bird.

# CRISP AND JUICY ROAST CHICKEN

A roast chicken is something every accomplished home cook should be able to turn
out with ease. In fact, think of this as something you can throw into the oven when
you don't even want to think about dinner.

1   chicken (about 3 1/2 pounds), giblets removed, all possible fat removed,
    rinsed under cold water, patted very dry with paper towels
    Salt and freshly ground black pepper, to taste
3   garlic cloves, smashed, with a thin layer of skin left on
2   fresh thyme sprigs or a pinch of dried
1   bay leaf
2   tablespoons olive oil
    Watercress sprigs, for garnish

**1.** Preheat the oven to 425°F. Choose a roasting pan in which the chicken fits com-
pactly. (I use an oval enameled cast-iron gratin dish.)

**2.** Season the chicken well with salt and pepper, inside and out, rubbing the seasonings into the flesh. (You can reach inside the cavity just to be sure the bird is
seasoned.) Tuck the garlic, thyme, and bay leaf into the cavity of the chicken.

**3. To truss:** Tie the wings together to hold in place or tuck under the back of the
bird. With kitchen string, tie the ends of the legs and tail skin together. Place the
chicken in the pan, scatter any giblets, including the neck, around the chicken, and
brush or rub with olive oil (I usually do this with my fingers, which are moisturized
by the oil). Place the trussed bird on its side, with a leg upward.

**4. Roast** for 25 minutes, without touching the bird. Holding the chicken with 2
spatulas or paper towels, very carefully turn it over onto its other leg. Baste once
with the pan juices and roast for 25 minutes longer. Carefully turn breast side up
and continue to roast, using a large metal spoon to baste the bird with the pan
juices every 5 minutes or so, until the breast is nicely golden. The bird is done
when you poke the thigh with a paring knife and the juices run clear and golden
with no trace of pink near the bone. This usually takes about 20 minutes from the
time you rearrange the bird breast up.

**5.** Remove the pan from the oven; place it on a stove-top burner. Carefully transfer the chicken to a serving platter. Cover loosely with foil and **let rest** for about 15 minutes before carving.

**6.** While the bird rests, carefully pour off and discard all possible fat from the roasting pan, leaving any browned pan juices in the pan. Add ⅔ cup water and cook over medium heat, scraping up all of the browned bits from the bottom of the pan (these bits have that great "roasted" flavor). Simmer the juices, uncovered, until reduced by not quite half. Carve the bird and arrange on a platter. Strain the juices over and serve hot, garnished with watercress sprigs.

**Letting roasted meats rest** is standard for any variety at all—chicken, beef, turkey, pork, whatever. You're allowing the hot and cooler juices to redistribute themselves, resulting in moister, juicier meat. If you cut right into the bird or meat as soon as it comes out of the oven, you'd let all the precious juices drain out immediately.

**Leftover roast chicken is** excellent for chicken sandwiches, soup, or chicken salad.

**How do I serve this?**
White rice or orzo and a small green salad would be my choices.

**Cooking the chicken on the bone with the skin adds delicious flavor. If** you're worried about fat, just remove the skin before serving.

**Sautéing the chicken first adds golden color to the skin, while baking evenly cooks the meat through to a moist doneness.**

# PAN-SAUTÉED CHICKEN BREASTS

This is an excellent (and easy) way to cook chicken breasts with the skin on—it becomes wonderfully crisp and crusty.

MAKES 4 SERVINGS

2 large whole chicken breasts, with skin and bone (12 to 14 ounces each), split in half, fat and excess skin removed

1 tablespoon olive oil, plus more as needed

1 large garlic clove, smashed

Salt and freshly ground black pepper, to taste

¼ teaspoon paprika, preferably Hungarian, hot or sweet, depending on taste

2½ to 3 cups sliced white mushrooms (or wild mushrooms, or a combination) (Mushroom Basics, page 21)

½ cup dry white wine or water

3 tablespoons snipped fresh chives or chopped fresh parsley

Lemon wedges, for serving

**1.** Preheat the oven to 400°F., with a rack positioned in the center. Rinse the chicken; pat thoroughly dry with paper towels.

**2.** Heat the olive oil and the garlic in a large, nonstick, ovenproof skillet over medium heat. Cook until the garlic is lightly golden, about 2 minutes; discard the garlic. Raise the heat to medium-high. Sprinkle the skin side of the chicken breast halves with salt and pepper to taste and the paprika. Place the chicken, skin side down, in the skillet. Salt and pepper the bone sides lightly. **Sauté,** shaking the pan once or twice to prevent sticking, until the skin is a rich golden brown, about 6 minutes.

**3.** Turn the breast halves over with tongs. Place in the oven and **bake** until the chicken is just firm (but not rubbery) when pressed with a fingertip and is no longer pink near the bone, usually 10 to 15 minutes. Carefully place the skillet on a stove-top burner; transfer the chicken to a plate, cover with foil, and set aside.

**4.** If there is less than 2 tablespoons of fat in the skillet, add enough olive oil to equal that amount; this should coat the bottom of the pan. Heat over medium-high heat. Add the mushrooms; sprinkle with salt and pepper. Let the mushrooms sizzle in the hot oil for about 1 minute. To finish the **sauce,** sauté, tossing, until the mushrooms begin to turn lightly golden, about 3 minutes. Add the wine and cook, scraping (Deglazing Basics, page 24) up any browned bits in the pan with a wooden spoon and stirring until the liquid has reduced by about half, 4 or 5 minutes. Stir in the chives or parsley.

**5.** Arrange the chicken breasts on dinner plates. Spoon the mushroom sauce over and around the chicken. Serve immediately with lemon wedges.

## VARIATION: CHICKEN FAJITAS

Prepare the chicken breasts as directed above. Trim away the bones. Cut the breast halves crosswise into slivers or strips. Heat a skillet, preferably cast-iron, with 1 tablespoon olive oil over medium-high heat. Add 1 large onion and 1 large red bell pepper, both cut in long slivers, plus 2 sliced, seeded fresh or pickled jalapeño peppers, if you like; sauté, stirring occasionally with a wooden spoon, until softened and lightly golden, usually 6 to 8 minutes. Add the chicken slivers and toss until heated through, about 2 minutes, no longer. Serve the chicken-vegetable mixture from its skillet, along with warmed flour tortillas (heat according to package directions), Fresh Salsa with Avocado (page 40), and sour cream. Garnish with lime wedges. Guests can assemble their own fajitas—that's half the fun.

This is the classic **pan sauce:** Ingredients are sautéed in the pan drippings; then the pan is deglazed with a flavorful liquid and the mixture is boiled or reduced to concentrate flavor and thicken the sauce.

Traditionally made with skirt steak that has been marinated, this version of **fajitas** is leaner since it uses chicken breast.

Grab the chicken skin with a paper towel for a firm grip and it will pull right off.

You can also cook breast halves on the bone; these may take slightly longer, usually 7 to 9 minutes in the oven. When they are cool, cut away and discard the bones. The bones help make the broth more flavorful.

Remember that the chicken will continue to cook slightly as it cools in its broth, so don't cook it a moment too long.

Reserve the poaching liquid for soups, stews, or for cooking rice pilafs. For an easy sauce, boil the poaching liquid in a saucepan until reduced by a half to two-thirds. Stir in a little heavy cream and your choice of seasonings.

Letting the chicken cool in its own cooking liquid keeps the chicken moist and infuses it with even more flavor.

# BASIC METHOD FOR OVEN-POACHED CHICKEN

Once you've mastered this easy technique with fish (page 92), there's no better way to cook moist chicken breasts. Simmering the chicken in chicken broth doubles the flavor—of both the chicken and the broth.

2 tablespoons chopped shallots or scallions (white and green portions)
Boneless chicken breast halves (any amount), skin and all possible fat removed, rinsed under cold water
Salt and freshly ground black pepper, to taste
1 cup canned chicken broth, or as needed
Watercress sprigs and lemon wedges, for garnish

**1.** Preheat the oven to 400°F., with a rack positioned in the center. Scatter the chopped shallots in a shallow baking pan or ovenproof skillet that will hold the chicken in a single layer. Arrange the chicken, without crowding, in the pan, with the smooth flesh side up. Season the chicken with salt and pepper. Pour enough of the **broth** around the chicken to come about two-thirds up it, then add enough cold water to come not quite to the top of the chicken. Cover with a buttered sheet of parchment or wax paper, buttered side down (this helps keep the breasts moist).

**2.** Place the pan on a stove-top burner over medium heat. Bring the liquid just to a boil, watching carefully. The moment it begins to boil, carefully transfer the pan to the oven. **Oven poach** until the chicken is just cooked—you're looking for the center of the breast to turn from translucent to opaque. This can take as little as 5 minutes or up to 7 minutes for thicker breasts. Don't overcook.

**3.** To serve the chicken hot, remove it from the broth right away. Serve the chicken as is, with or without a sauce, garnished with watercress and lemon. Or, to serve cool, remove the pan from the heat and let the **chicken cool in its broth** to luke-warm. With tongs, lift the chicken from the broth, draining all possible broth back into the pan. Serve cool, with an herbed mayonnaise.

## Other Uses for Oven-Poached Chicken

- Cut into slivers and toss with pasta dishes.
- Cut into slivers and toss with Stir-Fry of Rice and Vegetables (page 183).
- Serve cool, with a mustard vinaigrette, along with marinated potato salad, marinated steamed green beans, and salad greens—sort of a chicken version of salade niçoise.
- Arrange with Tri-Color Roasted Peppers (page 170), mozzarella, feta or ricotta salata cheese, plus kalamata olives for a light summer lunch.

### A GREAT CHICKEN SALAD SANDWICH

Cut the drained, cooled, oven-poached chicken into bite-size chunks. Add a little celery, strings removed (page 18) and finely diced, if you like, plus a little finely chopped red onion. Sprinkle with salt and pepper to taste and chopped fresh herbs —chives, tarragon (don't overdo it), parsley, dill, or combinations of any of these are all very nice. Very gently toss the ingredients in a bowl with a rubber spatula just to combine.

In a small bowl, stir together equal parts reduced-calorie mayonnaise and low-fat plain yogurt; if you like, stir in a spoonful of coarse-grained or Dijon mustard to taste (use judiciously). Add just enough of this dressing mixture to moisten the chicken without making it too gooey—start with less; you can always add more.

Pile the chicken salad onto whole wheat bread, toasted or not. Top with ripe tomato slices, well salted, and a piece of romaine or red leaf lettuce. Top with another slice of whole wheat, cut in half, and dig in.

To feed a crowd, just double the amount of ingredients.

Curry powder is not one spice, but actually a mix of spices—as many as 20—typically includ-ing cloves cumin coriander, cayenne, and turmeric for its characteristic yellow-orange color. If you're shopping for a commercially prepared mix, search for a spice store where spices will be fresher because of a higher turnover. Madras curry powder, usually packaged in a tin, is hotter than most other store-bought varieties. Since the flavors of a curry dish are pleas-antly complex and more often than not spicy hot, a variety of accom-paniments, ranging from sweet to spicy-sweet, are usually presented in small bowls to be spooned onto the plate with the curry.

Aromatic rices are long-grain white rices but are distinguished from ordi-nary white rice by their nutty aromas and flavors—in fact, they're often described as "popcorn" rice. Basmati and jasmine are two popular types in this family.

# CHICKEN AND VEGETABLE CURRY

This is not authentically Indian (but tasty nevertheless) and is loosely based on a dish that the late Bert Greene used to cook at The Store in Amagansett—arguably America's first gourmet take-out shop. Set out condiments to dress it up, if you like,

1    can (about 14 ounces) reduced-sodium chicken broth

$\frac{1}{2}$   cup cold water

4    skinless, boneless chicken breast halves (about $1\frac{1}{2}$ pounds total), fat and tendons removed

1    tablespoon vegetable oil

2    onions, thinly sliced

2    carrots, sliced on a sharp diagonal $\frac{1}{4}$ inch thick

1    celery rib, strings removed (Celery Stringing, page 18), sliced on a sharp diagonal $\frac{1}{4}$ inch thick

1    red bell pepper, cored, seeded (Bell Pepper Basics, page 16), and cut into short, thin slivers

2    garlic cloves, thinly sliced

2    teaspoons minced, seeded, fresh hot chili pepper (Hot Chili Pepper Basics, page 17, or canned jalapeño peppers [optional])

$1\frac{1}{2}$ to 2 teaspoons grated fresh ginger (page 20)

$1\frac{1}{2}$ to 2 tablespoons Curry Spice Mix (recipe, page 116) or good-quality **curry powder,** to taste

1    Granny Smith apple, peeled, cored, and diced

$\frac{1}{2}$   cup low-fat plain yogurt, plus more as needed

$\frac{1}{4}$   cup Coco Lopez or other canned sweetened coconut cream (optional)

$\frac{1}{2}$   cup dried apricots, cut into strips

$\frac{1}{4}$   cup dried currants or raisins

Grated zest of 1 small orange

Salt and cayenne, if needed

3   tablespoons chopped fresh cilantro and/or parsley

2   to 3 cups cooked rice, preferably basmati or jasmine

3   tablespoons chopped **crystallized ginger**, for garnish (optional)
    **Pappadams**, toasted almonds, and/or mango or other **chutney**, for
    accompaniments

**1.** Bring the broth and water to a boil in a wide skillet. Slip in the chicken. Lower
the heat, cover, and simmer **(poach)** just until firm and opaque in the center, about
8 minutes (the timing can vary; do not overcook). Remove from the heat, uncover,
and let the chicken cool slightly in the broth.

**2.** Heat the oil in a large nonstick skillet over medium-high heat. Add the onions,
carrots, celery, and bell pepper and cook, tossing with a wooden spoon, until crisp-
tender, 5 to 8 minutes. Add the garlic, chili (if using), and fresh ginger and sauté
until very fragrant, about 2 minutes. Sprinkle the Curry Spice Mix or curry powder
over the vegetables and cook, stirring, for 1 minute longer to mellow the flavor of
the spices.

**3.** With tongs, remove the chicken breasts to a plate. Add the chicken poaching
liquid plus the apple to the vegetable mixture. Bring to a boil. Lower the heat, cover,
and simmer until the vegetables are just tender, about 15 minutes.

**4.** Meanwhile, cut the chicken crosswise into ½-inch-wide chunks or strips; return
them to the plate.

**5.** With a slotted spoon or skimmer, transfer about 1 cup of the vegetables and a
little of the broth to a food processor or blender. Puree until smooth and stir back
into the broth to thicken. (If you'd like the sauce a little thicker, puree a bit more of
the solids.) Stir in the chicken plus any juices from the plate, the **yogurt,** coconut
cream, apricots, currants, and orange zest until blended. Gently heat through, but
do not allow to boil. Add salt and cayenne to taste and/or more yogurt to taste; the
sauce should be pale-colored with a mellow flavor but still with plenty of bite. Cover
and cook very gently over the lowest possible heat for 5 minutes. Check occasionally to make sure the mixture is not boiling. Stir in the cilantro and/or parsley, then
serve hot, over the rice. Scatter the chopped crystallized ginger over the top, if you
like, and arrange the accompaniments on the table.

Sweet-hot in flavor, crystallized ginger is made from coarsely chopped pieces of fresh ginger, cooked in syrup and then coated with sugar. You should be able to find it in jars in the spice section of your supermarket.

Pappadams are a very thin Indian bread, usu-ally round in shape and made with lentil flour. When deep-fried, they puff to double their size and are perfect for dunking into the deli-cious sauce in this dish.

Made from fruit, chut-ney is a spicy-sweet condiment that is fre-quently served with cur-ries since it cools the spicy heat.

Poaching the chicken, rather than browning it in fat as is often done in a curry dish, makes this dish lighter in terms of fat calories—plus the chicken stays moister.

Adding yogurt to the liq-uid in a pan at the end of cooking is an easy way to enrich a sauce without the addition of a lot of extra fat. Make sure the sauce doesn't come to a boil or the yogurt will separate.

**Toasting the spice mixture in a dry skillet cooks away the raw taste, making for a richer flavor.**

## CURRY SPICE MIX

You don't have to make this spice mix; you can simply use 1½ to 2 tablespoons of commercially prepared curry powder, to taste. But by toasting and grinding your own, you'll have a much more interesting, complex flavor. If you are using just the store-bought variety, also toast that in a dry skillet for more flavor.

MAKES ABOUT 3 TABLESPOONS

1½  tablespoons good-quality curry powder
  1  teaspoon coriander seeds or ground coriander
  1  teaspoon ground cinnamon
  ½  teaspoon mustard seeds or ground mustard
  ½  teaspoon allspice berries or ground allspice
  ½  teaspoon ground turmeric
  ½  teaspoon freshly grated nutmeg or mace
  ½  teaspoon cardamom seeds or ground cardamom

Place all the **spices** in a small, heavy skillet and heat **over medium heat,** shaking the skillet gently, until the first tiny wisp of smoke appears, 2 or 3 minutes. Cook, stirring constantly with a wooden spoon, until very aromatic and lightly colored, about 2 minutes more. Remove from the heat and let cool briefly; then grind in a spice grinder (unless you are using all preground spices). Place in a jar with a tight-fitting lid and store at cool room temperature for up to 4 months.

# CHICKEN PAPRIKA

This is a lightened version of the wonderful traditional Hungarian dish, which I ate in endless variation on two long visits to Budapest. The gravy is thickened only with a puree of its cooking vegetables, no flour—it makes for "purer" flavors. This recipe looks like it goes on forever, but it's actually a simple, easy braise (page 25)—you brown the meat first, then simmer it in a small amount of liquid, covered, until very tender. And it's even tastier if you make it ahead—the flavors will develop and marry.

MAKES 6 SERVINGS

4 to 4$\frac{1}{2}$ pounds chicken pieces (legs, thighs, breast halves), excess fat removed
   Salt, to taste
2 tablespoons vegetable oil or bacon fat
4$\frac{1}{2}$ cups chopped onions (4 or 5 medium)
4 carrots, trimmed, peeled, halved lengthwise, and sliced $\frac{1}{2}$ inch thick
3 celery ribs, strings removed (Celery Stringing, page 18), and sliced $\frac{1}{2}$ inch thick
2 red bell peppers, cored, seeded (Bell Pepper Basics, page 16), and cut into $\frac{3}{4}$-inch dice
1 green bell pepper, cored, seeded, and cut into $\frac{3}{4}$-inch dice
4 garlic cloves, minced
$\frac{1}{2}$ pound white mushrooms (or use wild or a combination of white and wild; Mushroom Basics, page 21), stems trimmed flush with caps, stems coarsely chopped and caps thickly sliced
$\frac{1}{3}$ cup medium-hot **Hungarian paprika** or $\frac{1}{4}$ cup sweet paprika plus 2 tablespoons hot paprika
1 can (about 1 pound) whole tomatoes, drained if in water but not if in puree, broken up
$\frac{1}{2}$ teaspoon dried marjoram
1$\frac{3}{4}$ cups homemade or reduced-sodium canned chicken broth
   Freshly ground black pepper, to taste
1$\frac{1}{3}$ cups sour cream
3 tablespoons chopped fresh parsley →

**How do I serve this?** Wide egg noodles or spaetzle (tiny noodles or dumplings) are perfect for soaking up the sauce and steamed green beans would add a touch of color to the plate.

**Hungarian paprika** has a haunting flavor that is more about the deep flavor of the red peppers rather than simple heat (though some Hungarian paprikas are hot indeed). This dish is not worth making without top-quality paprika imported from Hungary.

**Cooking the paprika (or toasting it in a dry skillet) removes its raw taste, adding depth of flavor. The same technique is used when cooking chili powder and curry powder.**

Braising the chicken pieces keeps them **moist and full of flavor.**

**1.** Pat the chicken pieces dry with paper towels; sprinkle with salt to taste. Heat the oil or fat in a nonreactive large skillet, preferably nonstick, over medium heat. When it is hot, add the chicken pieces (work in batches to avoid crowding the pan or get a second skillet going). Sauté until lightly golden, shaking the pan occasionally to prevent sticking and turning the pieces over with tongs, usually 8 to 10 minutes. Transfer the chicken pieces with tongs to paper towel–lined plates to drain. Discard all but 2 or 3 tablespoons of fat in the skillet.

**2.** Add the onions to the skillet; sauté over medium heat, tossing with a wooden spoon, until the onions begin to wilt, about 5 minutes. Add the carrots, celery, and bell peppers, tossing to coat with the fat. Sauté, tossing, until the vegetables begin to soften, about 5 minutes. Add the garlic and chopped mushroom stems; sauté, tossing, for 2 minutes. Add the **paprika** and cook, stirring, for about 2 minutes to mellow its flavor. Add the tomatoes and marjoram; cook, stirring and breaking up the tomatoes, until the mixture thickens somewhat, 2 to 5 minutes. Add the chicken broth, scraping up all browned bits in the bottom of the pan with a wooden spoon and stirring the mixture once or twice to combine. Season to taste with pepper.

**3.** Select a flameproof casserole or Dutch oven large enough to hold the chicken pieces in 2 layers. Arrange about one-third of the vegetable mixture in the bottom of the casserole. Arrange the chicken legs and thighs in one layer on top. Spoon half of the remaining vegetable mixture over, with some of its liquid. Top with the chicken breasts, skin sides up, and then with the remaining vegetable mixture and its liquid. The liquid should now come up to the bottom of the breasts; add chicken broth or water if necessary. Cover the casserole; bring to a boil over medium heat. Lower the heat and simmer or **braise,** covered, until the chicken is tender when poked with a fork and is no longer pink near the bone, 20 to 30 minutes. Remove from the heat. Degrease with a skimmer or large metal spoon, carefully spooning off and discarding all possible fat from the surface of the liquid. (The recipe can be prepared **in advance** to this point. Cool, then cover and refrigerate. When cold, remove the solidified fat from the top. Keep in mind this is an excellent way to remove fat from soups, stews, and casseroles, if you have the time.)

**4.** With a slotted spoon, transfer about 2 cups of the vegetables and a little of the broth from the casserole to a food processor or blender. Puree until nearly smooth. Stir the puree back into the stew **to thicken.** If the sauce doesn't seem thick enough, puree some more of the vegetables.

**5.** Return the casserole to the heat and bring to a simmer. Stir in the sliced mushroom caps; cover and simmer for 5 minutes. Spoon a little of the hot liquid into a small bowl. Stir in about ⅔ cup of the **sour cream** until well blended. Stir this mixture back into the casserole. The sauce should be a rosy salmon color; if it's too dark, add another spoonful or two of sour cream in the same manner. Taste and correct the seasonings, adding salt and pepper as needed. Return the stew to a simmer to gently heat through, but do not boil.

**6.** Stir the remaining ⅔ cup sour cream in a small bowl. Arrange the chicken pieces on 6 dinner plates, dividing equally. Spoon the chunky sauce over and around the chicken. Top with a dollop of sour cream, then sprinkle with chopped parsley. Pass the remaining sour cream at the table for extra garnishing.

**Thickening with vegetable purees** is a favorite technique of mine. It means you use less fat, no flour, and you get more flavor from the vegetables.

**Once sour cream** has been added to a sauce or other mixture for enrichment, be careful not to let the mixture boil, or the sour cream will separate.

**How do I serve this?**
Keep it simple for this one—small red potatoes, with skins on, boiled and tossed with a little butter and chopped parsley, and Quick Honey-Lemon Glazed Carrots (page 107).

For smaller appetites I would serve just half a hen per person. And for more than two diners, increase the number of hens accordingly.

Butterflying or flattening the hens allows all the surface on one side to be cooked evenly all at once.

Broiling works well for Cornish hens since the amount of meat on the bone is relatively small and cooks quickly, without drying out, under the high heat of the broiler. In this recipe, the high heat causes the bread crumb coating to get slightly crispy. The trick is to keep an eye on the bird so it doesn't cook too quickly.

# BROILED MUSTARD-CRUMBED CORNISH HENS

Here's a tasty treatment, made in minutes.

MAKES 2 SERVINGS

2 Cornish hens (about 1 pound each)
Salt and freshly ground black pepper, to taste
Olive oil, as needed
1½ tablespoons Dijon mustard
1½ tablespoons coarse-grained mustard
⅓ cup soft fresh bread crumbs (page 18)
Watercress or parsley sprigs, for garnish

**1.** Preheat the broiler, with a rack about 6 inches from the heat source. If you have access to a butcher, ask him to **butterfly** the hens, cutting out the backbone from each bird (freeze these for making stock or soup). Or do it yourself: With a boning knife or other sharp knife, simply cut along both sides of the backbone. Now place each hen, skin side up, on the work surface; press firmly with the palm of your hand, flattening the bird. Remove all excess fat from the birds; rinse in cold water and pat thoroughly dry with paper towels. (Wash your work surface well before using it for other ingredients.)

**2.** Line a jelly-roll pan or baking sheet that fits under the broiler with aluminum foil. Place the hens, skin side down (away from the heat), on the sheet. Salt and pepper the hens to taste; lightly brush with olive oil.

**3. Broil** until the bone sides begin to brown, 8 to 10 minutes. Remove the pan from the broiler; gently turn the birds over with tongs. In a small cup, stir together both mustards; spoon or brush the mustard over the entire skin sides of each bird. Sprinkle an even layer of bread crumbs over the skin. Drizzle with a little olive oil.

**4.** Return to the broiler, crumb sides up, and broil until golden, usually 2 or 3 minutes. Watch very carefully to prevent burning and gently shift the positions of the hens, if necessary, to prevent some spots from browning too quickly. Remove from the broiler and let stand for about 3 minutes before serving. Garnish with watercress or parsley sprigs.

## VARIATION: BAKED MUSTARD-CRUMBED CHICKEN

Cut a 3- to 3½-pound chicken into 8 parts: 2 drumsticks, 2 thighs, 2 breasts, 2 wings (or buy chicken parts). Preheat the oven to 400°F. Line a jelly-roll pan or baking sheet with foil; coat with nonstick cooking spray or rub with a little olive oil. Season the chicken with salt and pepper to taste. Place a layer of fresh bread crumbs in a pie plate next to the baking pan. Brush or spoon a mixture of equal parts Dijon and coarse-grained mustards on all sides of each piece of chicken. Then place a piece in the bread crumbs, turning it over to coat evenly. Shake off excess crumbs and place the chicken on the foil-lined sheet. Repeat, breading the remaining pieces.

**Bake,** without turning, until the crumbs are golden brown and the chicken is tender and no longer pink near the bone, usually 45 to 60 minutes. Serve hot.

This variation has all of the same flavoring elements as in the broiled hens, but since I'm using a whole chicken, cut up into parts, baking is much easier—I don't have to worry about turning all those parts over under the broiler and there is less likelihood the chicken, with more meat on the bone, will dry out since it cooks more slowly.

The chicken is delicious chilled—for picnic food, lunch boxes, or even midnight snacks.

**How do I serve this?**
Wide egg noodles, buttered, and a shredded cabbage salad on the side would be nice accompaniments.

Experiment with wild mushrooms such as shiitake, portobello, or cremini, or a combination of white and wild.

**Beer works just as well for braising** as it does as a beverage for accompanying food. It lends a mellow roundness of flavor to this chicken dish, and the sauce is then spiked with mustard. I also like beer for braising beef (page 135). This is one of those instances where light beer just won't work—you need the rich flavor of a full-bodied beer.

# ALSATIAN CHICKEN WITH BEER

This is based on traditional recipes for *coq à la bière*.

MAKES 4 SERVINGS

1 chicken (about 3½ pounds), cut into serving pieces, fat and extra skin removed
Salt and freshly ground black pepper, to taste
1 or 2 tablespoons unsalted butter
1 teaspoon vegetable oil
6 ounces quartered white **mushrooms** (about 2½ cups; Mushroom Basics, page 21)
2 tablespoons chopped shallots or the white portion of scallions
1 bottle (12 ounces) **beer** or ale (do not use "light" beer)
½ cup heavy cream
2 to 3 teaspoons whole grain mustard, to taste
Pinch of cayenne
2 tablespoons chopped fresh parsley

**1.** Pat the chicken pieces dry with paper towels. Sprinkle with salt and pepper to taste. Heat 1 tablespoon of the butter with the oil in a large, heavy skillet, preferably nonstick, over medium-high heat. Add the chicken pieces in a single layer (work in batches if necessary) and sauté, turning the pieces over once with tongs and shaking the pan to prevent sticking, until nicely browned, usually 15 to 18 minutes total. With a slotted spoon, transfer the chicken pieces to a plate, draining the fat back into the pan; set the chicken aside. If there is more than about 2 tablespoons fat in the pan, discard the excess.

**2.** Add the mushrooms to the pan and let sizzle for a moment over medium-high heat. Sauté, tossing with a wooden spoon, until lightly golden, about 4 minutes. With a slotted spoon, transfer to a plate and set aside. Pour off all but a thin film of fat, leaving any browned bits in the pan.

**3.** Add the shallots to the pan and cook, stirring, until softened slightly, 30 to 60 seconds. Add the beer or ale slowly; then add ¼ cup of the cream and bring to a boil, scraping up all of the browned bits from the bottom and sides of the pan with a wooden spoon (Deglazing Basics, page 24). Return the chicken to the skillet, cover, and lower the heat. Simmer or **braise,** turning the pieces over once, until the chicken is tender when poked with a fork and is no longer pink near the bone, about 20 minutes.

**4.** Meanwhile, preheat the oven to 250°F. (unless you're making this **in advance**). Transfer the chicken with tongs to a heatproof serving platter, cover loosely with foil, and keep warm in the oven.

**5.** Degrease the cooking juices, removing the fat from the surface with a skimmer or a large metal spoon. Add the remaining ¼ cup **cream** and the reserved mushrooms to the pan and bring to a boil. Boil vigorously, uncovered, until the sauce reduces by about half, 7 to 10 minutes. The sauce should coat the back of a spoon lightly but should still be quite liquid. Degrease the sauce again, if necessary, removing any fat from the surface. Stir in the mustard to taste, a pinch each of black pepper and cayenne, and any juices exuded by the chicken onto the platter. Taste and correct the seasonings, adding salt, black pepper, and cayenne, if needed. Remove the sauce from the heat and whisk in another tablespoon of butter if you like a sauce with a little more gloss. Pour the sauce over and around the chicken. Sprinkle with the parsley and serve immediately.

To make this dish **in advance,** leave the sauce slightly liquid when reducing it in step 5. Then place the chicken into the reduced sauce, cover, and set aside at cool room temperature. If storing for more than 1 hour, refrigerate. To serve, simply reheat the chicken and sauce together gently over medium heat, covered, until simmering, spooning the sauce gently over the chicken pieces as it heats.

Once **heavy cream** is added for the final enrichment, the sauce can be boiled without danger of separating, unlike the addition of sour cream or yogurt.

Use a fresh turkey within 1 or 2 days of purchase and keep refrigerated at all times.

Originally and traditionally made on the Portuguese island after which it is named, Madeira is a fortified wine, ranging in intensity from very dry to very sweet. It adds subtle flavors in cooking.

Roasting the turkey in a paper bag keeps it very moist during the initial cooking since it literally steams.

If you don't have a meat thermometer, the bird is done when you poke the thigh with a paring knife and the juices run clear and golden, with no trace of pink. The meat should not be pink near the bone.

To transfer the turkey to its platter, I usually pick up the turkey with a wad of paper towels in each hand—this way I get a firm grip and there's no risk of the bird sliding off the spatulas or whatever.

# TURKEY ROASTED IN A PAPER BAG

Just the idea of wrestling with a huge whole turkey probably throws you into a state of genuine panic. Actually, roasts are among the easiest of dishes, especially for a crowd—basically, you throw it in the oven and leave it there until it's done.

This is the most terrific dishes ever. I learned this method from the Levy's, the man whose Chicago restaurant, The Bakery, still lives on in happy memory. Did you know that the turkey was Ben Franklin's choice for our national bird?

MAKES 8 SERVINGS, WITH LEFTOVERS

1  **fresh turkey** (10 to 12 pounds), giblets removed and reserved
   Salt and freshly ground black pepper, to taste
¾  cup *each* diced onions, carrots, and celery
1  small turnip, peeled and sliced
3  garlic cloves, sliced
2  fresh thyme sprigs or a pinch of dried
   Chicken broth or water, as needed, plus 1 cup chicken or turkey broth, for the gravy
1  tablespoon unsalted butter, softened
1  tablespoon olive oil
⅔  cup dry **Madeira** wine

**1.** Preheat the oven to 325°F. Rinse the turkey inside and out; pat dry with paper towels. Salt and pepper the turkey lightly, inside and out. If stuffing the turkey (do it just before the turkey goes into the oven, no earlier), loosely spoon the stuffing into the neck cavity; then fold the neck skin over the opening and secure with a poultry pin. Spoon the stuffing loosely into the larger body cavity. Tuck the wings under the turkey. Scatter the onions, carrots, celery, turnip, garlic, and thyme in a roasting pan just large enough to hold the turkey (I like to use a disposable foil roasting pan—cleanup is a snap and in fact, the pan can be recycled). Scatter the turkey giblets (except the liver but including the neck) among the vegetables. Add chicken broth (better) or water to the pan to come to a depth of 1 inch. Rub the butter and olive oil over the turkey skin and carefully place it in a **brown paper bag.** (Try to find a bag with no printing on it. If you can't, use a special roasting bag.) Fold the top over and place the bag, turkey breast up, directly on the bed of aromatic vegetables in the pan.

**2.** Roast the turkey until an instant-read meat thermometer inserted in the thickest part of the leg but not touching the bone (carefully open the bag, watching out for escaping steam, and stick the thermometer in the bird) reaches 165° to 170°F., about 3 hours (or longer; the timing can vary). Carefully tear away and discard the paper bag. Raise the oven heat to 425°F. and roast for 30 minutes longer, basting with the pan juices every 5 minutes or so. The turkey should be golden brown and should now register 180° to 185°F. Remove the roasting pan from the oven. Carefully transfer the turkey to a platter, letting all of the juices run back into the pan. Cover the bird loosely with foil. Let it rest for 20 to 30 minutes before carving while you make the gravy.

**3.** Let the turkey pan juices rest for a few minutes; degrease, carefully spooning off and discarding all possible fat with a skimmer or a large metal spoon. Meanwhile, bring the Madeira to a boil in a nonreactive medium saucepan. Boil, uncovered, until reduced by about half. Strain the pan juices through a sieve into the Madeira, gently pressing on the solids to extract all possible liquid. Add an extra cup of chicken or turkey broth (see margin) and boil the juices, uncovered, until reduced by about a third, to concentrate their flavor. Taste and correct the seasonings, adding more salt and pepper, if needed. (If you like, finely **chop the cooked giblets,** including the neck, discarding any bones and gristle, and add them to the gravy. Yum.)

**4.** Carve the turkey and serve hot, spooning a little of the gravy over each portion. Pour the remaining gravy into a warmed sauceboat and pass at the table.

The **giblets help flavor the pan juices,** which are served with the turkey. They have a wonderful flavor—try chopping them and adding them to the pan gravy.

For what most people consider to be a **traditional gravy,** the pan juices are thickened, usually with a fat-and-flour roux, or sometimes with cornstarch, and then extra broth is added. Here's the method: Make a turkey broth with the giblets a day ahead—simmer the giblets without the liver in a saucepan of chicken broth or water for an hour or two. Strain the broth and chop the giblets. Then melt 3 tablespoons turkey fat (removed when you degrease the pan juices after roasting) or butter in a large saucepan. Add 3 tablespoons flour and cook, stirring, without browning, until smooth and thick, about 3 minutes. Add the degreased pan juices and the turkey broth and simmer for 20 to 30 minutes. Add the chopped giblets. Taste and correct the seasonings, adding more salt and pepper if needed.

Freshly grated nutmeg
is much more pungent
and aromatic than the
usual bottled ground
variety. Rub the hard
nutmeg seed against a
nutmeg grater, which is
a small handheld affair.
You will need much less
than what you are used
to from the jar.

# BRANDIED PECAN STUFFING

A stuffing in the American spirit, this is much lighter than many traditional stuffing
recipes, which often have meat plus eggs to bind them. You can spoon some of the
stuffing into the turkey as directed in the roast turkey recipe (page 124), but only
immediately before you put it into the oven to roast. Spoon the rest into a buttered
casserole and bake, uncovered, about halfway through the last 1½-hour segment of the
roasting time. I baste occasionally with the turkey pan juices—fatty and delicious.

MAKES ENOUGH TO STUFF A 10- TO 12-POUND BIRD,
PLUS EXTRA IN A CASSEROLE

2   cups pecan halves (or use a combination of pecans and macadamias)

4   tablespoons (½ stick) unsalted butter

2   large onions, coarsely chopped

3   celery ribs, strings removed (page 18), trimmed, and coarsely chopped

2   garlic cloves, minced

2   cups sliced white mushrooms (Mushroom Basics, page 21)

¾   teaspoon salt, or to taste

½   cup chopped fresh parsley

2   teaspoons chopped fresh thyme leaves or ¼ teaspoon dried

½   teaspoon paprika, preferably Hungarian, sweet or hot, depending
    on taste

¼   teaspoon **freshly grated nutmeg**

¼   teaspoon cayenne, or to taste (or use a large pinch of dried red pepper
    flakes)

¼   cup Cognac, Armagnac, or brandy
    Several grinds of black pepper

6   cups day-old Italian or French bread, white, whole wheat, or a
    combination, with some crusts left on, cut into ¾-inch dice or torn and
    coarsely crumbled

2   tart apples, such as Granny Smith, peeled, quartered, cored, and diced
    Juice of 1 large orange

½   cup dried currants

1   to 1½ cups canned chicken broth, as needed

1. **Toast** the pecans in a pie plate or baking pan in a preheated 375°F. oven until they are fragrant and lightly golden (this is hard to see; don't overtoast), usually about 8 minutes. Stir a couple of times with a wooden spoon as the nuts toast. Coarsely chop; set aside.

2. Heat 2 tablespoons of the butter in a large skillet, preferably nonstick, over medium-high heat. Add the onions and celery and cook, tossing occasionally with a wooden spoon, until slightly softened, about 6 minutes. Add the garlic, mushrooms, salt, 1/4 cup of the parsley, the thyme, paprika, nutmeg, and cayenne or red pepper flakes; cook, tossing, until the garlic is lightly golden, 3 or 4 minutes longer.

3. Remove the pan from the heat to avoid flareups and add the brandy. Return to the heat and boil for about 2 minutes to evaporate the alcohol. Transfer the mixture to a large bowl. Stir in the remaining 1/4 cup parsley, the black pepper, the bread, and the reserved chopped pecans. Melt the remaining 2 tablespoons of butter in the same skillet.

4. Toss the diced apples in the orange juice in a medium bowl (which helps prevent the apples from darkening). Add the apples with the juice, melted butter, and currants to the bread mixture in the bowl; stir until well combined. Then pour on enough broth to moisten the mixture, but don't let it become too mushy. Gently toss everything together. Taste and correct all of the seasonings, adding salt, pepper, and herbs and spices, if needed. Loosely spoon the stuffing into the neck and body cavities of the turkey, and spoon the remainder (or if no bird, all of the stuffing) into a baking dish. Bake alongside the turkey (or on its own) in a 425°F. oven for the last 30 minutes.

To **cool the stock quickly,** transfer to smaller bowls and stir with a spoon to aerate.

If time permits, **refrigerate the stock or soup overnight,** The fat will rise to the top and harden, making for easy removal.

## TURKEY STOCK

Whatever you do, don't throw out the turkey carcass after it's been stripped of the meat. It's the beginning of a delicious stock that can be used for any of your favorite soup recipes calling for chicken stock or broth.

MAKES ABOUT 8 CUPS

- 1 turkey carcass, with a little meat on the bones
- 8 cups water
- 2 carrots, trimmed and sliced
- 2 ribs celery, sliced
- 1 onion, sliced
- 1 large garlic clove, sliced
- 1 large fresh parsley sprig
- 1 bay leaf
- 2 teaspoons dried basil
- 1 teaspoon dried thyme

**1.** Cut the carcass into pieces with a large, heavy knife or meat cleaver if you have one; good heavy kitchen shears will also do the trick. Place in a nonreactive large stockpot. Add the water, carrots, celery, onion, garlic, parsley, bay leaf, basil, and thyme. Bring to a boil. Lower the heat; simmer, partially covered, for 3 to 4 hours. Skim any foam from the surface with a large spoon or skimmer, and discard.

**2.** Line a large colander with a double thickness of dampened cheesecloth and place over a large bowl. Carefully pour the stock through the colander. Discard the solids.

**3.** Use the stock at this point, or let **cool,** and then cover and **refrigerate** overnight. The next day, remove the solidified fat from the top and discard. Bring the stock to a boil in a large saucepan. Let cool. Refrigerate, covered, or freeze up to 2 months. Bring the stock to a boil before using.

# THE FOUR SEASONS CRANBERRY RELISH

I couldn't talk about turkey and stuffings without tossing in my favorite cranberry relish. This recipe is from New York's spectacular restaurant The Four Seasons, where American ingredients have been used inventively for over thirty-five years. It was created by Four Seasons Chef Christian (Hitch) Albin.

MAKES ABOUT 1 1/2 QUARTS

- 1 large navel orange
- 1 lime
- 1 tablespoon grated fresh ginger (page 20)
- 2 cinnamon sticks
- 1 dried hot chili pepper
- 1 vanilla bean, split lengthwise
- 2 cups sugar
- 1/4 cup plus 1/3 cup cold water
- 1 cup raisins
- 2 pounds fresh or frozen and thawed cranberries, picked over

**1.** Cut the orange and the lime, with their skins, into 1/4-inch dice. Tie the ginger, cinnamon sticks, chili pepper, and vanilla bean in a little **cheesecloth** bag.

**2.** Combine the sugar and the 1/4 cup cold water in a nonreactive, wide, heavy skillet. Heat over medium heat, stirring with a wooden spoon to dissolve the sugar and **brushing down** any crystals from the sides of the pan with a brush dipped in hot water, until all of the sugar dissolves. Raise the heat and bring the syrup to a boil.

**3.** Boil without stirring until the mixture **caramelizes** to a medium-dark amber color, about 5 minutes. Stir in the diced orange and lime and the bag of spices and cook over high heat, stirring constantly, for 5 minutes. Fold in the raisins and cranberries with a rubber spatula; gently stir in the 1/3 cup cold water to coat the raisins and cranberries with caramelized sugar. Cook over medium heat, stirring gently, until about half of the cranberries pop open, about 10 minutes. Remove the pan from the heat and cool.

**4.** Spoon the relish into sterilized jars (or use plastic containers after cooling the relish to lukewarm first). Cover tightly and refrigerate for 1 month before using. This relish keeps, refrigerated, for about 3 months.

Wrapping loose seasonings in **cheesecloth** lets you flavor a mixture without having to fish out the loose pieces at the end of the cooking.

**Brushing down** the sides of the pan dissolves any stray crystal, preventing it from slipping into the syrup and crystallizing the whole pot, resulting in a mess.

Heating sugar with water until it melts and turns brown is **caramelizing.** The resulting syrup has butterscotchlike flavor.

Six

# MAIN DISHES: MEAT

Filet Mignon with Wild Mushroom Sauce

**Techniques:** sautéing/deglazing/making a pan sauce

Beer-Braised Beef with Mushrooms

**Techniques:** sautéing/deglazing/oven braising/seasoning bag/thickening with browned flour

Skillet "Steak" au Poivre

**Techniques:** cracking peppercorns/sautéing/deglazing/making a pan sauce

"Sloppy Joes" from Scratch

**Techniques:** sautéing/simmering

Diner-Style Meat Loaf

**Techniques:** mixing ground meats/using bread crumbs for texture

Boiled Beef Dinner with Vegetables and Horseradish

**Techniques:** stove-top braising/Flame Tamer

Beef and Black Bean Chili

**Techniques:** sautéing/cooking spices/simmering/cooking with a pressure cooker

Seared Double Lamb Chops

**Techniques:** roasting garlic/searing cross-hatch grill marks/ deglazing/making a pan sauce

Braised Lamb Shanks with White Beans and Gremolata

**Techniques:** oven braising/tight seal for pan/reducing several liquids to concentrate flavor/making gremolata

Pork Chops with Mustard-Onion Gravy

**Techniques:** deglazing/stove-top braising/reducing liquid

Grilled Marinated Pork Tenderloin with Warm White Bean–Pepper Compote

**Techniques:** searing/roasting/grilling

Easy Choucroute with Smoked Pork Chops or Weisswurst

**Technique:** baking in casserole

**I don't eat red meat on a daily basis, but occasionally I do feel like a hit.** There's a long-established restaurant around the corner from my apartment in New York City: good jazz after nine o'clock, a bar menu out front, and white linen on the tables in the back. One of the specialties is large steaks, and large means feeding as many as twelve. I've watched those behemoths being carried out from the kitchen, but the furthest I go is the Cheddar-bacon burger, extra-crispy fries on the side, with a jar of Dijon for the burger. I've found that since I eat meat less frequently, I appreciate the taste a lot more, and I usually go after a few favorites.

The collection of recipes in this chapter reflects my preference for home-style cooking. Nothing's trendy here—just an assortment of honest, hearty preparations (some have been favorites for more than twenty years), with a leaning, I suppose, toward lean: lamb chops, pork tenderloin, lean ground beef, and large lean cuts of beef that cook by themselves—perfect for entertaining.

Here the beginning cook gets a chance to run through all of the basic techniques: sautéing, deglazing, reducing, braising, simmering, and the rest. Most of these dishes, however, begin by sautéing the meat to develop color and flavor. The high heat of the pan caramelizes the natural sugars in the meat, resulting in a rich, deep flavor as well as the characteristic browning. Many of the dishes are make-aheads and don't suffer if they have to stand a little longer than expected while guests find their way to the table. This makes it much easier on the cook.

To **expand** this luxurious meal for more guests, simply increase the amount of ingredients appropriately.

Oven-fried potatoes and a green salad with ~~vinaigrette dressing~~ ~~accompaniment~~ ~~this dish.~~

**Lean steak** is a proper choice for this kind of sauté since it cooks quickly.

Here is another example of creating a **pan sauce** by deglazing.

# FILET MIGNON WITH WILD MUSHROOM SAUCE

This is one of my favorite ways to cook—a quick sauté in which the ingredients are simply and quickly cooked, sauced with their own pan residues (here I use nothing more than water for the liquid) and served at once so their fresh tastes and textures are enjoyed to their optimum.

MAKES 2 SERVINGS

1   teaspoon plus 1 tablespoon olive oil
10  to 12 ounces **filet mignon,** in 1 or 2 pieces, well trimmed
    Salt and freshly ground black pepper, to taste
2   tablespoons chopped shallots
1½  to 2 cups sliced shiitake and/or other wild mushrooms (Mushroom Basics, page 21)
    Watercress or arugula sprigs, for garnish

**1.** Heat 1 teaspoon olive oil in a nonstick medium skillet over medium-high heat. Sprinkle both sides of the steak with salt and pepper to taste. Gently place the steak in the pan; lower the heat to medium. Sauté the steak until well browned, 6 to 9 minutes, adjusting the heat if necessary to maintain a gentle but steady sizzle. Turn the steak over with tongs and brown the second side, about 5 minutes. Transfer the steak to a plate, cover loosely with foil to keep warm, and set aside to rest.

**2.** Add the shallots to the skillet and cook over medium-high heat, stirring with a wooden spoon, until softened, about 2 minutes. Add the remaining 1 tablespoon olive oil; heat for a moment. Then add the mushrooms and sprinkle with salt and pepper to taste. Let the mushrooms sizzle in the hot oil for a minute or so, and then sauté, tossing, until lightly golden, about 4 minutes longer. Add ⅔ cup water, scraping (Deglazing Basics, page 24) up any browned bits from the bottom of the pan into the **sauce** with a wooden spoon; boil, uncovered, until the liquid reduces by nearly half, 4 or 5 minutes.

**3.** Meanwhile, thinly slice the steak across the grain. Arrange the slices, overlapping, on 2 warm dinner plates. Spoon the mushroom mixture with its juices over and around the meat. Garnish with the watercress or arugula and serve at once.

## VARIATION: OPEN-FACED DIJON STEAK SANDWICH

Toast 2 French rolls or an 8-inch length of French or Italian bread, split. Rub the toasted surfaces with a split garlic clove; spread with a little Dijon mustard. After you've sautéed the meat, prepare the pan sauce as above, with or without the mushrooms. Top the bread with the sliced steak and drizzle the pan juices over so that they cover the meat and toast.


# BEER-BRAISED BEEF WITH MUSHROOMS

I love this dish, which is mellow with the flavor of beer and onions. Guinness has both a slight bitterness and a sweetness that marry beautifully with the beef.

MAKES 6 SERVINGS

3   tablespoons vegetable or olive oil, or as needed
3   to 3$^1/_2$ pounds boneless lean beef, preferably shin, chuck, or bottom round, trimmed and cut into 2-inch cubes
    Salt or freshly ground black pepper, to taste
3   onions (about 1$^1/_2$ pounds), coarsely chopped
4   or 5 carrots, trimmed, peeled, and sliced $^1/_2$ inch thick
3   garlic cloves, thinly sliced
    Pinch of dried red pepper flakes
$^1/_4$   cup all-purpose flour
1$^1/_2$   bottles (12 ounces each) Guinness stout or dark beer, or as needed
1   tablespoon tomato paste
2   fresh thyme sprigs or a large pinch of dried thyme
5   fresh parsley sprigs
1   bay leaf
8   allspice berries
1   star anise
3   whole cloves
2   cups quartered white mushroom caps (Mushroom Basics, page 21)
3   tablespoons chopped fresh parsley  ➝

How do I serve this? This dish wants mashed potatoes, soft polenta, or wide noodles to soak up the juices. A green salad with tomatoes, if the season permits, dressed with a balsamic vinaigrette, is also a nice touch.

This is just another version of the **basic braising technique** (page 25). Like most braises, this dish cooks for a bit, but it does so unattended. Just check from time to time to make sure the mixture is not boiling—that can toughen the meat.

**What is star anise?** As the name suggests, this is a hard, star-shaped pod, a spice that adds flavor reminiscent of anise.

I usually use an **oven-proof casserole, plus an extra wide skillet,** to brown the meat and vegetables. Then I combine everything in the casserole, rinsing out and scraping up any browned bits from the bottom of the skillet with a wooden spoon, using some of the liquid, and add these juices to the stew in step 3.

The **browned flour** thickens the juices slightly, but not enough to make the stew pasty.

Tying **solid seasonings in cheesecloth** lets you fish them out easily after cooking.

I like simmering or braising stews **in the oven;** the all-around heat seems to bring the flavors together better, and you don't have to worry about any burning on the bottom of the pot.

As with all stews, this one **improves in flavor when made in advance and reheated,** plus the overnight refrigerating causes the fat to congeal on the surface for easy removal.

**1.** Preheat the oven to 325°F., with a rack positioned in the lower third of the oven. In a large **flameproof casserole** or Dutch oven, heat 2 tablespoons of the oil over high heat. Add enough meat to cover the bottom without crowding; sprinkle with salt and pepper to taste. Sauté, tossing occasionally with a wooden spoon, until well browned on all sides, 5 to 6 minutes. Transfer to a plate and brown the remaining meat in batches, adding oil as needed. Lower the heat slightly if the meat is sputtering violently. Set the meat aside on a plate.

**2.** Add the onions, carrots, garlic, and pepper flakes to the casserole, tossing to coat with the oil (add a little more oil if the pan is dry). Lower the heat to medium and sauté, tossing, until the vegetables are softened and lightly golden, about 12 minutes. Sprinkle the flour over the vegetables and cook over medium heat, stirring with a wooden spoon, **until the flour is** blended in and **lightly browned,** 3 to 5 minutes.

**3.** Add a little of the Guinness to the pan; stir and scrape up all possible browned bits from the bottom with a wooden spoon, stirring them into the liquid (Deglazing Basics, page 24). Stir in the tomato paste. Return the meat to the casserole, adding enough Guinness to come nearly up to the level of the solids. Meanwhile, **tie** the thyme, parsley sprigs, bay leaf, allspice berries, star anise, and cloves in a piece of **cheesecloth.** Tuck the cheesecloth bag into the stew.

**4.** Bring the mixture to a boil. Cover the casserole tightly with foil and then with the lid. **Place in** the lower part of **the oven;** immediately lower the heat to 300°F. Bake **(oven braise),** stirring occasionally, until the beef is tender, about 2 hours (start checking the meat after about 1½ hours). Check occasionally as the stew bakes; if it is boiling rather than simmering, immediately lower the heat further to 250° or 275°, so you maintain a gentle simmer. Boiling will toughen the meat.

**5.** Remove the casserole from the oven. If you have time, uncover and let the mixture cool to room temperature, then **refrigerate, covered, overnight.** The next day, lift off all possible solidified fat from the surface with a skimmer or a metal spoon. Bring the casserole to a simmer over medium heat. Remove and discard the spice bag, gently squeezing it to release all possible juices. Taste and correct the seasonings, adding salt, black pepper, and/or red pepper flakes if needed.

**6.** Heat the remaining tablespoon of oil in a nonstick large skillet over medium-high heat. Add the quartered mushroom caps and sprinkle with salt and pepper to taste. Let the mushrooms sizzle for a moment or two. Then sauté, tossing frequently, until lightly golden, about 5 minutes longer. Add the chopped parsley and toss to combine; spoon the mushrooms over each portion of stew and serve hot.

## VARIATION: BRAISED SHORT RIBS OF BEEF

Short ribs of beef are among my favorite cuts of meat—so tender, so packed with flavor. They're gelatinous, with a slightly chewy texture and a rich, beefy taste. When braised for a long time, they become meltingly tender. The orange juice, which cuts through the fatty meat nicely, is a touch borrowed from my friend, the estimable cook-author Barbara Kafka. This recipe is actually nothing more than a variation of the beer-braised beef above.

Substitute 3½ pounds beef short ribs for the boneless lean beef in the recipe above; have the butcher cut the ribs into segments about 4 × 2 inches; pat dry. Working in batches, sauté the ribs over medium-high heat, turning with tongs, until richly browned all over, about 15 minutes. Discard all possible fat. Decrease the onions to 2 and the carrots to 3. Add 2 strips of orange zest, removed with a vegetable peeler, to the spice bag. Braise in the oven until the beef is very tender, 2½ to 3 hours. You may need to lower the oven heat to 250° or 275° to maintain a gentle simmer, since the oven and pot can get overly hot during such a long period of cooking.

Remove the pan from the oven. Degrease the pan juices, removing any fat from the surface with a skimmer or a large metal spoon. (This works best on the next day, when the stew has been chilled and the fat solidifies on top for easy removal.) Remove the spice bag and discard. Add the juice of ¼ orange to the pan liquid, cover, and simmer for about 5 minutes. Taste and correct the seasonings with salt and pepper. Omit the mushrooms. Sprinkle with chopped parsley and serve hot.

**How do I serve this?** As with beer-braised beef, these ribs are very much at home with mashed potatoes, soft polenta, or wide egg noodles.

This is **delicious with Creamy Mashed Potatoes without Cream** (page 176).

If you are preparing **dinner for more than two**, this recipe is easily increased—just multiply everything by two.

Ground round holds its patty shape very well during cooking, without breaking up—the result is very "steaklike."

**Whole peppercorns are easily cracked** by placing them in a kitchen towel and whacking them with the bottom of a heavy skillet. Don't try to crack them in a food processor or blender—they'll just whirl around, making a lot of noise. And don't use a pepper mill—it grinds too fine. The point to this dish is to have an explosion of flavor when you bite down on a piece of pepper.

**Heavy cream,** unlike sour cream, can be boiled away without any danger of curdling or separation. When used for a pan sauce, the result is thick and glossy.

# SKILLET "STEAK" AU POIVRE

This is one of my favorite dishes when I'm craving red meat and want it quick. The recipe title may seem fancy, but this dish is nothing more than a peppered hamburger steak, with an elegant twist. The recipe takes practically no time to fix—perfect at the end of a busy day when I want something richly satisfying with lots of flavor. And there is no better example of the delicious results you can get using the techniques of sautéing and deglazing.

MAKES 2 SERVINGS

    1   pound ground **beef round**
    1   tablespoon **cracked black peppercorns**
        Salt, to taste
    2   teaspoons unsalted butter
    2   teaspoons olive oil
    ¼   cup dry red wine or 2 tablespoons brandy or Cognac
    ⅓   cup **heavy cream**

**1.** Divide the ground beef in 2 equal portions and form each portion into an oval patty about 5 inches long and 1 inch thick. Season both sides of each patty generously with cracked black peppercorns.

**2.** Just before cooking, sprinkle both sides of the patties with salt to taste. Heat together the butter and olive oil in an 8-inch heavy nonstick skillet over medium heat. When the butter begins to foam, add the patties to the skillet. Sauté until the undersides are well browned, about 4 minutes. Flip the patties over and continue cooking until the meat reaches the doneness you like—about another 4 minutes for medium-rare, 5 minutes for medium, and 5½ minutes for well done.

**3.** Remove the patties with a spatula to a plate; keep warm. Pour off the fat from the skillet. If using brandy, remove the skillet from the heat and then add the brandy to the skillet. Carefully return to the heat, keeping your face averted in case the brandy flames. Or carefully add the wine to the skillet while it's on the heat. Boil, scraping up any browned bits with a wooden spoon (Deglazing Basics, page 24), until the liquid is almost evaporated. Pour in the **heavy cream** and boil until the sauce is reduced to about ¼ cup and is thick enough to coat a spoon, about 1 minute. Pour the sauce over the steaks and serve.

# "SLOPPY JOES" FROM SCRATCH

Depending on where you grew up, "Sloppy Joes" can refer either to a savory ground beef mixture served on hamburger buns or to multilayered deli sandwiches served at catered parties (usually delivered wrapped in yellow cellophane). The version here is ground beef. More often than not, the mixture is actually made from a canned or powdered mix—almost never from scratch. I remember tasting Sloppy Joes when the commercial product was introduced at the 1964 New York World's Fair.

I first made this for a friend who missed the ones his mother used to make (probably from a can). Since then, I make this any time I want to tuck into a deliciously gooey quick supper.

MAKES 4 SERVINGS

- 1 tablespoon vegetable oil, or as needed
- 2 medium red onions, chopped
- 1 large red or yellow bell pepper, cored, seeded (Bell Pepper Basics, page 16), and chopped, or use 1 small pepper of each color
- 3 large garlic cloves, minced
- 1/2 teaspoon fresh thyme leaves or a pinch of dried
  Salt and freshly ground black pepper, to taste
- 1 1/2 pounds ground round or other lean ground beef
- 3/4 cup bottled chili sauce
- 1 cup beer (not light beer)
- 3 tablespoons Worcestershire sauce, or to taste
- 1/4 teaspoon hot pepper sauce, or more to taste
- 3 tablespoons thinly sliced scallion greens
- 4 lengths of French or Italian bread (4 to 6 inches), split lengthwise, or 4 seeded rolls, split

**1.** Heat the oil in a nonreactive wide skillet, preferably nonstick, over medium heat. Add the onions, bell pepper, garlic, thyme, and salt and black pepper to taste. Sauté, tossing occasionally with a wooden spoon, until the vegetables are softened but not browned, about 10 minutes. With a slotted spoon, transfer the vegetable mixture to a plate and set aside. ➝

**How do I serve this?**
Keep it simple—pickle slices, potato chips, and probably a bottle of beer for those eligible.

For a **Sloppy Joe party,** just increase the amount of ingredients to fit the size of your crowd.

**2.** Add a little more oil to the skillet if the pan is dry. Raise the heat to medium-high. Add the beef and cook, breaking it up with a wooden spoon, until browned but still partly rare, 3 or 4 minutes. Return the vegetable mixture to the skillet. Stir in the chili sauce, beer, Worcestershire, and hot pepper sauce. Bring the mixture to a simmer, stirring gently. Lower the heat, partially cover the skillet, and simmer until the sauce thickens lightly and the flavors blend, about 15 minutes. Stir in the scallions. Taste and correct all of the seasonings as needed, adding more thyme and salt and pepper. (The recipe can be **made ahead** up to this point. To serve, simply reheat over medium heat, stirring from time to time.)

**3.** Toast the cut sides of the bread or rolls briefly under a preheated broiler. Place on serving plates, cut sides up. Spoon the beef mixture over the toast and serve hot, with a knife and fork.

**How do I serve this? This makes a delicious midweek supper, accompanied by mashed potatoes and cornichons (tiny sour gherkins), which nicely offset the richness of the meat. If you like, you can serve the slices with a little warm Basic Chunky Tomato Sauce (page 62) spooned over them. This is also fine for a picnic or buffet table, or even sandwiches.**

# DINER-STYLE MEAT LOAF

It's the combination of ground meats—beef, veal, and pork—that makes this version special.

M A K E S   6   S E R V I N G S

- 1   tablespoon olive oil, plus more as needed
- 1   onion, chopped
- 1   carrot, trimmed, peeled, and chopped
- 1   celery rib, strings removed (Celery Stringing, page 18), trimmed and chopped
- 1   scallion (white and green portions), trimmed, halved lengthwise, and thinly sliced
- 4   or 5 white mushrooms, coarsely chopped (Mushroom Basics, page 21)
- 2   garlic cloves, minced
  Salt and freshly ground black pepper, to taste
  Pinch of dried thyme or 1 teaspoon chopped fresh thyme leaves

⅔   cup ketchup

Few drops of hot pepper sauce

2   large eggs, beaten

¼   cup chopped fresh parsley

½   cup soft fresh bread crumbs (page 18)

1½  pounds ground meat loaf mix (a combination of ground beef, veal, and pork), or use ¾ pound *each* ground beef and pork

**1.** Heat the olive oil in a large nonstick skillet over medium-high heat. Add the onion, carrot, celery, scallion, mushrooms, and garlic; sprinkle with salt and pepper to taste and the thyme. Sauté, tossing occasionally with a wooden spoon, until the vegetables begin to soften, about 6 minutes. Transfer the vegetable mixture to a plate and set aside to cool slightly.

**2.** Preheat the oven to 375°F. In a large bowl, whisk together the ketchup, hot pepper sauce, beaten eggs, and parsley. Stir in the bread crumbs. Add the ground meat; sprinkle with salt and pepper to taste. Combine with your fingers **without squeezing or compacting** the meat. Add the vegetable mixture and mix lightly, just until combined.

**3.** Pack the mixture into an 8 × 4-inch nonstick loaf pan (if the pan is not nonstick, oil it or coat it lightly with cooking spray). Tap the pan on the counter a couple of times to eliminate air bubbles. With moist fingertips, form a smooth surface on top, mounding the mixture slightly along the center of the length of the loaf. Rub the surface of the meat loaf with a light film of olive oil (about 1 teaspoon).

**4.** Bake until the meat loaf is lightly golden and a skewer inserted in the center of the loaf feels hot, usually about 1 hour. Spoon off any excess juices. Let the loaf stand for 5 or 10 minutes. Unmold and cut into thick slices. Serve hot.

**The trick to a light-textured meat loaf, in addition to the bread crumbs, is to handle the meat mixture lightly; avoid compacting or squeezing the mixture with your hands.**

This dish may seem **long cooking,** and it is. But remember, most of the simmering or braising is unattended. That's the value of these dishes—the cook ~~can go about other~~

Just check from time to time to make sure the liquid is simmering and not boiling, which can toughen the meat. And remember, there are leftovers for other dinners, hash, sandwiches, and so on.

I've given a recipe for **homemade horseradish,** which I find irresistible with boiled beef. Other possibilities include a **green sauce,** which is traditionally served with *bollito misto* in Italy— it's made with olive oil, vinegar, capers, chopped shallots, a touch of anchovy, and lots of chopped fresh green herbs.

A **Flame Tamer** is a great device for maintaining a slow steady simmer over a long period of time. You place the metal Flame Tamer over the burner (whether gas or electric) and then sit the pot on it. It prevents the liquid from boiling, which would toughen the beef.

# BOILED BEEF DINNER WITH VEGETABLES AND HORSERADISH

This is a great company dish—when was the last time you had boiled beef? And it couldn't be easier. I like serving the broth first, as a soup course—the broth has a haunting, homey quality that makes me think of all the legendary boiled beef served during the glory days of Vienna, Prague, and Budapest. My good friend Zanne Stewart, who is food editor at *Gourmet,* told me about her grandmother's midwestern boiled dinner, in which the vegetables were drizzled with brown butter, then sprinkled with vinegar. Yum.

MAKES 4 SERVINGS, WITH LEFTOVERS

- 1 piece (3 to 4 pounds) first-cut beef brisket, most of the fat trimmed
- 2 cans beef broth (about 14 ounces each), preferably reduced-sodium
- 4 cups cold water, plus more as needed
  Salt, to taste
- 1 bay leaf
- 6 leeks
- 6 small potatoes, scrubbed
- 6 carrots (or more, if they are very slim), trimmed and peeled
- 4 whole black peppercorns
- 1 medium head savoy cabbage, outer leaves removed, halved through the core, and cored

**Accompaniments** (any or all of the following)

Chopped fresh dill, chives, or parsley (if serving broth as a first course)

Coarse (kosher) salt or sea salt

Homemade Horseradish (recipe, page 144)

Coarse-grained mustard

Cornichons (French gherkins)

**1.** Choose a very large pot or casserole in which the beef will fit with plenty of extra room around and above it. Place the beef, broth, water, 1 teaspoon salt, and bay leaf in the pot. Cover and bring just to a boil over medium-high heat. Immediately lower the heat to maintain a gentle simmer (start timing now). Braise or simmer, covered, for 1½ hours. For the first 10 minutes or so, however, skim all possible foam from the surface with a large metal spoon. Then re-cover the casserole.

**2.** As the meat simmers, occasionally skim any foam or fat from the surface and adjust the heat if necessary to maintain a steady simmer (but never a boil).

**3.** Meanwhile, cut off the bottoms of the leeks, then cut off the tops, leaving the white portions with an inch or so of the green tops. Remove the tough outer layer if there is one. Clean the leeks well: Place the leeks on a cutting board. Make a slit lengthwise through the leek, starting about 2 inches up from the bottom or root end (which you leave joined) and cutting all the way through the top. If the leeks are thicker than an inch or so, make 2 slits, cutting the leek lengthwise in quarters, with the bottoms intact. Now let the leeks sit under lukewarm running water to remove all possible traces of sand and dirt. Let the water run cold until the leeks are completely clean. Set the leeks aside. With a vegetable peeler, remove a "racing stripe" of skin from each potato, cutting around the "equator."

**4.** When the meat has simmered for 1½ hours, slip the leeks into the broth around the meat. Tuck in the carrots and potatoes and add the peppercorns. If necessary, add more water to keep everything covered. Cover and simmer until the meat is very tender, and the vegetables are tender but not mushy, 30 to 40 minutes longer. If the vegetables are tender but the meat still offers resistance when poked with a paring knife, carefully remove the vegetables from the broth with tongs or a slotted spoon, set them aside on a plate, and continue to simmer the meat, covered, until it is very tender. (If you do this, return the vegetables to the broth to reheat once the meat is done.) If you are serving the meat now, skim off all possible fat from the surface of the broth with a large metal spoon or skimmer.

**5.** Shortly before serving time, bring a wide pot filled with 2 inches of water to a boil. Cut each cabbage half through the core end into 3 equal wedges or just in half again if not too large. Add salt to the boiling water and gently arrange the cabbage wedges in a steamer basket or metal colander over the water. Cover tightly and steam gently (the water should maintain a boil) until the cabbage is just tender but still has a little crunch when pierced with a knife and is still a nice bright green, about 10 minutes. Don't overcook.

**6.** If serving the broth as a separate first course, preheat the oven to 275° F. Regardless of what you plan to do with the broth, proceed with the next step. ➡

**Other accompaniments?** Sour rye bread or a coarse peasant bread is good with this for dunking in the broth.

**To make this dish ahead (a good idea):** At the end of step 4, when the beef and vegetables are all tender, set the pot on a wire rack (or a stove-top burner, off the heat) and let the meat, vegetables, and broth cool to room temperature (not lukewarm). Cover and refrigerate for several hours or preferably overnight.

The next day, or an hour or so before serving, lift all traces of solidified fat from the surface of the broth with a large metal spoon or skimmer. With a large spatula and spoon, lift the beef from the broth, letting the broth drip back into the pot, and place it on a carving board or work surface. With a large slicing knife or chef's knife, slice the cold beef about ¼ inch thick, cutting against the grain. Return the sliced beef to the casserole, tucking it into the broth. Bring the casserole to a simmer over medium heat. Then proceed with cooking the cabbage (step 5) and arrange everything as described in step 7.

Sometimes, when I'm slicing a very juicy piece of meat, I place it on a cutting board placed on a tray with sides or on a jelly-roll pan. The pan catches all the juices, which I then pour back into the casserole. Don't lose one drop of that flavorful liquid!

The **horseradish** is delicious with roast beef or any roast meat, for that matter, spread sparingly on hamburgers (or even mixed in with the ground meat mixture) or spooned lightly as a garnish on a strong-flavored soup, such as chicken or beef barley.

For **grating the horse-radish fine,** don't use those finger-cutting punched-out nailhole things on a four-sided grater. Go for the next size up so you get some shredding. And don't get your face too close—you want to avoid getting horserad-ish "spray" in your eyes.

**7.** With tongs and a large spatula, lift the beef from the broth, letting the broth drip back into the pot. Place the meat on a carving board or work surface and let it stand for a few minutes. Remove the bay leaf and the whole peppercorns, if you can find them, from the broth. Then, with a large slicing knife or chef's knife, **slice** the beef about ½ inch thick, cutting against the grain. Arrange the beef, overlapping the slices slightly, in the center of a very large warm serving platter. Remove the vegetables from the broth with a slotted spoon or tongs and arrange them in groups around the beef and at the ends of the platter. Lift the cabbage wedges from the water, draining off all water, and arrange them on the platter (the cabbage can also be served on a separate platter). Spoon a little of the broth over the meat and vegetables. If you are serving this without the broth as a soup, go ahead and place the platter on the table. Otherwise, cover the platter(s) with foil and place in the warm oven.

**8.** To serve the broth as a first course (the broth is one of the best parts of the meal), ladle in smallish portions into small bowls. For a nice touch, strain the broth through a fine-mesh sieve before serving. Add seasoning, if needed, and sprinkle each bowl of soup with a little chopped dill, chives, or parsley. Then serve the platter of meat and vegetables, passing coarse salt, horseradish, mustard, and corni-chons at the table.

## HOMEMADE HORSERADISH

MAKES ABOUT ²/₃ CUP

  6  to 8 ounces fresh horseradish (about the size of a smallish banana)

2½  teaspoons sugar, preferably superfine, or to taste

¾  teaspoon coarse (kosher) salt or sea salt, plus more to taste

    Juice of ½ lemon

¼  cup rice wine vinegar or white wine vinegar, or more to taste

**1.** With a paring knife, cut away the woody outer coating of the horseradish and discard. **Finely grate** it into a medium bowl; you should have about 1 cup or slightly more.

**2.** Add the sugar, salt, lemon juice, and vinegar, stirring to combine the ingredients. If you use white wine vinegar, you may need slightly less. Taste (the horseradish is very hot at this stage) and add more sugar and/or salt to taste. If necessary, add more vinegar; the mixture should be moist but not soupy. Cover with plastic wrap and refrigerate for at least 2 hours.

**3.** Taste and add more of anything to taste. I usually add a good pinch more salt, a pinch of sugar, if needed, and a drizzle more rice vinegar to moisten. Transfer the horseradish to a ramekin or small custard cup, cover with plastic wrap, and refrigerate until serving.

This sauce **keeps,** stored in a tightly covered jar, for at least 2 weeks; it becomes gentler with time.

**BONUS RECIPE**

## BOILED BEEF SALAD

Cut leftover sliced beef into wide slivers, and cut any leftover potatoes and vegetables into bite-size pieces. Make a fairly tart vinaigrette (page 194) with Dijon mustard, red wine vinegar, salt and pepper, and olive oil. In a large bowl, combine the meat, potatoes, and vegetables with enough of the vinaigrette to moisten, adding a few capers and some chopped fresh parsley. In a second bowl, toss a mix of bite-size salad greens with enough vinaigrette to coat.

Arrange the greens on a serving platter or on individual serving plates. Top with the meat-vegetable mixture and serve.

With corn bread and plenty of ice-cold beer, this is a great dish for a crowd. Feel free to double the recipe.

This is the ideal dish to rediscover the pleasures of cooking with a pressure cooker. My friend ~~...~~ ...

several pressure cooker cookbooks that are responsible for an entire generation of new users, has provided the basics for its use (Dried Bean Basics).

Look for **chili powder** that is nothing but ground chilies. Supermarket brands are a blend of chili powder, salt, sometimes cinnamon, and other spices.

# BEEF AND BLACK BEAN CHILI

Closely based on Deborah Madison's black bean chili, which, she notes, has been served at Greens, the great vegetarian restaurant overlooking the Golden Gate Bridge in San Francisco, every day since they opened in 1979. Deborah's use of seasonings is masterful: particularly as is her use of a small amount of chipotle chilies (smoked jalapeños, available dried and canned and pureed in adobo sauce or without the sauce), a touch that has been widely copied across the country.

MAKES  3  QUARTS,  ABOUT  8  TO  12  SERVINGS

| | |
|---|---|
| 5 | tablespoons vegetable oil |
| 3 | medium yellow onions, chopped |
| 4 | garlic cloves, peeled and chopped coarse |
| $\frac{1}{2}$ | teaspoon coarse (kosher) salt or sea salt, or to taste |
| 4 | teaspoons cumin seeds |
| 4 | teaspoons dried oregano leaves |
| 4 | teaspoons paprika, preferably Hungarian |
| $\frac{1}{4}$ | to $\frac{1}{2}$ teaspoon cayenne, or to taste |
| $\frac{1}{4}$ | cup best-quality **chili powder,** or more or less to taste |
| 1 | can (28 ounces) whole tomatoes, chopped, with juices |
| 2 | teaspoons chopped chipotle chilies, or to taste |
| $1\frac{1}{2}$ | pounds beef shin or chuck, cut in $\frac{3}{4}$-inch cubes |
| 2 | cups dried black beans, sorted and soaked overnight, then drained (Dried Bean Basics, page 17) |
| 1 | bay leaf |
| $1\frac{1}{2}$ | tablespoons rice wine vinegar or cider vinegar, or to taste |
| $\frac{1}{4}$ | cup chopped fresh cilantro or parsley |

**Garnishes**

Sour cream

Lime wedges

Cilantro sprigs

Grated Muenster or Monterey Jack cheese

Ripe avocado wedges (optional, but good)

1. Heat 3 tablespoons of the oil in a large skillet over medium heat. Add the onions; toss to coat and sauté, tossing, until they soften, about 8 minutes. Add the garlic, salt, cumin seeds, oregano, paprika, cayenne, and chili powder and cook, stirring, for 5 minutes longer to cook the chili and spices. Add the tomatoes with their juices plus about 1 teaspoon of the chipotle chilies. Simmer everything together for 10 minutes.

2. In a large casserole or Dutch oven and working in batches if necessary to avoid crowding the pan, brown the beef in the remaining 2 tablespoons oil over medium-high heat, about 1 minute. Sprinkle with salt and turn the beef cubes frequently until they are well browned on all sides, usually about 15 minutes.

3. Add the vegetable-tomato mixture to the beef, along with the drained beans and the bay leaf. Stir everything to combine. Add enough cold water to the pot to cover everything by about 3 inches. Cover the pan and bring the liquid to a boil. Lower the heat and simmer, stirring occasionally, until the beans and beef are tender, usually about 1½ to 2 hours. Use a Flame Tamer (page 142) if you have one.

4. When the beans are cooked, degrease the chili, removing all the fat from the surface with a large metal spoon or skimmer. The chili can be **made ahead** to this point.

5. Taste the chili and stir in another teaspoon of chopped chipotles, if you like. Season with the vinegar, more salt if needed, and the chopped cilantro. Remove the bay leaf and discard. Serve with bowls of the garnishes.

If you're preparing the chili **in advance**—a good idea, as it will improve and mellow in flavor—cool to room temperature. Then cover and chill overnight. Any solidified fat will lift right off.

**To cook with a pressure cooker** (a godsend for making chili), first brown the meat in the oil in the pressure cooker pot. Drain off excess fat. Then add all the other ingredients, except the salt. Lock the lid in place. Over high heat, bring the cooker to high pressure. Lower the heat just enough to maintain high pressure and cook for 30 minutes. Reduce the pressure with the quick-release method by running under cold water. Remove the lid, tilting it away from you to let steam escape. If the beans aren't done, partially cover the pan (but don't lock) and simmer over conventional heat until they're done. Stir in the salt.

**How do I serve these?**
My choice—plain mashed potatoes to soak up the garlic sauce and asparagus if in season or broccoli. Open a special bottle of cabernet or red Bordeaux

to be on good terms with your butcher. Ask him (or her) to cut the double chops from the rack and to **french the bones,** which is nothing more than scraping the meat away from the ends of the bones, leaving them clean—a nice touch for presentation.

When meats or vegetables are cooked at high temperatures, as in **searing,** the natural sugars break down or caramelize, resulting in browning and the development of a wonderful deep, rich flavor.

Using a ridged skillet lets you form a professional-looking **cross-hatch pattern** on the meat.

# SEARED DOUBLE LAMB CHOPS

Your butcher can cut the double chops for you if you order them a day in advance. This recipe also shows you how to achieve a restaurant-style grill cross-hatching.

MAKES 2 SERVINGS

2 double-rib lamb chops, about 1½ inches thick, bones frenched
Salt and freshly ground black pepper, to taste
Olive oil
Fresh or dried rosemary leaves, to taste
8 to 12 garlic cloves
⅓ cup water or ¼ cup *each* dry white wine and water
Watercress sprigs, for garnish

**1.** Preheat the oven to 400°F. Place the chops on a plate; sprinkle with salt and pepper to taste. Drizzle with olive oil and sprinkle with a few rosemary leaves; rub these seasonings into the chops on all sides; use your hands—it's okay. Let the chops stand to marinate while you roast the garlic.

**2.** Peel the garlic cloves, leaving a thin skin on each one. Place in a pie pan and drizzle with a little olive oil. Roast until tender when pierced with a paring knife, about 15 minutes. Raise the oven heat to 450°. Set the garlic aside to cool.

**3.** Heat a cast-iron ridged stove-top grill or heavy ridged skillet over high heat. Add the chops and **sear** the lamb, forming a **cross-hatch pattern** of grill marks. Here's how: First, place the chops at a diagonal to the ridges and let sear for a minute or two, or until there are ridge lines on the chops. Then rotate them one-quarter turn (without turning them over) and let sear for another moment or two until that side is browned and there is a cross-hatch pattern. Turn the chops over and brown the second sides, rotating a quarter turn as with the first side. Holding the chops on edge with tongs, brown the meaty edges of the chops. All this browning should take about 5 minutes total. Transfer the chops to a small roasting pan or flameproof pie plate so that they are resting on their bones. Place in the oven.

**4.** For medium-rare, roast the chops until an instant-reading meat thermometer registers 130°F., 10 or 11 minutes. Meanwhile, peel the roasted garlic cloves. If they are very large, cut them lengthwise in half. Transfer the chops to a plate and let stand for 5 minutes or so before serving.

**5.** Now make a little pan juice: Pour off any fat from the roasting pan or pie plate used for the chops. Place the pan directly on a stove top burner over medium heat. Add the water or wine and water and boil, scraping up any browned bits from the pan with a wooden spoon (Deglazing Basics, page 24), until reduced to a few tablespoons of concentrated juices. Remove from the heat and stir in the roasted garlic.

**6.** To serve, cut 1 double chop into 2 single chops. Arrange on 2 dinner plates. Spoon the juices, with the garlic, over and around the chops. Garnish with watercress and serve immediately.

## VARIATION: LAMB WITH ROASTED GARLIC-CABERNET SAUCE

Make chops as above, but replace step 5 sauce making with this recipe.

½ teaspoon olive oil
1 small onion, chopped
½ carrot, trimmed, peeled, and chopped
½ celery rib, strings removed (Celery Stringing, page 18), chopped
1 garlic clove, smashed
Pinch of dried or fresh thyme, plus more as needed
⅓ cup good cabernet sauvignon or red Bordeaux
⅔ cup rich veal stock or chicken broth
Salt and freshly ground black pepper, to taste
Roasted garlic (page 19)

**1.** Place the oil, onion, carrot, celery, garlic, and thyme in a nonreactive small saucepan over medium heat. Cover and sweat (page 79) or cook, tossing once or twice with a wooden spoon, until the vegetables are tender, 5 to 10 minutes (add a spoonful of water if the vegetables start to stick to the pan).

**2.** Uncover the pan; add the wine and boil until nearly dry. Add the stock or broth and boil gently until reduced by not quite half. Strain into a clean pan, pressing firmly on the solids in the strainer with the back of a spoon. Skim off any fat from the surface of the sauce with a large metal spoon or skimmer. Taste and correct the seasonings, adding salt, black pepper, or thyme, if needed. Stir in the roasted garlic; keep covered. If necessary, rewarm just before serving. Spoon over the lamb chops.

**How do I serve this?** If you like, instead of serving the shanks with the beans, serve them on a bed of Potatoes Boulangère (page 178) for a special treat—the potatoes will soak up the rich juices from the lamb. For an easier approach, wide egg noodles are fine or just plain white or brown rice. For a little crunch, a vegetable salad, such as blanched cauliflower or green beans, would be ideal.

If you have difficulty finding enough **shanks** to prepare this dish, buy them as you see them, then freeze until you have collected enough.

*Herbes de Provence* is a blend of dried herbs commonly used in the cooking of the south of France. Large supermarkets carry it in their spice section.

**Gremolata** is a handy seasoning to know about. Sprinkle it on pork tenderloin and chops—or practically any meat, for that matter. It's also good on soups and stews and even salads.

# BRAISED LAMB SHANKS WITH WHITE BEANS AND GREMOLATA

Lamb shanks are a wonderfully gelatinous cut, treasured by smart cooks (and they're inexpensive). Currently, they are enjoying a vogue on restaurant menus.

MAKES 4 SERVINGS

2 tablespoons olive oil

4 **lamb shanks** (about 1 pound each), knob end of bone cut off by your butcher
  Salt and freshly ground black pepper, to taste

1 onion, chopped

2 carrots, trimmed, peeled, halved lengthwise, and sliced crosswise $\frac{1}{4}$ inch thick

2 celery ribs, strings removed (Celery Stringing, page 18), sliced crosswise $\frac{1}{4}$ inch thick

6 garlic cloves, thinly sliced

3 tablespoons Cognac or brandy (optional, but good)

$\frac{1}{2}$ cup dry white wine

1 can (28 ounces) whole tomatoes in thick puree

$\frac{3}{4}$ teaspoon *herbes de Provence,* or a mixture of dried basil, thyme, rosemary, and fennel seed

2 strips orange zest (removed with a vegetable peeler)

1 bay leaf

1 cup canned reduced-sodium chicken broth, or more as needed

**Gremolata**

  Grated zest of $\frac{1}{2}$ orange

  Grated zest of 1 small lemon

$\frac{1}{4}$ cup chopped fresh parsley

1 small garlic clove, minced

3 to 4 cups cooked flageolets or white beans (Dried Bean Basics, page 17), or 2 cans (about 19 ounces each) cannellini beans, drained and rinsed

$\frac{1}{2}$ cup chopped fresh parsley

1. Heat the olive oil in a nonreactive heavy, flameproof casserole or Dutch oven over medium heat. Season the shanks with salt and pepper to taste. Add them to the casserole and brown well on all sides, turning several times, 15 to 20 minutes total. Transfer to a plate; if there is excess fat, pour off all but a thin film from the casserole.

2. Preheat the oven to 325°F., with a rack positioned in the lower third of the oven. Add the onion, carrots, and celery to the casserole. Cook, stirring now and then with a wooden spoon, until the onions begin to soften, about 8 minutes. Add the garlic and cook, stirring, until the garlic is lightly golden, about 2 minutes.

3. Add the Cognac and **boil until nearly dry.** Add the white wine and boil until nearly dry. Add the tomatoes, *herbes de Provence,* orange zest, and bay leaf. Cook, crushing the tomatoes with a wooden spoon, until they reduce to the consistency of a thick tomato sauce, about 10 minutes. Stir in the broth and bring to a boil.

4. Place the lamb shanks in the liquid, adding any juices from the plate. The mixture in the casserole should reach halfway to two-thirds of the way up the lamb shanks; add more broth or cold water, if needed. **Cover** the casserole with foil to guarantee a tight seal and then cover with the lid.

5. Place the casserole in the oven and lower the heat to 300°. Braise until the lamb is very tender when poked with a paring knife, 2 to 3 hours. As the lamb cooks, turn the shanks over occasionally. If the liquid should begin boiling, lower the oven heat to 250° or 275° to maintain a gentle simmer (boiling the meat will toughen it).

6. Remove the casserole from the oven. Carefully remove the foil without letting any condensed liquid fall from the foil back into the pan. Remove and discard the bay leaf (and the orange zest, if you can find it). If you have time, let the casserole cool to room temperature; cover and refrigerate overnight. The solidified fat will lift easily off the surface. Or, if you don't have the time to refrigerate the pot overnight, gently transfer the lamb shanks with a large slotted spoon to a plate, letting the juices fall back into the casserole. Cover the lamb shanks with foil and keep warm while you finish the sauce.

7. With a large metal spoon or skimmer, spoon off and discard all possible fat from the surface of the liquid. Place the casserole on a stove-top burner over medium-high heat. Boil, uncovered, until the juices thicken slightly, about 8 minutes. ➝

**Boiling or reducing the brandy and wine separately until nearly dry adds layers of concentrated flavor.**

**For long simmering or braising, whether on top of the stove or in the oven, first covering the top of the pan snugly with aluminum foil and then the lid ensures that practically no liquid will be lost during the cooking.**

**If you have leftover gravy from these shanks, toss it with penne or other short pasta for a quick midweek supper.**

**8.** Meanwhile, in a small bowl, combine the **gremolata** ingredients; set aside.

**9.** Add the cooked beans to the thickened liquid in the casserole; lower the heat, cover the pan, and simmer gently to heat through and combine flavors, about 10 minutes. Stir in the parsley. Taste and correct the seasonings, adding salt and pepper, if needed.

10. Place the shanks on warm dinner plates, pouring any exuded juices from the shanks into the beans. Spoon some of the beans next to or around each shank, spoon the juices over and around the shanks. Sprinkle with the gremolata mixture and serve hot.

# PORK CHOPS WITH MUSTARD-ONION GRAVY

The Guinness and onion mixture produces a slightly sweet, meaty gravy. This is actually a quick braise (page 25)—you brown the meat, then simmer it gently in a little liquid until tender. Cooking these chops on the bone adds flavor, too.

MAKES 2 SERVINGS

> 4 center-cut loin pork chops, cut 1 inch thick (about 2 pounds)
> Salt and freshly ground black pepper, to taste
> 1 tablespoon vegetable oil or olive oil
> 2 medium to medium-large onions, halved and sliced lengthwise through the root end
> 2 large garlic cloves, minced
> Pinch of dried thyme
> 1 cup Guinness stout or dark beer, or more as needed
> 1 to 1½ teaspoons coarse-grained mustard, or to taste
> ¾ teaspoon balsamic or red wine vinegar, or to taste
> 1 tablespoon chopped fresh parsley (optional)

**1.** Pat the chops dry with paper towels. Season with salt and pepper to taste. Heat the oil in a nonreactive wide, heavy skillet, preferably nonstick, over medium-high heat. Gently slip the chops into the skillet and sauté, shaking the pan occasionally

**How do I serve this?** Mashed potatoes seem the best choice here—spoon a little gravy over them. And for most of my friends, I would offer a glass of dark beer as the beverage.

to prevent sticking, until the chops are nicely browned on each side, about 6 minutes per side. Transfer the chops to a plate.

**2.** Add the onions, garlic, and thyme to the skillet. Sprinkle lightly with salt and toss to coat. Cover and sweat (page 79) or cook for about 5 minutes, stirring once or twice with a wooden spoon. Uncover and continue to cook, tossing, until the onions soften, 3 or 4 minutes. Add the Guinness, scraping up (Deglazing Basics, page 24) the flavorful browned bits from the bottom of the pan with a wooden spoon; bring to a boil. Tuck the chops back into the pan, spooning some of the onions and liquid over the chops. (The chops should be about halfway covered with liquid; add more if necessary.) Adjust the heat to maintain a simmer (don't let the liquid boil or the meat will toughen; use a Flame-Tamer if you have one).

**3.** Cover the pan with foil and then with a lid. Simmer or **braise,** basting the chops once or twice with the pan juices, until the chops are very tender, usually about 45 minutes from the time they start to simmer. Turn the chops over once about halfway through the cooking time. (Don't overcook or the chops will become dry. Also, don't let the condensed moisture on the foil drip into the gravy when uncovering the pan.)

**4.** Transfer the chops and onions to warm serving plates, covering them loosely with foil to keep warm. Tilt the pan to one side and degrease the pan juices, spooning off the fat with a large metal spoon or skimmer. Raise the heat and **boil the gravy down,** uncovered, until it is concentrated in flavor and thickened, 2 to 4 minutes. Stir in the mustard and vinegar to taste plus the parsley. Taste and correct the seasonings, adding more salt, pepper, and vinegar, if needed. Pour the gravy over the chops and serve hot.

Since pork is now bred particularly lean, it's easy to overcook—you'll end up with a dry piece of meat. Since **braising** is a moist cooking technique, this danger is lessened—plus the pork picks up all the delicious flavors of the braising liquid.

**Boiling liquids down** concentrates flavor and can slightly thicken the consistency, without adding flour, cornstarch, or any other thickener. In this recipe, be careful not to overreduce the sauce—you want enough to spoon over the chops and mashed potatoes (if you follow my suggestion).

**Pork tenderloins**—the small band of tender flesh inside the loin, corresponding to the filet mignon of beef—are a wonderful but underused cut. They're very low in fat and ten~~der~~ ~~. . . . .~~ ~~. . . . . . .~~ ~~. . . . . .~~ both for grilling the pork (this is a great cut for the grill) and also for a combination technique, starting the pork on top of the stove and then finishing it in the oven.

# GRILLED MARINATED PORK TENDERLOIN WITH WARM WHITE BEAN–PEPPER COMPOTE

This recipe looks involved but isn't—it's actually an easy, hearty supper.

MAKES 4 SERVINGS

Marinade and Pork

- ¼ cup fresh orange juice
- 1½ tablespoons reduced-sodium soy sauce
- 1 teaspoon olive oil or vegetable oil
- 2 large garlic cloves, smashed
- 2 fresh rosemary sprigs or a small pinch of dried
  Freshly ground black pepper, to taste
- 1 to 1¼ pounds **pork tenderloins** (usually 2 pieces), scrupulously trimmed of all surface fat

**Warm Bean Compote**

- 2 teaspoons vegetable oil or olive oil
- 1 *each* medium red, yellow, and green bell pepper, cored, seeded (Bell Pepper Basics, page 16), and coarsely chopped
- 2 garlic cloves, minced
- 2 cups cooked white beans, such as Great Northern (Dried Bean Basics, page 17), or 1 can (19 ounces) cannellini beans, drained and rinsed
- 3 tablespoons finely chopped red onion
- 1 scallion (green portion only), thinly sliced on a sharp diagonal
- 1 ripe plum tomato, cored, seeded (Tomato Basics, page 22), and cut into ¼-inch dice
- 3 roasted garlic cloves (Garlic Basics, page 19), peeled and thinly sliced
- 2 tablespoons fresh lemon juice, plus more to taste
- 1 tablespoon sherry vinegar or red wine vinegar
  Freshly ground black pepper and salt, if needed
- 3 tablespoons chopped fresh parsley
- 1 tablespoon olive oil
  Fresh rosemary sprigs, for garnish

1. **To make the marinade:** In a sealable plastic bag, combine the orange juice, soy

sauce, oil, garlic, rosemary, and pepper. Add the pork and seal the bag. Turn the bag around to coat the pork thoroughly. Refrigerate for at least 1 hour.

**2. To make the warm bean compote:** Heat the oil in a nonreactive medium skillet, preferably nonstick. Add the bell peppers and sauté, stirring occasionally with a wooden spoon until softened, usually about 6 minutes. Add the garlic and sauté for 1 minute. Transfer to a bowl and add the drained cooked beans, onion, scallion, tomato, roasted garlic, lemon juice, vinegar, and pepper and salt if needed. Toss gently with a rubber spatula to combine all of the ingredients; set aside at cool room temperature (or refrigerate).

**3.** Remove the pork from the marinade, reserving the marinade. Pat the pork dry with paper towels.

**4. To roast:** Preheat the oven to 375°F. Heat a ridged stove-top grill over high heat (or a nonstick skillet over medium-high heat). Oil the ridged grill or skillet very lightly. Sear the pork tenderloins on all sides, turning 2 or 3 times, until browned all over, 4 to 5 minutes (it will not be cooked through). Transfer the tenderloins to a roasting pan or shallow baking dish and roast in the oven, basting occasionally with the reserved marinade, until just cooked through but still very juicy, usually 20 to 25 minutes. (The timing can vary based on the thickness of the tenderloins. Do not overcook.) Remove the pork to a cutting board and let rest for 5 minutes.

**5. To cook on a charcoal or gas grill:** Preheat the grill or charcoals until hot. Oil the grill rack very lightly. Grill the pork, turning frequently with tongs and basting occasionally with the reserved marinade, until golden brown on all sides and no longer pink in the center, 20 to 25 minutes. (The pork should be firm in the center but not too springy when cooked through, and it should still be very juicy.) Remove the pork to a cutting board and let rest for 5 minutes.

**6.** While the pork is resting, place the bean-pepper compote in a saucepan over medium heat. Cook, stirring with a wooden spoon, until warmed through but not hot. Stir in the parsley and olive oil plus a little more lemon juice and freshly ground pepper. Taste and correct all of the seasonings, if needed.

**7.** To serve, slice the pork diagonally about ¼ inch thick. Arrange several slices of pork on each warm serving plate, overlapping the slices slightly in a curved pattern. Spoon the juices from the roasting pan over the pork. Spoon some of the bean compote next to the pork slices. Garnish the plates with rosemary sprigs and serve hot.

**How do I serve this?**
Just a huge green salad
and lots of peasant-style
crusty bread. And of
course, a crisp Alsatian
white wine.

If you live near a Polish
or Ukrainian butcher it
buys Manhattan's East
Village's own sauerkraut
sold in bulk. Otherwise,
purchase it in plastic
bags in the refrigerated
section of your
supermarket.

You can **double** the
**sauerkraut recipe** (prepared through step 3)
and keep some in the
freezer for a cold night.
This is also an effortless
dish for a large winter
party—just multiply the
amount of ingredients
appropriate for your
number of guests.

**Weisswurst** or veal
sausage is deliciously
subtle; you'll find it
in butcher shops,
delis, and many
supermarkets.

# EASY CHOUCROUTE WITH SMOKED PORK CHOPS OR WEISSWURST

This is a very manageable version of Alsace's gift to the food world. Served with either smoked pork chops (delicious) or weisswurst (also delicious), this is fragrant and won-derful. The grated apple adds sweetness, the grated potato gives body and flavor, and it all dissolves into the sauerkraut juices as they cook. Baking the meat right in the pre-pared sauerkraut infuses both their flavors together in a delectable symbiotic exchange.

MAKES 4 SERVINGS

- 4  slices bacon, cut into 1-inch squares
- 2  onions, halved through the root end and sliced crosswise
- 2  garlic cloves, thinly sliced
- 2  pounds prepared **sauerkraut,** rinsed in a colander under cold water for several minutes, then drained well
- 2  small-medium sweet apples, such as Golden Delicious, peeled, quartered, cored, and coarsely grated
- 1  potato (all-purpose or russet), peeled and coarsely grated
- 1  cup dry white wine, plus more if needed
- $\frac{1}{2}$  cup apple cider or apple juice
- $\frac{1}{2}$  cup chicken broth or water
- $\frac{1}{2}$  teaspoon dried thyme
- 1  bay leaf
- 8  juniper berries, bruised with the back of a knife, or 1 tablespoon gin
- 3  whole cloves

   Salt, if needed
- 4  smoked pork chops, cut 1 inch thick (10 to 12 ounces each), or 8 **weisswurst** (about $1\frac{1}{2}$ pounds total)
- $1\frac{1}{2}$  teaspoons vegetable oil or butter, for weisswurst

   Freshly ground black pepper, to taste, for weisswurst

**Accompaniments**

   Boiled potatoes

   Coarse-grained mustard

   Cornichons (French gherkins)

If it's more convenient, you can also simmer the sausages in the sauerkraut on top of the stove.

1. Place the bacon in a nonreactive, large, heavy casserole or Dutch oven over medium heat; cook, stirring, until golden brown, 3 to 5 minutes. With a slotted spoon, transfer the bacon to a paper towel–lined plate, letting all possible fat drain back into the pan.

2. Pour off all but a thin film of fat from the casserole. Add the onions and cook, stirring with a wooden spoon, until the onions soften but are not browned, about 7 minutes. Add the garlic and toss until fragrant, 1 or 2 minutes. Add the sauerkraut, apples, and potato, stirring with 2 large wooden spoons to combine. Add the wine, cider or juice, broth, thyme, bay leaf, juniper berries, and cloves. Add salt if needed (it probably won't be). Cover the casserole and bring the mixture to a boil. Lower the heat and simmer steadily, covered, stirring from time to time, for 35 minutes. Stir in the reserved bacon.

3. The sauerkraut is now ready. If not cooking it with the meat right away, let it cool completely and then refrigerate. If you'd like to freeze some of it, cool that portion; freeze in a tightly sealed, labeled container.

4. **To serve with smoked pork chops:** Preheat the oven to 350°F. Choose a baking dish in which the chops will fit in a single layer. Spoon a bed of sauerkraut (it's okay if it's still cold) with its juices into the pan. Place the chops on top; top with the remaining sauerkraut and juices. Cover the pan tightly with foil. Bake until the chops are very hot and tender, 45 to 50 minutes (add 10 minutes or so if the sauerkraut came right out of the refrigerator). Serve the chops with the sauerkraut alongside, with boiled potatoes, mustard, and cornichons.

5. **To serve with weisswurst:** Preheat the oven to 350°F. Prick the weisswurst all over with the point of a paring knife—this prevents split or burst skins. Heat 1½ teaspoons vegetable oil or butter in a nonstick skillet over medium-high heat. Place the sausages in the pan and sauté, turning several times with tongs, until golden on all sides, 8 to 10 minutes. Tuck the sausages into the sauerkraut in the casserole (or in a shallow baking dish), covering them completely. Cover the casserole and bake for 30 minutes. Add black pepper, to taste. Serve the sausages with the sauerkraut alongside, with boiled potatoes, mustard, and cornichons.

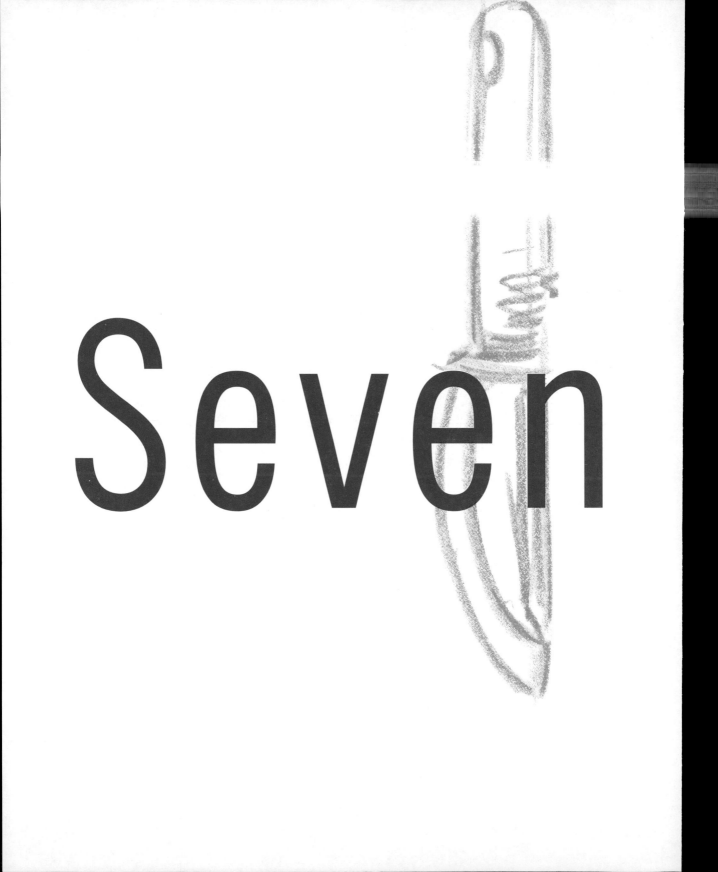

Seven

# VEGETABLES, RICE, BEANS, AND OTHER GRAINS

Basic Method for Parboiling Green Vegetables

Basic Method for Steaming Green Vegetables

Basic Method for Microwaving Green Vegetables

Sautéed Mushrooms with Garlic and Parsley

**Technique:** sautéing

Quick Honey-Lemon Glazed Carrots

**Technique:** preparing a glaze

Basic Method for Leafy Greens

**Techniques:** steaming/sautéing

Roasted Winter Vegetables

**Technique:** roasting

Tri-Color Roasted Peppers

**Technique:** broiling peppers

Baked Balsamic Beets

**Techniques:** baking/marinating

Corn and Cheese Pudding

**Techniques:** removing fresh kernels/cooking in a water bath

Corn on the Cob

**Technique:** boiling

Boiled Golden Potatoes

Technique: boiling

Creamy Mashed Potatoes without Cream

**Techniques:** mashing through food mill/mixing in cooking liquid

One-Step Crusty Red Potatoes

**Technique:** cooking to evaporate liquid

Potatoes Boulangère

**Technique:** baking in a gratin dish

A Perfect Baked Potato

**Technique:** baking

Oven-Fried Potatoes

**Technique:** oven frying

Diner Hash Browns

**Technique:** browning in a heavy skillet

Basic Method for Perfect Rice Pilaf

**Techniques:** stirring rice in oil or fat/cooking rice/stir-frying/
steaming/flavoring oil

Basic Cooking Method for Dried Beans

**Techniques:** overnight soaking/quick soaking

|  | Basic Method for Cooking Lentils |
| --- | --- |
|  | Lentil and Rice Pilaf |
| **Technique:** | cooking grains and beans together |
|  | Bulgur Pilaf |
| **Techniques:** | soaking bulgur/cooking bulgur |

**While vegetables or a rice and bean dish may not be the first thing I reach for when I'm starving, they are among my favorites.** I was raised on fresh-picked Jersey corn on the cob, and at my house while growing up, vegetables were considered good food. And we've become increasingly more aware of this fact. The U.S. Department of Agriculture, the Department of Health and Human Services, and the National Cancer Institute have recommended that we eat three to five servings of vegetables every day. The new food pyramid from the USDA underscores the importance of vegetables as well as grains and beans in our daily menu planning.

It's for these reasons, as well as what I consider their natural affinity for each other, that in this chapter I decided to mix together vegetables with beans and grains—they work well together in a wide variety of dishes. And on their own, we all know their virtues.

With the vegetables I explore basic cooking techniques—roasting, sautéing, blanching, steaming, baking, and even microwaving—that are easy and bring out the natural flavor of the vegetables themselves. The important rule is not to overcook. Even though I use a specific technique for a particular vegetable, the technique is easily applied to other similar vegetables.

What I like about beans and rice and other grains is that although they have their own rich flavor and texture, they offer a neutral background against which other flavors can dance. Cooking dried beans from scratch does require a little forethought, but most of the work is unattended. And if you're really in a rush, rinsed and drained canned beans can be substituted.

Although most of the recipes in this chapter are designed as side dishes to round out a meal, with a little bread on the side they work well as a light lunch or supper, or even as a small plate for a midafternoon break.

This technique can save you last-minute "timing panic," since the vegetables can be cooked in advance, drained, and cooled. Then, just before serving, toss them in a skillet with a little butter or oil to heat through.

When testing for doneness, rinse the vegetable under cold running water before taking a bite—no burned tongues.

Refreshing vegetables means tossing the hot cooked vegetables in a colander under cold running water (or plunging them into a bowl of ice water) to stop the cooking in order to retain crispness and set the color.

If you're serving the beans right away, omit the refreshing under cold water in step 3. Just drain the beans well and proceed to step 4.

If you'd rather serve the vegetables cold, drizzle them (after refreshing under cold water) either with a squeeze or two of fresh lemon juice and olive oil or with a vinaigrette.

# BASICS FOR GREEN VEGETABLES

# BASIC METHOD FOR PARBOILING GREEN VEGETABLES

[...] tage? Nutrients are leeched out into the cooking liquid—so you may want to hang onto the liquid for soups, stews, sauces, or whatever. While this recipe is for green beans, it is a basic method that can be used for many other green vegetables; some specifics follow.

MAKES 4 SERVINGS

Generous sprinkle of salt
1 to 1½ pounds slender green beans, ends trimmed
Unsalted butter or olive oil
Freshly ground black pepper, to taste
Lemon wedges, for serving

**1.** Bring a large saucepan of water to a boil. (If you cover the pan, the water will boil more quickly.) Uncover and add a generous sprinkling of salt.

**2.** Add the green beans by handfuls so the water continues to boil. Boil gently, uncovered, until the vegetables are crisp-tender to the bite, usually about 2 to 4 minutes. If the beans are quite slender, they can be done in as little as a minute. Go by feel, not by time. And don't overcook—or undercook.

**3.** Drain the beans in a colander and **refresh** under cold running water. Now you can place them on a paper towel–lined plate, cover, and refrigerate until serving time.

**4.** Heat a little butter or olive oil in a large nonstick skillet or saucepan over medium heat. Add the blanched beans and toss just until heated through, usually about 3 minutes. Add a grind or two of pepper and serve hot, with a lemon wedge.

**BROCCOLI** Cut the florets from the stems of the broccoli, reserving the stems for soup, stir-fries, and other dishes. Parboil the florets until crisp-tender, 3 to 4 minutes.

**SUGAR SNAP PEAS** Remove the strings. Parboil the peas until crisp-tender, about 2 minutes.

## ASPARAGUS, THE EASY WAY

Forget all those complicated directions for using asparagus steamers and for tying asparagus into bundles. The best way is also the easiest. Here's how.

MAKES 4 SERVINGS

   1  **pound asparagus**
      **Salt, to taste**
      **Lemon wedges, for serving**

**1.** Bring a wide skillet of water to a rolling boil.

**2.** Meanwhile, trim off the woody bottoms of the asparagus stalks with one swipe of a chef's knife. With a vegetable peeler, carefully peel a thin layer from the bottom halves of the stalks. Be careful not to take off too much.

**3.** Salt the boiling water, then drop in the asparagus. (If they vary in size, add the thickest stalks first; cook for 1 or 2 minutes and then add the rest.) Boil, uncovered, just until crisp-tender, 3 or 4 minutes. With tongs, transfer the asparagus to a paper towel–lined plate to drain. That's it. Serve with lemon wedges.

## VARIATION: ROAST ASPARAGUS WITH SHAVED PARMESAN

This easy, unusual method comes from my friends Johanne Killeen and George Germon, chef-owners of Al Forno restaurant in Providence, Rhode Island.

MAKES 4 SERVINGS

   1  **pound asparagus**
      **Fruity extra-virgin olive oil**
      **Fresh lemon juice**
      **Freshly ground black pepper, to taste**
      **Shavings of Parmesan cheese**

**1.** Preheat the oven to 500°F. Trim and peel the asparagus stalks as above. Place the asparagus in a shallow baking dish and drizzle with the olive oil.

**2.** Roast just until crisp-tender, 8 to 10 minutes, turning occasionally with tongs; the spears will be slightly spotted with black. Serve immediately, with a squeeze of lemon and freshly ground pepper. **A few shavings of Parmesan,** scraped from a room-temperature wedge of cheese with a vegetable peeler, makes a nice touch.

Serve hot, as is, with a squeeze of fresh lemon juice and a grind or two of black pepper. Or top with olive oil or a pat of butter plus a squeeze of lemon. To serve cool or lukewarm, dress with a vinaigrette or olive oil and lemon, or serve with an herb mayonnaise on the side.

Thinly shaved curls of Parmesan cheese are a nice garnish for salad, all kinds of cooked green vegetables, soups, and of course, pasta dishes.

**Serve hot, seasoned with salt and freshly ground black pepper and a squeeze of lemon juice, if you like. Or refresh in a colander under cold water to** ~~stop the cooking, pat~~ ~~dry, then drizzle with~~ ~~lemon juice and olive oil~~ ~~or a vinaigrette, and~~ **serve at room temperature.**

# BASIC METHOD FOR STEAMING GREEN VEGETABLES

You can steam green vegetables to preserve more of their nutrients—cooking vegetables in lots of water removes the nutrients.

~~MAKES ...~~

Salt, to taste

1 to 1½ pounds green beans, ends trimmed

**1.** Bring about 1 inch of water to a boil in a wide saucepan with a tight-fitting lid. Add a sprinkling of salt; arrange a collapsible steamer in the pan.

**2.** Scatter the beans in the steamer basket in an even layer—stacking the beans on top of each other in a dense layer results in uneven cooking. Cover the pan tightly and steam (Steaming Basics, page 25) over vigorously boiling water just until the beans are crisp-tender but still bright green, usually about 7 minutes—go by feel, not strictly by time. Slender beans will steam in as little as 4 minutes.

**BROCCOLI** Trim the woody broccoli stem bottoms and discard. Cut off the florets from the tops of the stems and set aside. Cut the stems into ½-inch lengths. Place the stems in an even layer in the steamer over vigorously boiling salted water; cover tightly. Steam for 3 minutes. Add the florets and steam until everything is crisp-tender but still bright green, about 5 minutes longer. Drain; rinse under cold running water to stop the cooking and set the color. Drain well; place on paper towels to dry.

**SUGAR SNAP PEAS** Remove the strings (page 20). Arrange in an even layer in a steamer basket over boiling salted water. Cover tightly and steam until just crisp-tender and still bright green, usually about 2 minutes.

**ASPARAGUS** Prepare the asparagus as directed on page 163. Arrange in an even layer in a steamer basket over boiling salted water. Cover tightly and steam until just tender (with a hint of crispness remaining) but still bright green, usually 4 to 7 minutes.

## BASIC METHOD FOR MICROWAVING GREEN VEGETABLES

Cooking vegetables is one of the things the microwave oven does best. Basically, you are steaming. Microwaving preserves plenty of nutrients because it is so fast, practically no extra liquid is used (no chance for nutrients to dissolve into the liquid), and it cooks to a fairly precise degree of doneness. (But don't overcook—you can always stick it back in for another 30 seconds.)

**GREEN BEANS** Snip off the ends. Place in a shallow baking dish; sprinkle with water and cover tightly with plastic wrap. For $\frac{1}{2}$ pound green beans (2 or 3 servings), the timing usually ranges from 4 to 6 minutes. Slender beans will microwave in as little as 4 minutes.

**BROCCOLI** Trim the woody broccoli stem bottoms and discard. Cut the broccoli into florets, with some of the stalk on each piece. Place in a shallow baking dish; sprinkle with water and cover tightly with plastic wrap. For $\frac{1}{2}$ pound broccoli (2 to 3 servings), microwave generally for 3 to 4 minutes.

**SUGAR SNAP PEAS** Remove the strings (page 20). Place the peas in a shallow baking dish; sprinkle with water and cover tightly with plastic wrap. For $\frac{1}{2}$ pound sugar snap peas (2 to 3 servings), microwave for about 2 minutes.

**ASPARAGUS** Prepare the asparagus as directed on page 163. Place in a shallow baking dish; sprinkle with water and cover tightly with plastic wrap. For $\frac{1}{2}$ pound asparagus (2 to 3 servings), microwave for $2\frac{1}{2}$ to 3 minutes.

**How do I serve this?**
Alongside grilled meats, spooned over baked or mashed potatoes, or as a topping for burgers.

# OTHER VEGETABLES

## SAUTÉED MUSHROOMS WITH GARLIC AND PARSLEY

This is a quick, basic method—use it for any type of mushrooms, regular, wild, or a combination. You can also toss this mixture with fettuccine or linguine (see the variation that follows) or use it to top polenta.

MAKES 4 SERVINGS

> 2 tablespoons olive oil
>
> 6 ounces shiitake, Golden Oak, portobello, or other mushrooms, wiped clean and thickly sliced
>
> 6 ounces white mushrooms, wiped clean and thickly sliced (Mushroom Basics, page 21)
>
> Salt and freshly ground black pepper, to taste
>
> 1½ tablespoons minced garlic
>
> 3 tablespoons chopped fresh parsley and snipped fresh chives

**1.** Heat the oil in a large skillet, preferably nonstick, over medium-high heat. Add the mushrooms; sprinkle with salt and pepper to taste.

**2.** Let the mushrooms sizzle in the hot fat for a minute or so (which will give them that sautéed flavor). Then continue to sauté (Sauté Basics, page 24), tossing frequently with a wooden spoon, for about 3 minutes. Add the garlic and cook, tossing, until the mushrooms are tender and lightly golden, about 4 minutes longer. Add the parsley and chives; toss for a few moments and serve hot.

### VARIATION: PASTA WITH MUSHROOMS

MAKES 2 OR 3 SERVINGS

Cook ½ pound fresh or dried fettuccine or linguine until tender, reserving a little of the pasta cooking liquid. Meanwhile, when you sauté the mushrooms in the above recipe, add a few spoonfuls of dry red or white wine or chicken broth along with the parsley; let cook for a few moments. Drain the pasta, toss with the mushrooms in the skillet, and serve hot, sprinkled with freshly grated Parmesan cheese and a few grinds of black pepper.

# QUICK HONEY-LEMON GLAZED CARROTS

This easy recipe uses the method of the French classic, carrots Vichy—carrots are covered with Vichy water and the water boils away as it cooks the carrots.

MAKES 4 SERVINGS

1 bunch (about 1 pound) carrots, green stalks removed, trimmed, peeled, and cut diagonally into ¾-inch lengths

1 strip lemon zest, removed with a vegetable peeler

1 tablespoon honey
   Pinch of dried cumin (optional)
   Pinch of coarse (kosher) salt or sea salt
   Juice of ½ lemon, or to taste
   Freshly ground black pepper, to taste

**1.** Place the carrots, lemon zest, honey, cumin, and salt in a sauté pan or low-sided saucepan. Add enough cold water to not quite cover the carrots. Bring to a boil.

**2.** Cook, uncovered, stirring once or twice and adjusting the heat as necessary to maintain a fairly vigorous but not violent boil until the liquid has nearly evaporated, about 14 minutes. If the carrots are not yet tender, lower the heat slightly. (The recipe can be **made ahead** to this point. Cool and then cover and refrigerate. Reheat when needed, adding a couple of spoonfuls of water if the carrots seem dry.)

**3.** Lower the heat and toss gently with a wooden spoon until the liquid reduces to form a light, syrupy **glaze,** usually a couple of minutes. Remove the lemon zest. Stir in the lemon juice and pepper and serve hot.

I serve these with roast chicken or almost any fish or meat.

As the liquid cooks down the carrots become tender. In the final stage of cooking, the concentrated honey mixture forms a glaze on the carrots.

**If not cooking right away,** place the spinach, with the water clinging to its leaves, in a large plastic bag and refrigerate (for up to 8 hours or so) in the crisper drawer.

~~I know it might look like you're starting with way too~~

**much spinach,** but remember, it quickly cooks down to a very small amount. If you are doubling or tripling the recipe, make sure your pots are big enough or work in batches.

# BASIC METHOD FOR LEAFY GREENS

Broccoli rabe and Swiss chard are also good cooked this way. This method—actually a combination of steaming and sautéing—works well with tougher greens, such as beet, collard, and mustard, all nutrient-packed powerhouses. Just remember they ~~need a little more water and slightly longer cooking time to become tender.~~

~~MAKES 4 SERVINGS~~

1   to 1½ pounds fresh **spinach**
1½  tablespoons olive oil
1   large garlic clove, thinly sliced
    Salt and freshly ground black pepper, to taste (or a tiny pinch of dried red pepper flakes)
2   or 3 gratings of fresh nutmeg (optional)
    Lemon wedges, for serving

**1.** Place the spinach in a colander in the sink under lukewarm running water. Remove the large, tough stems and swish the leaves around under the water to wash them very well. Change the water to cold and continue to wash all traces of grit from the leaves.

**2.** Place the spinach, with the water clinging to its leaves, in a nonreactive large pot over medium-high heat. Cover tightly. Steam (Steaming Basics, page 25) until the spinach is just wilted but still bright green, usually about 3 minutes. As the leaves steam, carefully uncover the pot and turn the spinach over once with a wooden spoon to combine the cooked and raw portions—but don't leave the cover off too long.

**3.** Pour the contents of the pot into a colander in the sink. With a large skimmer or spoon, gently press the spinach to remove all excess water.

**4.** Heat the olive oil in the same pot over medium heat. Add the garlic and red pepper flakes, if you are using them. Sauté (Sauté Basics, page 24), stirring once in a while, until the garlic begins to turn very pale gold, 2 or 3 minutes. Add the spinach; sprinkle with salt and black pepper and nutmeg and turn the leaves over with 2 spoons to separate and coat them with oil. When they are heated through, after a minute or two, serve immediately, with a wedge of lemon.

# ROASTED WINTER VEGETABLES

Roasting vegetables in a hot oven helps bring out the flavor—their natural sugars caramelize, developing a rich, mellow flavor.

MAKES 4 SERVINGS

- 2 tablespoons extra-virgin olive oil
- 2 garlic cloves, smashed
- 3 Yukon Gold or Yellow Finn potatoes, peeled, quartered, and cut into 1-inch wedges
- 3 carrots, trimmed, peeled, halved lengthwise, and cut into 2-inch lengths
- 1 parsnip, trimmed, peeled, halved lengthwise, and cut crosswise into 2-inch-long chunks
- 1 onion, cut into 6 wedges
- 5 white mushrooms, wiped clean and quartered (Mushroom Basics, page 21)
- 1 teaspoon fresh thyme leaves or ½ teaspoon dried
  Salt and freshly ground black pepper, to taste
- 1 tablespoon chopped fresh parsley

**1.** Preheat the oven to 450°F. Pour the oil into a large gratin dish or roasting pan, preferably metal. Add the garlic and place the pan in the oven for 5 minutes to heat the oil. Carefully add all of the vegetables, sprinkle with the thyme and salt and pepper, and gently turn the vegetables over with a spatula and large spoon to coat them with the oil.

**2.** Roast the vegetables, turning occasionally with a spatula, until golden and fork-tender, about 40 minutes. Sprinkle with the parsley and serve hot.

I like to serve these with broiled or grilled meats and rich creamy casseroles.

Once you've roasted vegetables this way, you can use this method for any single vegetable or for any combination that you like. Two tips to remember, however: Keep the size of the vegetable pieces uniform for even cooking, and if using more than one ingredient, be sure the consistency and textures are similar, again for even cooking.

Once you have them on hand, roasted peppers can serve as an appetizer, on their own or interleaved with mozzarella or goat cheese. They can be warmed and served as a vegetable course or used to add flavor and color to soups, salads, rice, and pasta dishes.

I usually roast a big batch of peppers at once, since roasted peppers keep, refrigerated, for several days. You can also layer them between sheets of aluminum foil and freeze them until ready to marinate and serve.

Use all one color of pepper or a different mix than the three colors suggested.

The peppers are actually roasted by charring them under a broiler or on a grill.

# TRI-COLOR ROASTED PEPPERS

Roasted peppers are such a nice thing to have on hand, and they're easy to fix, with a minimal amount of forethought.

MAKES A SIDE-DISH SERVINGS

2 red bell peppers

1 *each* of yellow bell pepper and green bell pepper

**1.** Preheat the broiler or prepare a charcoal grill, with the rack adjusted so the peppers will be as close as possible to the heat. If using the broiler, place the peppers on a foil-lined baking sheet. Broil or grill the peppers, turning with tongs, until charred on all sides, 8 to 15 minutes total. Wrap the foil around the peppers, crimping the edges to seal shut (or place in a brown paper bag and close); set aside for about 10 minutes, letting the steam loosen the skins further.

**2.** Working over the foil or a bowl to catch the roasted pepper juices, carefully peel the charred skins from the peppers with a small paring knife and your fingers (do not rinse). Remove the stems, seeds, and ribs. Cut the peppers in strips about 1 inch wide (or narrower, if you prefer); arrange the peppers on a platter. Strain some of the reserved pepper juices over the peppers. Serve at room temperature.

## VARIATION: HERBED MARINATED ROASTED PEPPERS

1 garlic clove, halved

   Tri-Color Roasted Peppers (above)

2 tablespoons shredded fresh basil leaves

   Salt and freshly ground black pepper, to taste

1½ to 2 tablespoons balsamic vinegar

1 tablespoon olive oil

**1.** Rub a platter or shallow dish with the cut sides of the garlic; leave the garlic in the dish. Arrange the roasted pepper strips in an even layer, alternating groups of each color. Drizzle the reserved pepper juices over the pepper strips. Season with the basil and salt and pepper to taste. Drizzle with the balsamic vinegar and olive oil.

**2.** Cover and marinate at room temperature for 1 to 2 hours or for up to 2 or 3 days in the refrigerator. Remove the garlic clove halves and serve at cool room temperature.

# BAKED BALSAMIC BEETS

The sweetness is twofold here: The beets caramelize during baking, becoming wonderfully sweet, and the slight sweetness of the balsamic vinegar then underscores them.

MAKES 4 SERVINGS

2 bunches beets (10 to 12 small-medium)

¼ cup balsamic vinegar

Salt and freshly ground black pepper, to taste

**1.** Preheat the oven to 400°F. Trim off the leafy tops of the beets, but leave about an inch of the stem attached. Wash the beets well, scrubbing them with a vegetable brush, but leave them unpeeled.

**2.** Tear off large sheets of aluminum foil. Place 2 or 3 beets on each piece and gather the foil up and around the beets. Crimp together, sealing well. Repeat, forming several foil packages; place on a baking sheet.

**3.** Bake until the beets are tender, 1 to 1½ hours. (To test, slide the baking sheet out of the oven, carefully open one of the packages—stand away from the steam—and poke a beet with a paring knife.) When done, remove from the oven and partially open the foil packages. Let the beets cool to room temperature.

**4.** With a paring knife, **pull the skins off** the beets and discard. Slice the beets, letting them fall into a soufflé dish or serving bowl. Add the balsamic vinegar and a sprinkling of salt and pepper. Toss gently with 2 soup spoons and let marinate for at least an hour at room temperature, stirring from time to time. Serve at cool room temperature.

You can **double** this recipe; if you're going to the trouble of baking beets, you may as well have them on hand, since they are a delicious and colorful addition to many dishes. Dice or slice and add to a salad; cut into julienne, toss with butter in a skillet, and serve as a side dish or garnish; or marinate them in vinegar, as in this recipe, and serve as part of an antipasto plate. For a vivid puree to accompany grilled or broiled meats and poultry, puree baked beets until smooth or coarse, season with a touch of nutmeg, and work in a little unsalted butter.

An added bonus: After the beets have been baked this way, **peeling them is a snap** and there is no danger of getting crimson stains all over your kitchen.

**To store** these balsamic beets, cover with plastic wrap and refrigerate for 2 or 3 days (remove the beets from the refrigerator about 15 minutes before serving).

This makes a wonderful **side dish** with grilled meats and poultry or fish.

To **remove corn kernels** from the cob, hold the husked cob upright at an angle by the stem end with the blossom or opposite end in a bowl. Using a small paring knife and beginning at the stem end, cut under the kernels into the cob all the way from one end to the other, releasing the kernels and some of the corn "milk" from the cob into the bowl. Continue turning the cob and cutting until all the kernels have been removed.

If **fresh corn on the cob is not available,** I prefer using canned whole kernel corn to frozen. Just substitute cup for cup. One 12-ounce can equals 1¾ cups drained kernels, which is the equivalent to fresh kernels cut from about 3 medium ears.

The small amount of **cornstarch** binds the pudding mixture, preventing it from curdling as it bakes.

# CORN AND CHEESE PUDDING

MAKES 6 SERVINGS

2 cups fresh **corn kernels** with pulp (cut from 5 or 6 ears)
3 tablespoons cornstarch
1 teaspoon unsalted butter
½ cup thinly sliced scallions (green and white portions)
3 large eggs
1 cup milk
½ cup chicken broth
1 teaspoon salt
1 teaspoon sugar
Freshly ground black pepper, to taste
Pinch *each* of freshly grated nutmeg and cayenne
½ cup *each* ¼-inch dice Monterey Jack and sharp Cheddar cheese, plus ¼ cup shredded Cheddar

**1.** Preheat the oven to 375°F. Bring a kettle of water to a boil and set aside. Thoroughly butter an 8-inch square baking pan or 9-inch round pie or cake pan. Puree 1¼ cups of the corn kernels with the cornstarch in a food processor or blender; set aside.

**2.** In a small skillet, heat the butter over low heat. Add the scallions and cook slowly until softened slightly, about 5 minutes. Set aside to cool briefly.

**3.** In a large bowl, whisk together the eggs, milk, chicken broth, salt, sugar, a generous grind or two of pepper, the nutmeg, and cayenne. Stir in the pureed corn mixture, the remaining ¾ cup whole corn kernels, and the diced cheeses. Pour the mixture into the baking pan or pie pan. Sprinkle the shredded Cheddar on top.

**4.** To make a water bath, place the baking pan in a larger roasting pan; set on the center oven rack. Pour enough of the boiling water into the larger pan to reach halfway up the sides of the pudding. Bake until lightly golden and just set, about 45 minutes; the top should be just firm but still jiggly. Serve hot.

## VARIATION: CORN PUDDING WITH CHILIES

4 fresh **poblano** or **Anaheim chili peppers** (Hot Chili Pepper Basics, page 17), preferably a combination of green and red chilies, or 1 small can (about 4 ounces) chopped green chilies, preferably mild, drained

**1. Char** (page 170) the fresh chilies, turning with tongs, directly over a gas flame or under a hot broiler until charred on all sides, about 4 minutes. Wrap the chilies in foil or seal in a paper bag and set aside to cool. This helps steam the skins loose. Peel and trim away the stems, ribs, and seeds. Cut the flesh into ¼-inch dice.

**2.** Stir the fresh-roasted or drained canned chilies into the pudding mixture along with the corn kernels and cheeses in step 3 of the Corn and Cheese Pudding recipe. Proceed with the recipe as directed.

# CORN ON THE COB

I put the shucked ears of corn in a large pot of boiling water (without salt). Some people like to add a teaspoon of sugar for each ear of corn—but I find the new sweet hybrids plenty sweet as is. Return the water to a boil; turn off the heat. Let the corn sit for about 5 minutes, then drain well. (If necessary, you can hold the corn in the water for a little while longer, off the heat.) Serve with salt and unsalted butter. There's nothing better.

## VARIATION: MICROWAVE CORN ON THE COB

You can microwave the corn with the husks still on, which keeps them moist and adds flavor. But frankly, once the corn is cooked, I find it easier not to handle the hot ears beyond sprinkling with salt and spreading with a little butter.

Or, use my "cheating method": Husk 2 ears of corn; place them in a shallow baking dish and cover tightly with plastic wrap. Microwave at high power for 6 minutes. Remove from the oven and let stand for a couple of minutes; then cut away the plastic wrap, transfer the corn to dinner plates, sprinkle with salt, and spread with butter.

Here is a rundown on a few of the **most commonly found fresh chili varieties.** The poblano is dark green, wide, and tapers to a length of about 5 inches; it is mild to mildly hot. Anaheims are bright green, about 7 inches long, and mildly hot. The **jalapeño** is about 2 inches long and ¾ to 1 inch in diameter, with a rounded top; it is medium to dark green, turning red when ripe, and hot. The smoked and dried version is called a **chipotle.** The **serrano** is dark green and smaller, thinner, and hotter than a jalapeño.

Until the new hybrid sweet corns were developed, the only way to enjoy truly sweet corn was to put a pot of water on to boil, run out to the field and pick the corn, and rush it to the waiting pot. While this is no longer necessary, you still want to keep both storage and cooking times to a minimum.

**I love this as a light supper with a green salad and it certainly goes well with any grilled meats, as well as scrambled eggs for breakfast or brunch.**

If not serving right away, drain the potatoes in a colander or strainer. **To reheat, place about 1 tablespoon butter or olive oil in a nonstick skillet or saucepan over medium heat. Add the potatoes and toss gently with a wooden spoon until heated through. Toss in 1 tablespoon chopped fresh parsley, if you like, and serve hot.**

## POTATOES

## BOILED GOLDEN POTATOES

Try this basic method with any of the many potato varieties now found at our markets.

1 to 1½ pounds Yukon Gold or Yellow Finn potatoes, scrubbed but left unpeeled, quartered or halved
Salt, to taste
Unsalted butter, to taste
Freshly ground black pepper, to taste
1 tablespoon chopped fresh parsley (optional)

**1.** Place the potatoes in a saucepan in which they fit comfortably in a single layer. Add enough cold water to cover by 1 or 2 inches. Bring to a boil; add a sprinkling of salt.

**2.** Boil the potatoes gently, uncovered, until they are tender when pierced with a knife blade or a fork, usually about 15 minutes. Drain in a colander. Serve, topping each portion with a pat of butter and a sprinkling of freshly ground pepper. Add a sprinkling of parsley, if desired. Let each person gently mash the butter into his or her own potatoes on the plate.

### BONUS RECIPE

### GOLDEN POTATO CAKE

Make this when you have leftover boiled potatoes on hand.

MAKES 4 SERVINGS

3 tablespoons olive oil, or as needed
1 small onion, chopped
2 garlic cloves, minced, or 4 roasted garlic cloves (Garlic Basics, page 19), sliced
3½ cups (about) cut-up cooked potatoes, preferably Yukon Gold or Yellow Finn

**Salt and freshly ground black pepper, to taste**

1 **tablespoon chopped fresh parsley (optional)**

**1.** Heat 1 tablespoon of the oil in an 8- to 10-inch nonstick skillet over medium high heat. Add the onion and cook, stirring, until wilted and beginning to turn lightly golden, 6 to 8 minutes. Add the garlic and cook, stirring, for about 2 minutes longer.

**2.** Add 1 tablespoon more olive oil to the skillet. Add the potatoes, salt them, and grind a generous amount of pepper over them. Stir and turn the mixture, breaking up some of the potatoes and combining the ingredients for a couple of minutes (add a little more olive oil if the pan seems dry). Flatten the mixture with a wide spatula so that it covers the bottom of the pan. Cook the cake over medium to medium-high heat; adjust the heat as necessary so that the cake sizzles steadily but not furiously. Shake the pan from time to time to prevent sticking. It should take the cake 8 to 10 minutes to brown on the bottom (you can peek by lifting it with the spatula).

**3.** Now comes the fun part: inverting the potato cake onto a plate. Place a dinner plate upside down on top of the skillet and hold it in place with a kitchen towel. Decisively turn the whole thing over, skillet and plate. You've just flipped the cake onto the plate. Remove the skillet. Set the pancake aside; return the skillet to the heat and add the remaining 1 tablespoon olive oil. Slide the cake back into the pan, browned side up. Cook the second side, shaking the pan now and then to prevent sticking, about 8 minutes longer. Cut the cake into wedges, sprinkle with parsley if you like, and dig in.

**Mealy-textured potatoes such as russets or Idahos are best for baking or anytime you want dry, fluffy flesh. These high-starch potatoes are also good for mashing.**

Forcing the potatoes through a food mill or sieve makes for lump-less mashed.

**Mashing the potatoes with some of the reserved cooking water is the secret to the creamless potatoes.**

# CREAMY MASHED POTATOES WITHOUT CREAM

Who would think no cream or milk in these potatoes—but maybe the pat of butter helps

MAKES 4 SERVINGS

1   russet (baking or Idaho) potatoes, peeled, quartered lengthwise, and thickly sliced
3   or 4 garlic cloves, smashed
    Salt, to taste
    Freshly ground black pepper, to taste
    Freshly grated nutmeg (optional)
1   tablespoon cold unsalted butter

**1.** Place the potatoes, garlic, and salt in a pan with enough cold water to cover the potatoes. Partially cover and bring to a boil. Boil gently until the potatoes are very tender when poked with a knife, about 30 minutes.

**2.** Drain, reserving the cooking liquid. Press the potatoes and garlic through a **food mill,** or push through a coarse sieve with a large metal spoon or wooden pestle, into a bowl. Moisten the puree with enough (usually ½ to 1 cup) of the **reserved cooking liquid** to make a creamy consistency—these potatoes should be somewhat runny. Season with pepper, a little nutmeg, and more salt, if needed; stir in the butter. Serve hot.

### VARIATION: **MASHED SWEETS**

Just substitute sweet potatoes for the russets and proceed as directed.

# ONE-STEP CRUSTY RED POTATOES

These potatoes cook in shallow water until tender; once the water boils away, the potatoes brown in the same pan until golden.

MAKES 4 SERVINGS

1¼ to 1½ pounds red-skinned new potatoes, scrubbed and quartered
   lengthwise (if larger, cut in 6 wedges)
1½ tablespoons olive oil
   Salt, to taste
2 garlic cloves, smashed and peeled
   Freshly ground black pepper, to taste
   Chopped fresh parsley or rosemary (optional)

**1.** Place the potatoes in a wide, heavy nonstick skillet. Add enough cold water to come about two-thirds of the way up the potatoes. Add the olive oil, a sprinkling of salt, and the garlic. Bring the water to a boil.

**2.** Adjust the heat to maintain a steady but not violent boil. Cook, uncovered, until the water **evaporates,** 15 to 18 minutes; turn the potatoes over with a slotted spoon or tongs 2 or 3 times as they cook.

**3.** When the liquid has evaporated, raise the heat slightly to medium-high. Sauté the potatoes, tossing frequently or turning with tongs, until golden and crusty, 7 to 10 minutes longer. Remove the garlic. Season with pepper, the herb, plus more salt, if needed.

**How do I serve these?** With grilled or roasted meat, on a brunch table with eggs and sausage and all those other no-no's, or even with a club sandwich for a fancy weekend lunch when the mood strikes.

Once the water **evaporates,** the softened potatoes will begin to turn a golden, crusty brown.

This is delicious served with roasted meats and poultry—and I've been known to eat a sizable portion of this for lunch, with a few pieces of crusty bread and a glass of red wine.

A gratin dish is a wide shallow baking dish exposing a large surface for crusting and allowing moisture to dispense for proper browning.

# POTATOES BOULANGÈRE

This is an offshoot of the bourgeois French classic *gratin dauphinois* (a richer version of our scalloped potatoes), in which sliced potatoes are bathed in cream and baked until golden and irresistible. This version flavors the potatoes with broth instead of the richer cream and this preparation is an especially appropriate side dish for meats and poultry. In French, this dish is called *pommes de terre à la boulangère,* or "potatoes, baker's wife–style." Housewives would often bring casseroles like this to be baked in the village baker's oven.

MAKES 4 SERVINGS

1 tablespoon olive oil, plus more as needed

1 onion, halved, then cut into thin slivers

1 bay leaf

Salt and freshly ground black pepper, to taste

4 garlic cloves, thinly sliced

3 or 4 russet potatoes (1½ to 1¾ pounds), peeled and sliced into thin rounds

Freshly grated nutmeg, to taste

1 to 1½ cups reduced-sodium chicken broth, as needed

1 tablespoon finely chopped fresh parsley

**1.** Preheat the oven to 425° F. Position a rack in the center of the oven. Heat the olive oil in a large nonstick skillet over medium-high heat. Add the onion, bay leaf, and a sprinkling of salt and pepper. Cook, stirring often with a wooden spoon, until the onion is lightly golden, 6 or 7 minutes. Add the garlic and cook, tossing, for 2 minutes longer.

**2.** Rub a 10- or 12-inch oval **gratin** dish, preferably metal, with olive oil. Layer one-third of the potatoes in the dish, scattering them randomly. Season lightly with salt, pepper, and a tiny bit of nutmeg. Top with half of the onion mixture. Arrange a second layer of potatoes, season, then top with the remaining onions. Arrange a top layer of potatoes neatly in overlapping layers like roof tiles. Pour on enough chicken broth to come not quite to the bottom of the top layer of potatoes. With your fingers, rub the top layer of potatoes with a little more olive oil.

**3.** Bake the potatoes for 30 minutes. Lower the oven heat to 400° F. and continue to bake until the potatoes are nicely browned and tender when poked with a paring knife and most of the liquid is absorbed, anywhere from 25 to 45 minutes longer. (The timing can vary because of the size and shape of various baking dishes. If the potatoes are browning too fast, lower the heat to 350° or 375°.)

**4.** Remove the pan from the oven and let the potatoes sit for about 5 minutes. Sprinkle with the parsley and serve hot.

# A PERFECT BAKED POTATO

So simple and so sublime—good anytime.

**Baking (russet or Idaho) potatoes, any number**

**1.** Preheat the oven to 425° F. Scrub any number of potatoes with a vegetable brush. Pat dry with paper towels and place on a pie plate or other shallow baking dish (I keep an old metal pie plate just for baking potatoes). Prick the skin in a few places with a fork to prevent bursting. (Do not wrap the potatoes with foil, which steams them and prevents the skins from crisping.)

**2.** Bake the potato(es) until the pulp is tender when poked with a knife and the skin is becoming very crusty, 1¼ to 1½ hours. Cut a cross in the top of each potato. Covering your hands with a kitchen towel, grasp each end and gently push toward the center to pop open the top. Serve hot.

## VARIATION: BAKED SWEETS

Just substitute sweet potatoes for the baking potatoes and proceed as directed.

Of course the fun of a baked potato is the topping—play: anything from sour cream (it can be full-fat, reduced-fat, or nonfat) mixed with horseradish; any kind of grated cheese, including crumbled goat or feta; or just plain yogurt mixed with a little Dijon mustard.

These are **ideal with** many of my favorites: hamburgers, sautéed liver, pork tenderloin, roast chicken, and even a turkey sandwich.

# OVEN-FRIED POTATOES

Classic French French fries or *pommes frites* are usually deep-fried twice in beef fat, lard, or oil. But by baking instead of frying, you can make them with only a fraction of the usual fat. Turn the potatoes often as they cook, so all of the sides brown evenly. While they are still hot, sprinkle them with coarse salt.

MAKES 4 SERVINGS

4   **long russets, Idahos, or sweet potatoes, unpeeled, scrubbed, and patted dry**

2   **tablespoons vegetable oil**
    **Coarse (kosher) salt or sea salt and freshly ground black pepper, to taste**

**1.** Preheat the oven to 425°F. Cut the potatoes into long wedges; rinse with cold water and drain. Spread on a double thickness of paper towels and top with another double layer; press to dry thoroughly.

**2.** Place the potatoes in a bowl; add the oil and toss to coat evenly. Spread in a single layer on a large baking sheet or jelly-roll pan.

**3.** Bake for 20 minutes. Remove the pan from the oven and carefully turn and rearrange the potatoes with tongs. Sprinkle with salt and pepper. Bake until golden brown, rotating the baking sheet once to insure even browning, 15 to 20 minutes longer. Sprinkle with the salt while hot; serve right away.

# DINER HASH BROWNS

Nowadays, these are usually called "home fries." Hash browns (or technically "hashed browns") are often grated—and there are even frozen toaster versions. But these are the real thing.

MAKES 4 SERVINGS

10  small-medium red (or other waxy) potatoes (1 to 1¼ pounds), boiled in salted water until tender but not mushy, preferably left unpeeled

2  tablespoons *each* bacon fat and unsalted butter, or olive oil and butter, plus more as needed

1  onion, chopped (about 1 cup)

1  garlic clove, minced (optional)
   Salt and freshly ground black pepper, to taste
   Paprika (optional)

**1.** Halve the potatoes lengthwise; cut crosswise into fat wedges or chunks. Heat 3 tablespoons of the combined fats in a **wide, heavy skillet** over medium heat. Place the potatoes, onion, and garlic in the pan, tossing with a wooden spoon to combine and coat with fat. Cook without stirring, shaking the pan occasionally to prevent sticking and adjusting the heat as necessary to maintain a steady, not violent sizzle. From time to time, press the potato mixture down gently with a wide spatula. When the bottom of the potatoes are golden, usually after about 8 minutes, you're ready to start turning.

**2.** Add the remaining 1 tablespoon fat to the center of the skillet; season the potato mixture with salt and a generous grind or two of pepper. Now cut through the mixture with the spatula; turn the potato mixture over, about one-quarter of the mixture at a time. As you turn, press that portion down into the fat. Continue to do this every 2 minutes or so, cutting, folding, and pressing as the mixture becomes nicely browned and crusty. Add a little more fat as needed to keep the potatoes lightly coated. The potatoes should be well browned in about 10 minutes from the time you start turning. If using the paprika, add a sprinkling toward the end of the cooking time, combining it with the potatoes as you turn them. Taste and correct the seasonings, adding more salt, pepper, and paprika, if needed. Serve immediately, piping hot.

A couple of **cooking notes:** In many restaurants, the cooks boil a big batch of new potatoes at the end of the previous day's shift, so they'll have cooked potatoes to start with. Some recipes start you off with raw potatoes, but I find the timing trickier and not as authentic to that real diner taste.

The **skillet** approximates a well-seasoned griddle. A cast-iron skillet substitutes well, though any heavy skillet will do. A nonstick skillet works fine as long as it's heavy (though you'll still need most of the fat; grease is part of the essence of real hash browns). Neither garlic nor olive oil are traditional, but they add good flavor; a dusting of paprika for color is up to you.

**What's a pilaf?** While pilaf is of Persian origin, examples are also found in Greek and Indian cooking. The rice is first cooked in oil or butter and then is simmered, covered, in a liquid or other liquid. A pilaf can be as simple as rice in combination of rice and cooked onion or it can be an elaborate concoction, containing meat and vegetables.

**White rice** comes in three different lengths: long-grain cooks into separate, fluffy grains; medium-grain, commonly used in risotto and paella, cooks moist and tender with a slight stickiness; and short-grain, often referred to as sushi rice, is sticky.

If, at the end of the cooking time, **the rice is not tender but all of the liquid has been absorbed,** what to do? Add a little more liquid, cover the pot, and continue to cook until tender. If, however, the rice is tender but still liquidy, continue cooking, uncovered.

# RICE, BEANS, AND OTHER GRAINS

These should be among the mainstays of a healthy diet. Following are a few basics. If you have one of the new generation of pressure cookers, it makes quick, easy work of dried beans and grains. I must say I've been very impressed, both with their ease and the rich complex flavored foods cooked in them.

## BASIC METHOD FOR PERFECT RICE PILAF

MAKES 4 SERVINGS (ABOUT 2 1/2 CUPS COOKED RICE)

- 1 tablespoon unsalted butter
- 3 tablespoons chopped onion
- 1 cup **long-grain white rice**
- 1 can (about 14 ounces) reduced-sodium chicken broth
    Salt and freshly ground black pepper, to taste
- 2 tablespoons chopped fresh parsley (optional)

**1.** Heat the butter in a heavy saucepan over medium heat. Add the onion; sauté, stirring, until the onion begins to wilt, about 3 minutes. Add the rice; stir to coat. Cook, stirring, until the grains of rice are starting to turn translucent, about 2 or 3 minutes.

**2.** Add the broth all at once, along with a pinch of salt. Raise the heat, cover the pan, and bring the broth to a boil. Stir once, then lower the heat to maintain a steady but gentle simmer. Cook, covered, until the rice is tender and the liquid has been absorbed, usually about 17 minutes. Remove the pan from the heat.

**3.** Cover the pilaf and let stand for 5 minutes. Season with salt (if needed) and pepper, plus the parsley; fluff with a fork and serve hot. A little cold butter, stirred in at the end, is a tasty touch.

### VARIATION: VEGETABLE RICE PILAF

To the onion in step 1, add 1 or 2 carrots, halved lengthwise, then thinly sliced crosswise; 1 celery rib, thinly sliced; plus, if you like, a little minced garlic and chopped mushrooms (stems work fine). Sauté for about 3 minutes and then add the rice and continue as directed.

## STIR-FRY OF RICE AND VEGETABLES

Based on what my old, dear friend, chef-author-restaurateur-amazing human crea-
ture Barbara Tropp cooks for herself and her husband Bart at home, this is a terrific
use for leftover rice. It's a fresh, healthy homemade dinner in minutes.

This is a master recipe; have fun with whatever ingredients you have on hand.

MAKES 2 SERVINGS

- 1 teaspoon vegetable oil
- 1 large garlic clove, minced
- ½ teaspoon minced, peeled, fresh ginger (optional)
- 2½ cups (approximately) cut-up fresh vegetables (such as 1 small red or
  yellow onion, slivered; 1 red or yellow bell pepper, slivered; 1 diagonally
  cut carrot; 1 or 2 handfuls of ½- to 1-inch lengths green beans or
  asparagus; sugar snap or regular peas)
- 3 cups cooked rice (such as long-grain white or brown rice, or basmati)
- 2 teaspoons flavored oil
- 2 scallions (both green and white portions), trimmed and thinly sliced on
  a sharp diagonal
- 1 tablespoon chopped fresh parsley and/or other fresh herbs (optional)
  Salt and freshly ground black pepper, to taste
  Optional addition for a main course: slivered leftover chicken, meat, or
  seafood (about 8 ounces)

**1.** Heat the oil in a large nonstick skillet or wok over medium-high heat. Add the
garlic and ginger; heat, tossing with a wooden spoon, until fragrant, about 20 seconds. Add the firmer vegetables (onions, peppers, carrots) and cook, stir-frying and
tossing, for about 3 minutes.

**2.** Add the quicker-cooking and green vegetables plus a spoonful or two of water.
Cover and steam for 2 minutes. Uncover and add the rice. Lower the heat to medium
and cook, stirring gently, to combine the ingredients and heat everything through,
about 4 minutes. Stir in the oil, scallions, and any other additions; heat through. Taste
and correct the seasonings, adding more salt and pepper, if needed. Dig in.

By the way, you can **substitute** 3 cups of cooked short **pasta** (shells, elbow macaroni) for the rice.

Here's the procedure for **flavoring oils:** Gently heat olive oil, peanut oil, or other oil in a saucepan, usually about 3 to 5 minutes. Mean-while, place fresh herb sprigs, herb leaves, chilies, or crushed pep-percorns in clear glass jars—figure about 2 or 3 sprigs, a tablespoon or so of herb leaves, 1 chili, or 1 teaspoon peppercorns for each cup of oil. Pour the oil into the jars. Let cool, cover, and let steep for about 1 week. Store in a cool, dark place for up to 6 months.

Unless you're rushed, the **overnight soaking method** is preferred, since it generally helps the beans retain their shape and not split or crumble.

Or, if you're in a hurry, use the **quick-soaking method.** Place beans and enough water to cover by 2 inches in a large saucepan. Bring to a boil; turn the heat to medium and simmer, uncovered, for 2 minutes. Cover and let stand for 1 hour. Drain and cook, proceeding with step 3, or according to whatever recipe you are using.

Note that **salt is added only at the end.** Any earlier, and it can toughen the beans, preventing them from becoming tender. If you plan to use chicken broth for part of the cooking liquid, try to use a no-sodium version to avoid toughness.

# BASIC COOKING METHOD FOR DRIED BEANS

Use this method for any variety of dried beans or legumes, except lentils and split peas, which need no soaking. Also, specialty beans (sometimes called "new crop" beans) may not require soaking; check the package instructions. (See Dried Bean Basics, page 17.)

Dried Beans

Onion, peeled (optional)

Bay leaf (optional)

Salt, to taste

**1.** Place the beans in a colander and rinse with cold water; sort and pick out any discolored beans.

**2.** Place the beans in a large bowl; add cold water to cover by at least 2 inches. **Soak overnight** (refrigerated if your kitchen is very warm). The next day, drain the beans, discarding the liquid.

**3.** Place the beans in a large pot with fresh cold water to cover by 2 inches. If you like, add the onion and bay leaf. Cover and bring to a boil; lower the heat and boil gently until the beans are tender, usually 1 to 1½ hours. Salt after cooking. Remove the bay leaf and discard, and chop the onion and add to the beans if you'd like.

## VARIATION: PRESSURE COOKER METHOD

This technique I borrow from my good friend Lorna Sass—the person most responsible for the renaissance of the pressure cooker. Her several pressure-cooker cookbooks would be a good addition to your library if they're not already there.

In her *Cooking Under Pressure,* Lorna recommends the following:

Cook 1 cup of beans (presoaked or unsoaked) with 4 cups of water plus 1 tablespoon of oil (the oil controls the foaming so the vent won't clog). For each additional 1 cup of beans, add 3 cups of water and 1 tablespoon of oil.

- Do not fill the cooker above the halfway mark.
- For firm-cooked beans, check for doneness after minimum time indicated. For soft-cooked (mushy beans), add 2 extra minutes under high pressure.
- When the cooking time is up, quick-release the pressure by placing the cooker under cold running water.
- Drain immediately.

Here are Lorna's cooking times:

| Beans (1 cup dried) | Minutes Under High Pressure | |
| --- | --- | --- |
| | Soaked Overnight | Unsoaked |
| Black (turtle) | 9–11 | 20–25 |
| Cannellini | 9–12 | 22–25 |
| Chickpeas | 10–12 | 30–40 |
| Great Northern | 8–12 | 25–30 |
| Lentils | | 7–10 |
| Pinto | 4–6 | 22–25 |
| Red kidney | 10–12 | 20–25 |

**BONUS RECIPE**

## QUICK BEAN RAGOUT WITH ROASTED PEPPERS

MAKES 4 SERVINGS

- 1 tablespoon olive oil
- 3 tablespoons finely chopped red onion
- 1 garlic clove, minced
- 1 large red or yellow bell pepper, roasted (Bell Pepper Basics, page 16) and diced
- 2 cups cooked (method above) white beans, such as Great Northern (Dried Bean Basics, page 17), or 1 can (19 ounces) cannellini beans, drained in a sieve and rinsed under cold water
- 1 ripe plum tomato, cored, seeded (Tomato Basics, page 22), and cut into ¼-inch dice (optional)
- 2 tablespoons sherry vinegar or wine vinegar, or to taste
  Salt, if needed
- 3 tablespoons chopped fresh parsley
- 1 scallion (green portion only), thinly sliced on a sharp diagonal
  Freshly ground black pepper, to taste →

**Serve this with** slices of rye bread and a simple spinach salad—and that's it.

**A ragout,** derived from the French *ragoûter*, meaning "to awaken or stimulate the appetite," is a rich, stewlike dish traditionally made with meat or poultry. Contemporary recipes have taken license with this definition—often meat is nowhere to be found, as in this dish with vegetables and beans.

**1.** Heat the oil in a nonreactive medium saucepan over medium heat. Add the onion and garlic; cook, stirring with a wooden spoon, until wilted, about 6 minutes. Stir in the diced roasted pepper (with a spoonful of the roasting juices, if you have them), the drained cooked beans, tomato, vinegar, and salt, if needed.

**2.** Stir gently over medium heat until very warm but not quite hot. Stir in the parsley, scallion, and black pepper. Taste and correct all of the seasonings, adding more vinegar and salt and pepper if needed, and serve.

## BASIC METHOD FOR COOKING LENTILS

DePuy lentils from France, now available in specialty food shops, are particularly good. You may have to adjust their cooking time slightly.

MAKES 6 SERVINGS

$1\frac{1}{2}$  cups (about 12 ounces) raw **lentils**, picked over

1   small onion, peeled

1   sprig fresh thyme or $\frac{1}{4}$ teaspoon dried

1   bay leaf

$3\frac{1}{2}$  cups cold water

Salt and freshly ground black pepper, to taste

**1.** Place the lentils in a saucepan with the onion, thyme, bay leaf, and water. Cover and bring to a boil. Lower the heat so that the water boils gently. Cook, covered, until the lentils are tender but not mushy, 30 to 40 minutes (the timing can vary).
**2.** Drain the lentils; discard the liquid and aromatics (onion, thyme sprigs, bay leaf). Season the lentils with salt and pepper and serve hot.

**How do I serve these?** With roast meats. And they're wonderful as a light meal by themselves, with crusty bread and a green salad. A glass of red wine would be okay, too.

**Lentils,** unlike most other beans, require no soaking and in fact cook quickly. Watch carefully to avoid overcooking, which results in a mushy texture.

## VARIATION: LENTILS VINAIGRETTE

This is ubiquitous in Lyons restaurants in France, where you'll be served a hot slice of juicy sausage with lentils as you look over the menu. Here are instructions for lentils vinaigrette, with and without sausage.

MAKES 6 APPETIZER SERVINGS, OR MORE

1 recipe lentils, cooked according to Basic Method (opposite)

**Vinaigrette**

¼ cup red wine vinegar

1 teaspoon Dijon mustard

Salt and freshly ground black pepper, to taste

½ cup plus 2 tablespoons olive oil, or a combination of olive and vegetable oils

⅓ cup chopped fresh parsley, or more to taste

¼ cup finely chopped shallots, or more to taste

**1.** Prepare the lentils as directed in the Basic Method.

**2. To make the vinaigrette:** In a medium bowl, whisk together the vinegar, mustard, and salt and pepper. Gradually whisk in the olive oil. Taste and correct the seasonings and vinegar/oil balance, if needed. Whisk in the parsley and shallots. Add the drained lentils while they are still warm; stir gently. Set aside and let cool to room temperature.

## VARIATION: LENTILS VINAIGRETTE WITH SAUSAGE

1 fresh sausage (about 2 pounds), such as fresh (unsmoked) kielbasa, skin **pierced with the point of a paring knife in several places**

1 recipe Lentils Vinaigrette (above)

**1.** Simmer the sausage in water to cover in a saucepan until tender and cooked through, about 45 minutes (the timing can vary).

**2.** Remove the sausage with tongs to a cutting surface. Slice the sausage and serve hot on a bed of Lentils Vinaigrette.

**Piercing the sausage skin** prevents the sausage from bursting during cooking.

I'd **serve** this with a green salad and toasted pita bread—and that would be it for a light supper.

A nonmeat or vegetable-derived source of pro-____ __ _____ __ _____ __ ____ ___ _____ ____ __ amounts of the nine essential amino acids needed for proper growth. But when two incomplete proteins are combined and not nec-essarily in the same meal, the body regards them as one complete protein. Grains and beans together form a **complementary protein.**

Letting the **pilaf stand** helps dry it out a little, resulting in more sepa-rate grains.

# LENTIL AND RICE PILAF

Combining grains and beans works very nicely with pilafs.

MAKES 4 SERVINGS

- 1 tablespoon olive oil
- 1 small-medium onion, chopped
- 1 garlic clove, thinly sliced
- ¾ cup (about 5 ounces) raw lentils
- 2 cans (about 14 ounces each) no-sodium or reduced-sodium chicken broth
- ¾ cup long-grain rice (basmati is good here)
  Salt and freshly ground black pepper, to taste
- 2 tablespoons chopped fresh parsley (optional)

**1.** Heat the oil in a heavy saucepan over medium-high heat. Add the onion and cook, stirring, until slightly wilted, 3 or 4 minutes. Add the garlic; stir for a few moments, or until aromatic.

**2.** Stir in the lentils and broth and bring to a boil. Lower the heat to maintain a steady simmer. Cover the pan and cook without stirring for 25 minutes. (Check occasionally to be sure the liquid is simmering, not boiling—lift the lid very quickly to avoid losing heat.) Stir in the rice, cover, and simmer until the **rice and lentils** are tender and the liquid has been absorbed, about 20 minutes longer. Remove from the heat.

**3.** Let the pilaf **stand,** covered, for 5 minutes. Season with salt, if needed, and pep-per, plus the parsley. Fluff with a fork and serve hot.

# BULGUR PILAF

MAKES 4 SERVINGS

|   |   |
|---|---|
| 1 | cup bulgur |
| 2½ | cups boiling water |
| 2 | teaspoons olive oil |
| 1 | small-medium onion, chopped |
| 1 | garlic clove, thinly sliced |
| ⅔ | cup chicken broth |
|   | Salt and freshly ground pepper, to taste |
| 2 | tablespoons chopped fresh parsley (optional) |

**1.** Combine the bulgur and boiling water in a heatproof bowl. Set aside and let **soak** for 30 minutes (if you are using coarser bulgur, soak for 45 minutes). Drain in a fine strainer, gently pressing the bulgur with a spoon without crushing to remove all excess water.

**2.** Heat the oil in a heavy saucepan over medium-high heat. Add the onion and sauté, stirring, until the onion wilts slightly, 3 or 4 minutes. Add the garlic; stir for a few moments, or until aromatic. Add the broth and drained bulgur, stirring to combine. Bring to a boil, stirring occasionally. Cover, lower the heat, and **simmer for 5 minutes.**

**3.** Season with salt (if needed) and pepper, plus the parsley. Fluff the bulgur with a fork and serve hot.

## VARIATION: BULGUR PILAF WITH CURRANTS

Add ¼ cup dried currants with the broth in step 2.

---

I'd **serve** this in all of the same places as rice.

**Bulgur** is cracked wheat that has been partially steamed. (To confuse matters, there is another type of cracked wheat that is not steamed. What you want for this should be labeled bulgur.) Organic bulgur, sold in health food stores, has infinitely more flavor than the supermarket variety—it explodes with nutty whole wheat flavor.

Note that once you **soak** bulgur, which has been presteamed, it needs to be cooked for only a few minutes. This recipe is a good example of a grain cooked in the simplest possible way, bringing out its earthiness just right.

If you are using **organic bulgur,** which is available in health food stores, it is often coarser than supermarket brands. Increase the boiling water to 3 cups and soak it for 45 minutes instead of 30 in step 1.

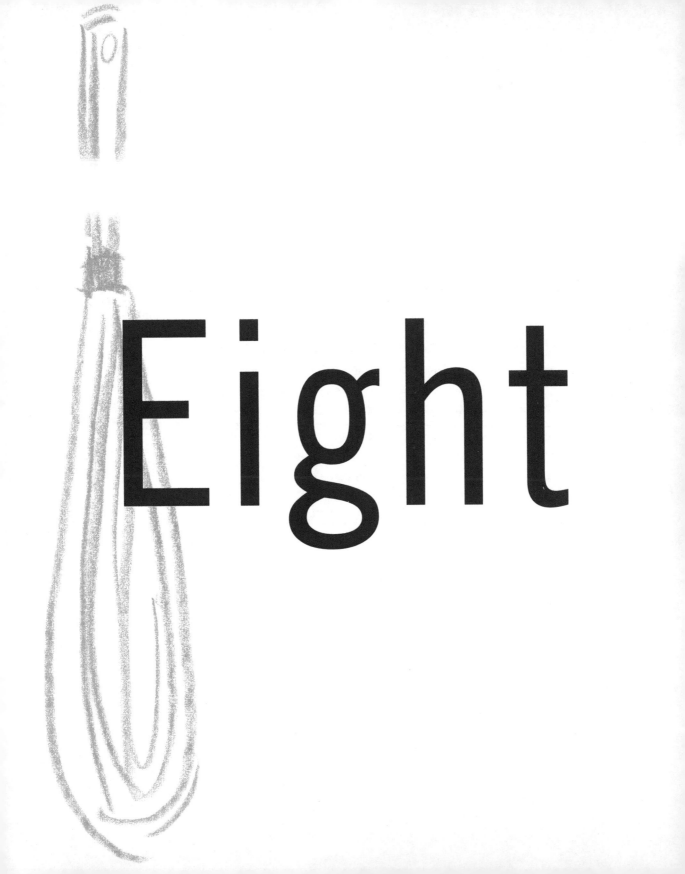

# Eight

# SALADS

| | |
|---|---|
| **Techniques:** | Basic Chicken Salad<br>poaching/cooking spices |
| Techniques: | Seafood Salad with Dill Dressing<br>cooking hellfish poaching fish |
| **Technique:** | Cold Sesame Noodle Salad<br>toasting sesame seeds |

Tips on Serving Cheese

**For me a salad can be a lot of things.** The simplest depends on the most perfect ingredients. A plump, August-ripe tomato, sliced, lightly salted, and drizzled with a gutsy olive oil, is the best—a sublime summer lunch, with a baguette and a cool glass of chardonnay. For any cook, including a beginner, my advice is always to pay attention to the quality of the ingredients, especially when there is little else to hide behind. If the produce is only mediocre, then pass it by.

In this chapter I've included recipes for a few of my favorite salads—some I grew up with and have made over and over again throughout the years and some I've collected from travels. One thing, however, is the same for all of them—each time I prepare one it's never the same. I'm always altering and improvising, depending on my mood and what looks good in the market. You should do the same.

Supermarkets now offer a startling array of fresh salad greens, many grown by local farmers, some of them organic (a far cry from the iceberg only, just a few years ago). Many markets even stock baby greens, all trimmed and washed and ready to go. I always marvel at the huge produce areas in many of the chain supermarkets in Los Angeles—shelf after shelf of baby vegetables of all kinds, inspiring new salad combinations that had never occurred to me before.

Panzanella, potato salad, or even tossed greens, with good-quality bread, can easily be a "small plate." There's no reason to just have salad sandwiched between other courses as part of a supper.

# TOSSED GREEN SALAD WITH BALSAMIC VINAIGRETTE

Preparing a well-made green salad is one of those basics that every home cook must master. It couldn't be simpler, but you have to do it right—and that means paying attention to details. Drying the lettuce makes all of the difference in a crisp salad.

MAKES 4 SERVINGS

- 1 head of Boston or other soft lettuce
- 1 head of red-leaf lettuce or radicchio
  Additional greens: arugula or watercress, stems removed (optional)
- 1½ tablespoons chopped fresh parsley and/or other fresh herbs, such as tarragon or chives (optional)

**Dressing**
- 1½ tablespoons balsamic vinegar
  Salt and freshly ground black pepper, to taste
- 2 tablespoons olive oil

**1.** To prepare greens: Trim off the cores and thick stems from the lettuces and greens. Separate the heads into leaves, discarding any bruised leaves. Wash the greens well (page 194), especially the arugula since it may be sandy. Drain well and dry thoroughly in a salad spinner (a good investment). Place the leaves between sheets of paper towels, roll up, place in plastic food storage bags, and refrigerate.
**2.** At serving time, tear the lettuces into bite-size pieces and place in a salad bowl with the herbs, if using.
**3.** For the dressing, **drizzle the greens** with the vinegar, sprinkle with salt and pepper, and finally, drizzle with olive oil. Toss gently with wooden spoons or forks just until the leaves are well coated with the dressing. Taste and correct the vinegar-oil balance and add more salt and pepper, if needed. Serve immediately on salad plates or in bowls.

There's a reason for drizzling the greens with the vinegar—oil coats the leaves and allows nothing else to stick.

Most liquids added to oil will form droplets without combining unless the oil is slowly stirred or whisked into the other liquid so the droplets are broken and the liquids combine to form a smooth, creamy emulsion—a salad dressing. How about that?

You can also make a dressing in a jar with a screw-top. Place all of the ingredients in the jar, cover securely, shake vigorously, and there you have it. The dressing will keep, refrigerated, for about 3 days. But don't let the garlic sit in the dressing for more than about 15 minutes or the dressing may become too strongly flavored with a raw garlic taste.

## BASIC MUSTARD VINAIGRETTE

Actually, the most basic vinaigrette is made without mustard, but this is a good, all-purpose dressing. For a milder dressing, leave out the garlic.

MAKES ENOUGH FOR 4 SERVINGS

1 tablespoon red wine vinegar, or to taste

1 teaspoon Dijon mustard

1 garlic clove, smashed (optional)

Salt and freshly ground black pepper, to taste

2½ to 3 tablespoons good olive oil

In a glass measuring cup or small bowl, whisk or stir together with a fork the vinegar, mustard, garlic, and salt and pepper. Slowly whisk in the olive oil until smooth and **emulsified** or creamy. Taste and correct the vinegar-oil balance. Remove the garlic clove before serving.

## BASICS FOR SALADS
### WHAT GREENS TO CHOOSE

Don't combine all the same "flavored" greens. Develop a knack for mixing; toss a bitter lettuce, such as endive, chicory, or arugula, with a soft lettuce, such as Boston, and a crisp one, such as romaine, and maybe even a red-leaf variety for color.

### BASIC METHOD FOR CLEANING SALAD GREENS

To clean most greens, you can just rinse them in a colander under cold running water to remove any dirt. Be sure to separate the leaves for thorough cleaning—nothing is more annoying than a gritty salad. For greens that tend to be very sandy—which is anything you buy at a farmers' market or is otherwise freshly picked, and even unbagged spinach and arugula in the supermarket—first plunge them into a sink or dishpan of warm water; this relaxes the leaves, loosening the dirt for easier rinsing. Then lift the leaves to a colander and rinse under cold water. If the leaves are still limp, crisp them in several changes of cold water.

A salad spinner is one of the few kitchen gadgets that I find indispensable. It makes quick and easy work of what can be a tedious chore. If there's no spinner, shake the greens vigorously in a colander over the sink and then place the leaves in a single layer on several layers of paper towels. Blot each leaf dry with paper towels. See how easy the spinner makes it? So splurge if you don't have one. Another alternative is to wrap the washed greens in several clean towels or a clean pillowcase (or there are specially designed cloth salad drying bags), step into the backyard (if you have one), and spin the greens overhead as if you were a helicopter. It's best to do this technique in sunny weather. And why is all this drying important? If wet, the salad dressing won't cling to the leaves and you'll have a big puddle at the bottom of the bowl.

## BASIC METHOD FOR STORING SALAD GREENS

To store as well as crisp, roll up the washed and dried greens in clean kitchen towels or paper towels, place in plastic food storage bags, and refrigerate in the crisper section where they will keep for a day or two.

## BASIC SALAD DRESSING

For a simple oil and vinegar dressing, first sprinkle the greens with vinegar, then oil. If drizzled first, the oil would coat the leaves and the vinegar would run off into the bottom of the bowl.

**The key to dressing a salad is that you want just enough dressing to coat the leaves, without any drippy excess.**

If you're preparing the slaw more than 1 hour before serving, store the vegetables and dressing separately and don't combine the two until 1 hour before—this avoids souping out."

# MULTICOLOR SLAW

There's lots of color in this version. Choose either dressing.

MAKES 4 SERVINGS

½   head of green cabbage, (halved through the core)

½   head of red cabbage (halved through the core)

1   small red bell pepper, cored, seeded (Bell Pepper Basics, page 16), and
    cut into long, thin slivers

1   small yellow pepper, cored, seeded, and cut into long, thin slivers

3   carrots, trimmed, peeled, and coarsely grated (about 2 cups)

3   scallion greens, thinly sliced on a sharp diagonal

¼   cup chopped fresh parsley
    Salt and freshly ground black pepper, to taste
    Creamy Mustard-Dill Dressing or Light Sweet-and-Sour Dressing (recipes
    opposite page)

**1.** To shred the cabbage, cut the green cabbage half in half again through the core. Remove the outer leaves. Cut away the core with a large chef's knife. Cutting cross-wise, cut the cabbage in long, thin shreds. Transfer the shredded cabbage to a large mixing bowl. Repeat with the red cabbage. Add the red and yellow bell peppers, the carrots, scallions, parsley, and salt and pepper. Toss gently with your hands or 2 large spoons until all of the ingredients are evenly distributed.

**2.** Pour whichever dressing you choose over the vegetable mixture and toss with your hands or 2 large spoons to combine. Taste and correct the seasonings, adding more salt and pepper, parsley, or scallion greens, if needed. Cover and chill for at least 1 hour.

## CREAMY MUSTARD-DILL DRESSING

This dressing is for those who like a creamy traditional coleslaw dressing with a nice mustardy edge.

MAKES ABOUT 1 1/2 CUPS

- 2/3 cup reduced-calorie or light mayonnaise
- 1/2 cup plain low-fat yogurt
- 2 tablespoons fresh lemon juice
- 3 tablespoons cider vinegar or rice vinegar, or to taste
- 1 to 2 tablespoons sugar
- 2 tablespoons Dijon mustard, or to taste
- 2 tablespoons coarse-grained mustard (or substitute 1 tablespoon more Dijon)
- 1/3 cup chopped fresh dill
  Salt and freshly ground black pepper, to taste
  Pinch of cayenne (optional)

In a medium bowl, whisk all of the ingredients together until very well blended.

## LIGHT SWEET-AND-SOUR DRESSING

MAKES ABOUT 1 1/2 CUPS

- 1/2 cup rice vinegar
- 1/2 cup cider vinegar
- 3 tablespoons cold water
- 3 tablespoons olive oil
- 1/4 cup sugar
  Salt and freshly ground black pepper, to taste
  Pinch of cayenne

In a medium bowl, whisk all of the ingredients together until the sugar dissolves and the oil is well blended.

Both of these dressings can be made a day or two ahead and refrigerated. But for the creamy mustard, you may want to wait until serving time to stir in the dill to avoid the strong dill flavor that will develop as it sits in the refrigerator.

If you want to nutrition-
ally streamline this
salad even further,
you're halfway there.
Switch the mayonnaise
to fat-free and use just
the hard-cooked egg
whites.

For hard-cooked eggs
(with no greenish line
around the yolks), I like
Shirley Corriher's
method: bring-to-a-boil-
then-sit. Place the eggs
(any number) in a
saucepan in which they
fit comfortably. Cover
completely with luke-
warm water and bring
to a boil over medium
to medium-high heat.
The moment the mix-
ture starts to boil
(watch carefully),
remove the pan from
the heat. Now let the
eggs sit in the hot water
for 10 or 11 minutes.
Drain, then cover with
cold water and allow to
cool before peeling.

Marinating the potatoes
while they are still
warm allows the flavors
to permeate and infuse
them.

If you make this ahead,
remove from the refrig-
erator about 15 minutes
before serving so the
chill doesn't dull the
flavor.

# LITTLE RED POTATO SALAD

This is great for the classic American picnic or with grilled foods.

MAKES 4 SERVINGS

1¼ to 2 pounds small red potatoes, peeled

Salt to taste

5 large eggs

3 tablespoons red wine vinegar

1 tablespoon olive oil

Freshly ground black pepper, to taste

3 small dill pickles, chopped

¼ cup chopped red onion

⅓ cup chopped fresh parsley, or a mixture of parsley and fresh dill

½ cup plain low-fat yogurt

⅓ cup reduced-calorie mayonnaise

2 teaspoons Dijon mustard

**1.** Place the potatoes in a large saucepan with enough cold water to cover by about 2 inches. Bring to a boil, then add a teaspoon or two of salt. Boil gently, uncovered, for 12 minutes. With a large slotted spoon, gently lower the eggs into the water. Cover the pan and simmer steadily until the potatoes are tender when poked with a knife, about 12 minutes longer. The eggs will be **hard-cooked** at this point. Remove the eggs with a slotted spoon to a colander and rinse with cold water to cool. At the same time, drain the potatoes in a second colander and rinse with cold water until cool enough to handle but still quite warm. Quarter the potatoes (or cut in eighths if quarters are too large for bite-size). Place the warm potatoes in a large mixing bowl. Drizzle **while still warm** with the vinegar and oil and add a few grinds of black pepper. Toss very gently with a large rubber spatula and a wooden spoon until the potatoes are well coated. Let sit until cooled to room temperature.

**2.** Carefully peel the eggs under cold running water. Coarse chop and add to the potatoes along with the pickles, onion, and parsley. Toss gently without breaking up the eggs too much.

**3.** In a bowl, combine the yogurt, mayonnaise, and mustard; stir together with a fork until smooth. Add the dressing to the potatoes; fold the ingredients together very gently, using a large rubber spatula and a wooden spoon, until all of the ingredients are evenly coated. Taste and correct all of the seasonings, adding more salt, pepper, vinegar, onion, and mustard as needed; cover with plastic wrap. Serve at cool room temperature or refrigerate until ready to serve.

## VARIATION: POTATO SALAD WITH OLIVES

My grandmother used to slice a few pimiento-stuffed olives and add them to the potato salad, one of her unforgettable specialties. Nice touch.

# HUNGARIAN-STYLE MARINATED CUCUMBERS

I brought this recipe back from Budapest several years ago, and it's become a favorite at my house.

MAKES 4 SERVINGS

2 large cucumbers, preferably seedless, peeled and thinly sliced

1½ teaspoons coarse (kosher) salt or sea salt

⅓ cup rice vinegar, or more to taste

1 tablespoon cold water

1½ teaspoons superfine sugar

1 garlic clove, smashed

2 tablespoons chopped fresh dill (optional)

Freshly ground black pepper, to taste

**1.** Layer the cucumbers and **salt** in a colander set over a bowl. Let the mixture stand for about 1 hour.

**2.** Squeeze the cucumbers gently in the colander with your hands or the back of a spoon to extract the liquid. Place the cucumbers in a glass serving bowl. Add the vinegar, cold water, sugar, garlic, dill, and pepper, stirring to combine. Cover and refrigerate until ready to serve, draining off some of the juices as you serve the cucumbers.

Try this with Soy-and-Ginger-Glazed Salmon (page 94) or other strongly flavored dishes that would welcome a crisp, cooling accent.

Salting the cucumber slices removes excess liquid, making them crisp and refreshing.

# THE BEST RIPE TOMATO SALAD

When ripe tomatoes are at their peak, the less that's done to them, the better. When they're in season, I've been known to eat this salad just about every day.

Tomatoes, as ripe as possible (any number)

Coarse (kosher) salt or sea salt, to taste

Freshly ground black pepper, to taste

Fresh basil leaves (optional)

Extra-virgin olive oil, to taste

**1.** Core the tomatoes with a small knife, then thickly slice them with a serrated bread knife.

**2.** Sprinkle the tomato slices fairly generously with salt and arrange them in a shallow dish, overlapping them slightly. Sprinkle the tomatoes with a few grinds of black pepper and then top with fresh basil leaves, if you like. Drizzle with a little extra-virgin olive oil.

**3.** Let the tomatoes stand at room temperature for at least 30 minutes. Dig in.

**BONUS RECIPE**

## GRILLED TOMATO, MOZZARELLA, AND BASIL SANDWICH

The now-ubiquitous *insalata caprese*—tomatoes, mozzarella, and basil, from Capri—can be made as an open-face grilled sandwich. When summer tomatoes are at their peak, this is one of the best things imaginable—sometimes I call it dinner.

MAKES 1 SANDWICH

2 tomatoes, cored, sliced, and prepared as for The Best Ripe Tomato Salad (recipe above)

1 length (6 inches) Italian or French bread, whole wheat or white, split horizontally in half

3 or 4 ounces **mozzarella** cheese, preferably fresh

A few small fresh basil leaves

Freshly ground black pepper, to taste

Olive oil, to taste

Although the recipe is for just one sandwich, set up an assembly line and you can make any amount you want.

Of course, I'm spoiled because I can easily get freshly made mozzarella in New York. Look for it in cheese shops and Italian markets.

1. Prepare the tomatoes as for the salad.

2. In a broiler or toaster oven, toast the cut surfaces of the bread until only very lightly toasted. Place the bread on a baking sheet (if using the broiler) or on a sheet of foil (if using a toaster oven). Overlap slices of tomato and mozzarella on each piece of bread; tuck 2 or 3 basil leaves into the slices on each sandwich.

3. Broil or toast until the cheese melts and begins to bubble slightly, no longer. Sprinkle with a few grinds of pepper and drizzle with a little olive oil. Serve hot, with a knife and fork.

Slowly savoring this
salad with a glass of
wine is a wonderful way
to while away a sum-
mer afternoon.

Look for a firm bread
that can hold up to the
chewing that all dish
use a good sourdough,
which, while not tradi-
tional, is tasty prepared
this way.

Peel the cucumber
lengthwise with a veg-
etable peeler. Trim off
the ends and then cut
the cucumber in half
lengthwise. Scrape out
the seeds with the tip of
a teaspoon or a small
melon baller.

For both flavor and tex-
ture in a salad, I like to
use the kalamata, a
ripe, purple-black,
brine-cured Greek olive.
These are now available
in the deli departments
of better grocery stores.

# PANZANELLA (TUSCAN SUMMER BREAD AND VEGETABLE SALAD)

This is an ingenious and delicious way to use up yesterday's bread. Many cuisines transform day-old bread into similar salads, as well as bread soups and more.

With real Tuscan bread, which is firm and dense, the bread is soaked in cold water, then squeezed dry. Because most bread we get here is less dense, I've soaked the bread more quickly and then marinated it in a vinegar and olive oil dressing, which soaks in nicely.

MAKES 2 SERVINGS OR MORE

1 long loaf (12 inches) good Italian bread, day-old

1 cucumber, peeled, halved lengthwise, seeded, and sliced

1 small red bell pepper, cored, seeded (Bell Pepper Basics, page 16), and cut into thin slivers

½ red onion, halved and cut into thin slivers

8 to 12 kalamata or oil-cured black olives

2 or 3 tablespoons capers, drained and rinsed

¼ cup extra-virgin olive oil, plus more for serving

¼ cup red wine vinegar, or 2 tablespoons *each* red wine vinegar and balsamic vinegar, plus more for serving

1 garlic clove, minced (optional)

2 tablespoons torn fresh basil leaves (do not use dried)

2 to 3 teaspoons chopped fresh thyme leaves (do not use dried)

1 tablespoon snipped fresh chives or chopped fresh parsley
   Salt and freshly ground black pepper, to taste

2 large ripe tomatoes, cored, seeded, and diced (Tomato Basics, page 22)

**1.** With a long serrated bread knife, cut the loaf of bread into cubes. Place the bread in a large bowl and drizzle with very cold water, tossing gently and using just enough to lightly coat all the cubes, without drowning the bread. Let the bread stand until it is moistened but not mushy. This can take as little as 3 minutes or as long as 10 for denser bread. Working with a handful at a time, gently squeeze out all possible excess water from the bread; place it in a bowl or on a large plate. The bread should still remain in pieces, not be mashed to a mush. Set the bread aside while you prepare the vegetables.

**2.** Place the cucumber, bell pepper, onion, olives, and capers in a large bowl and toss with a wooden spoon to mix. In a 2-cup glass measure, measure out the oil and vinegar and add the garlic, herbs, and salt and pepper. Whisk or stir vigorously with a fork to blend. Stir in the diced tomatoes.

**3.** Place about half of the bread in a glass serving bowl or salad bowl. Top with half of the vegetables. Give the tomato dressing another stir and pour half of it over everything. Repeat, layering the remaining bread, vegetables, and dressing. Cover with plastic wrap and refrigerate for 1 to 2 hours.

**4.** Remove the salad from the refrigerator a few minutes before serving. Toss the ingredients gently with a large rubber spatula. Taste and correct all seasonings, adding more salt, pepper, basil, thyme, and chives, if needed. Serve, passing cruets of olive oil and vinegar plus a pepper mill at the table.

Poaching helps tenderize food, keeps it moist, and eliminates the need for any fat during the cooking. The food cooks immersed in a liquid—water, broth, wine, whatever—in a covered pot, usually with a tight top cover. Adjust the heat as necessary to maintain a gentle simmer—boiling will toughen the food.

Save the flavorful poaching liquid for soups or deglazing a skillet for a sauce (Deglazing Basics, page 24). To concentrate the flavor, you can reduce the liquid in a saucepan over high heat.

Briefly cooking the curry powder, as with most spices, eliminates any raw or "musty" taste if the spice is being added to a dish that is uncooked.

# BASIC CHICKEN SALAD

The trick for any delicious chicken salad is to make sure that the chicken remains moist. To ensure that result, I poach the chicken—the perfect cooking method for foods that may have a tendency to dry out, such as chicken white meat or fish.

MAKES 4 SERVINGS

2   cans (about 14 ounces each) reduced-sodium chicken broth or 4 cups water plus 1 tablespoon salt

4   boneless, skinless chicken breast halves (about 5 ounces each)

**Dressing**

2   teaspoons vegetable oil (if using curry powder)

2   teaspoons curry powder (optional)

½   cup mayonnaise or reduced-fat mayonnaise

1   medium red onion, diced ¼ inch (about ½ cup)

4   celery ribs, strings removed (Celery Stringing, page 18) and finely diced (about 2 cups)

2   teaspoons celery seed or dill seed

1   small head Bibb lettuce, separated into leaves, washed, and dried

6   to 8 cherry tomatoes, halved

4   hard-cooked eggs, cut into quarters (page 198)

1.  Heat the broth or water and salt in a 3-quart saucepan to simmering. Slip the chicken breasts into the simmering liquid. Adjust the heat so the liquid stays at a simmer. **Poach** the chicken breasts until there is no trace of pink in the thickest part, about 8 minutes. Remove the chicken with a slotted spoon from the liquid to a plate, cover with wax paper, and cool to room temperature.

2.  **Meanwhile, make the dressing:** If you are using the curry powder, heat the oil in a very small skillet or saucepan over medium heat. Stir in the **curry powder** and **cook for 10 seconds.** Let cool completely.

3.  Stir together the mayonnaise, onion, celery, and celery seed in a medium bowl until blended. Stir in the curry mixture if using.

**4.** Cut the chicken into 1-inch cubes; you should have about 3½ cups. Fold the chicken into the dressing. Let stand at room temperature for 30 minutes or refrigerate for up to 4 hours before serving. If refrigerated, **let the salad stand** at room temperature for 30 minutes before serving.

**5.** Arrange the lettuce leaves over 4 serving plates. Spoon the chicken salad over the leaves. Arrange the cherry tomato halves and hard-cooked eggs on either side of the salad and serve.

**Letting the salad stand** for a bit before serving allows the chicken to absorb both flavor and moisture from the dressing.

Since **refrigerating a dish will dampen or mute the flavor,** it is important to let it stand at room temperature before serving so the flavors will develop.

An easy way **to extend this salad** is to add cold, diced boiled potatoes or drained, rinsed canned cannellini or garbanzo beans.

I like **serving** this over a few well-washed arugula leaves—the sharp flavor nicely complements the seafood—and with a glass of chilled Alsatian Riesling

When purchasing mussels, be sure the shells are closed, or if open, they close when pressed and stay closed. Discard any that won't stay closed. **Culti-vated mussels are** sweeter and much less gritty than wild mussels. (See Shellfish Basics, page 21.)

**Coarsely chopped fresh dill** looks more like dill than finely chopped, which sometimes can create a gritty texture.

If you like, **reserve the cooking liquid** for soups and stews.

# SEAFOOD SALAD WITH DILL DRESSING

Fresh dill is a classic seasoning partner for seafood, especially salmon. For best flavor, serve this salad as soon after making as possible.

MAKES 2 MAIN COURSE SERVINGS OR 4 FIRST COURSE SERVINGS

3/4  pound medium whole shrimp, in the shell (about 25 to the pound)

1  pound medium **mussels** (about 14), preferably **cultivated**

1/2  cup cold water

1/2  pound skinless salmon fillets, cut into 1-inch cubes or equal amount lump crabmeat or cooked lobster meat

2  celery ribs, strings removed (Celery Stringing, page 18) and cut into 1/3-inch dice

Basic Mustard Vinaigrette (page 194)

1/4  cup **coarsely chopped fresh dill**

Salt, to taste

Freshly ground pepper, to taste

**1.** Peel and devein shrimp (see Shrimp Basics, page 22). Cut the shrimp crosswise into 2 or 3 pieces.

**2.** Pull the wiry beard, if any, from the flat side of the mussels. Rinse the mussels well under cold water and drain. Combine the mussels and 1/2 cup cold water in a 2-quart saucepan. Set over high heat and cover the saucepan. Steam (Steaming Basics, page 25) the mussels until they have opened, about 3 minutes, shaking the pan vigorously once or twice to help the mussels cook evenly. Remove the mussels with a slotted spoon, draining them thoroughly over the saucepan, to a separate bowl. Let them stand until cool enough to handle. Discard any that have not opened.

**3.** Strain the cooking liquid into a bowl through a paper coffee filter or fine-mesh sieve lined with a double thickness of dampened cheesecloth. Return the liquid to the saucepan.

**4.** Pour any liquid accumulated in the bottom of the mussel bowl back into the saucepan. Heat the liquid to a simmer. Add the salmon. Cover the pot and simmer or poach until the salmon is cooked through, about 3 minutes; the flesh of the salmon should be opaque in the center. Remove the salmon pieces with a slotted spoon, letting them drain thoroughly over the saucepan, and transfer them to a separate bowl.

**5.** Reheat the seafood cooking liquid to boiling. Stir in the shrimp. Remove the saucepan from the heat; cover and let stand until the shrimp are cooked through—curled and opaque in the center—about 5 mintues. Drain the shrimp thoroughly and discard the liquid. Add the shrimp to the bowl with the salmon.

**6.** Pick the cooked mussels from their shells; you should have about ⅔ cup. Add them to the bowl with the salmon and shrimp. Add the celery, vinaigrette, and dill; toss well with two large spoons to coat the seafood with the dressing. Check the seasoning, adding salt and pepper to taste.

There are so many ways I like to serve this: for lunch, a light dinner with a green salad, a snack, and even breakfast. If serving leftovers, remember to let the salad stand at room temperature so the flavors will become more pronounced and the oil in the dressing will liquefy.

You can **toast sesame seeds** very quickly in a dry skillet. Heat the skillet over medium heat, toss in the sesame seeds, and stir constantly, watching closely, since they can go from lightly toasted to black in just a brief moment.

# COLD SESAME NOODLE SALAD

A salad like this would be made in Japan with Udon (buckwheat) noodles or in China with thick fresh egg noodles—certainly use these noodles if available, preparing them according to package directions. Spaghettini, sometimes called thin spaghetti on the package, works especially well, but it should be rinsed before adding the cooked spaghettini to the dressing; rinse the noodles under cold running water and then drain well.

MAKES 6 SERVINGS

Salt, to taste

8 ounces spaghettini

¼ cup smooth peanut butter

3 tablespoons soy sauce

2 tablespoons chopped, peeled, fresh ginger

2 tablespoons rice vinegar

1 tablespoon dark Asian sesame oil

¼ teaspoon hot-pepper sauce

¼ cup very hot water

3 scallions, trimmed, green and white parts separated, and each very thinly sliced

3 tablespoons **sesame seeds, toasted** (optional)

1 tablespoon chopped fresh cilantro (optional)

**1.** Bring a large pot of water to a boil for the pasta. Add a little salt. When the water is boiling, add the spaghettini, stirring. When the pasta is tender, drain well in a colander. Rinse very thoroughly under cold running water. Drain the pasta well.

**2.** Meanwhile, combine the peanut butter, soy sauce, ginger, vinegar, sesame oil, and hot-pepper sauce in a food processor. Process until all the ingredients are blended, stopping the machine once or twice to scrape down the sides of the work bowl with a rubber spatula. Add the very hot water and process until the sauce is smooth, again stopping the machine once or twice to scrape down the sides of the work bowl. Scrape the sauce into a medium bowl.

**3.** Add the white part of the scallions and the cooled and drained spaghettini to the sauce. Toss gently with 2 forks to thoroughly coat the pasta. Let stand at room temperature for 30 minutes, tossing once or twice.

**4.** Before serving, taste the salad and adjust the seasoning if needed with a little more soy sauce, hot pepper sauce, and/or sesame oil. Garnish with the scallion greens and with sesame seeds and cilantro if desired.

## TIPS ON SERVING CHEESE

With a green salad I often serve a selection of cheeses, and instead of a dessert, I'll sometimes bring out an array of cheeses for sampling.

A few things to keep in mind: Fresh cheeses such as farmer's or fresh mozzarella (not the rubbery version from the supermarket refrigerated case) may be served slightly chilled, while all others are best at room temperature for full aroma and flavor. Let stand for about 1 hour at room temperature if taking directly from the refrigerator. Allow a separate cheese knife for each variety to prevent the transfer of flavors.

To prepare an intriguing sampling, select 3 to 5 varieties of cheese, keeping in mind different shapes, textures, and flavors and figuring on 2 to 3 ounces per person. For instance: Offer a hard, mild cheese, such as Swiss, with a softer, stronger-flavored cheese, such as a Brie, and a very aromatic, tangy Gorgonzola. Keep the accompaniments simple—plain unflavored crackers for crunch or crusty French or Italian bread. Fruits and nuts are also good choices and, if doable within your dinner plans, a glass of wine. For the wine, here's a few guidelines (meant to be broken once you've discovered your likes and dislikes): fresh and mild cheeses go well with light red and white wines; strong-flavored varieties need a young, robust red; and mellow cheeses match well with mature reds. But don't think that contrasting combinations can't be delicious: Try a sweet dessert wine with a very intense blue cheese.

# QUICK BREADS

|  |  |
|---|---|
|  | Buttermilk Biscuits |
| **Technique:** | preparing dough with food processor or by hand |
|  | Sweet Potato Biscuits |
| **Techniques:** | patting out dough/cutting biscuits |
|  | Bill Neal's Skillet Corn Bread |
| **Technique:** | making bread in a skillet or cake pan |
|  | Cornmeal-Berry Muffins |
| **Techniques:** | sifting flour/mixing batter/using paper liners/ doneness test |
|  | Lemon-Ginger Muffins |
| **Techniques:** | mixing batter/using paper liners/doneness test |
|  | Cranberry-Orange Quick Bread with Nutmeg-Rum Glaze |
| **Techniques:** | greasing and flouring pans/sifting flour/mixing batter/doneness test/glazing |

**Good bread is one of those things I can't do without; while reading a book, I've been known to tear off pieces from a baguette until there is nothing left.** Fortunately, in New York where I live, I have a huge variety of quality breads available close by. But this is now true for most home cooks regardless of where they live with the advent of supermarket bakeries, farmer markets (even during the winter months) and specialty bakeries in small towns (I remember one in a small coastal Maine fishing village that has some of the best sourdough bread I've ever tasted). So in our busy lives we can still enjoy the pleasures of good-quality yeast-risen loaves, although a Saturday morning is the perfect time for this satisfying hands-on labor at home. And the aroma of baking bread is practically its own reward.

But there is always time for muffins, biscuits, and quick breads, even for the beginning cook. The techniques are simple. For biscuits, you simply cut butter into a flour mixture and add a little liquid; muffins and quick breads are as easy as stirring a liquid into dry ingredients—not exactly brain surgery. These baked home-made touches are always a welcomed treat for a dinner with friends or on their own as a stress-reduction snack, with a smear of butter and a glass of hot tea.

My choices in this chapter are just a handful, meant to start you on your way. Master these with their short array of basic techniques, and surprisingly you'll encounter them again when you make certain desserts, such as piecrusts, cookies, cakes—but that's another book.

# BUTTERMILK BISCUITS

These are one of the mainstays of fine Southern home cooking.

MAKES 1 DOZEN

1½  cups all-purpose flour
1½  tablespoons sugar
 1  teaspoon baking powder
 ½  teaspoon baking soda
 ½  teaspoon salt
 4  tablespoons (½ stick) cold unsalted butter, cut into pieces
 ⅔  cup buttermilk, or as needed (or substitute ⅓ cup plain yogurt mixed with ⅓ cup skim milk or cold water)

**1.** In a **food processor,** combine the flour, sugar, baking powder, baking soda, and salt, pulsing once or twice with an on-and-off motion. Add the butter and process, pulsing, until the mixture is crumbly. Drizzle most but not all of the buttermilk over the dry mixture; pulse to combine, **without overworking** the dough. The dough should hold together and be moist but not sticky. If necessary, add more buttermilk, pulsing to combine. Scrape the dough with a rubber spatula onto a floured work surface. With your hands, gather the dough together, pulling it together to form a cohesive disk of dough.

**2.** Preheat the oven to 425°F. On a lightly floured surface, pat the dough out to an even thickness of ¾ inch. Use a floured 2¼- to 2½-inch biscuit cutter to cut out rounds of the dough (reflour the cutter as needed to avoid sticking); transfer the rounds to a well-buttered (or nonstick) baking sheet. Gently gather the scraps of dough together, pat out, and cut out more biscuits.

**3.** Bake for 14 to 16 minutes, or until golden brown. Serve hot, with butter.

## VARIATION: MINIATURE CHEESE BISCUITS

Make the biscuit dough as directed above, but cut the biscuits in smaller rounds, about 1 inch in diameter. Place on the baking sheet as directed. Brush the surfaces very lightly with beaten egg and then sprinkle with a thin layer of freshly grated Parmesan cheese mixed with a tiny pinch of cayenne, if you like. Bake at 400°F until golden brown on top and baked through, usually about 10 minutes.

These are actually a snap as long as you remember one thing—**don't overhandle biscuits at any stage.** Gentle kneading stimulates the gluten in the flour, giving the biscuits a little extra boost in the oven. Anything more results in a tougher biscuit.

If a food processor is not part of your kitchen *batterie de cuisine,* here's how to make the dough by hand: Combine the dry ingredients in a medium bowl, stirring together with a fork or wire whisk to thoroughly blend. Drop the pieces of butter into the mixture, and with a pastry blender, 2 knives held scissors fashion, or your fingertips, quickly work it in until the mixture resembles coarse bread crumbs. Drizzle in the buttermilk, tossing the mixture with a fork, until the dough comes together. (It can be **made several hours in advance.** If so, wrap in floured plastic wrap or wax paper and refrigerate until needed.)

Cheese biscuits are **wonderful with soups,** such as homemade mushroom or tomato soup.

These make a **nice addition** to roast pork or chicken and are also delicious for breakfast or a brunch—top with a pat of butter, spread with apricot jam, or drizzle with honey.

Save any mashed sweets for stirring into soups or just reheating for a snack break.

Wondering why you have to **stir in the pepper?** If you are using freshly ground black pepper, it's too coarse to pass through the holes in the sifter.

**Gradually add the milk**—you can always add more, but once you've added too much, you'll have to add more flour, and maybe more liquid, and so on, back and forth.

**To cut out the biscuits,** press the cutter straight down firmly and pull it straight up; don't use a twisting motion, which may mash the sides, making for a less high biscuit when it comes time for rising.

# SWEET POTATO BISCUITS

The sweet potatoes keep these golden biscuits moist and flavorful.

MAKES 1 DOZEN

4 sweet potatoes (10 to 14 ounces total), baked (A Perfect Baked Potato, page 179)

2 cups all-purpose flour

1 tablespoon baking powder

2 teaspoons packed light brown sugar

¼ teaspoon freshly grated nutmeg

Large pinch *each* of salt and freshly ground black pepper

6 tablespoons (¾ stick) cold unsalted butter, cut into pieces

Milk, as needed

1 large egg, well beaten

**1.** Preheat the oven to 425°F. When the baked sweet potatoes are cool enough to handle, peel and mash in a medium bowl with a potato masher or ricer. Measure 1 cup of the mashed sweet potatoes and set aside; save the remainder for other uses.

**2.** Sift the flour, baking powder, brown sugar, nutmeg, and salt into a medium bowl. **Stir in the pepper.** Scatter the pieces of butter over the flour mixture. With a pastry blender, 2 knives held scissors fashion, or with the tips of your fingers, quickly work in the butter until the mixture resembles coarse bread crumbs. Make a well in the center of the mixture and scrape the cup of mashed sweet potatoes into the well. Gently stir the mixture together with a fork just until the dry ingredients are evenly moistened. **Drizzle in enough milk,** 1 tablespoon at a time, tossing with a fork, to make a sticky dough but one that can be worked without impossibly sticking to everything.

**3.** Scrape the dough onto a floured surface and pat out to a thickness of ¾ inch. Use a floured 2¼- to 2½-inch biscuit cutter to **cut out** rounds of the dough; transfer to a well-buttered (or nonstick) baking sheet. Gently gather the scraps of dough together and cut out more rounds. Lightly brush the tops of the biscuits with the beaten egg.

**4.** Bake for 14 to 16 minutes, or until the biscuits are golden brown. Serve hot, with sweet butter.

# BILL NEAL'S SKILLET CORN BREAD

Bill Neal was a pioneer in the rediscovery of traditional Southern cooking. He owned a restaurant and produced three excellent cookbooks. He also loved gardening and raised three children.

This is Bill's "Company Corn Bread," from his outstanding book, *Biscuits, Spoonbread, and Sweet Potato Pie* (Knopf, 1990). This corn bread, with a higher proportion of cornmeal to flour than in most, was a staple when I had a summer house. Bill died in 1991, but by baking his recipes, I like to think I'm remembering him.

MAKES 4 TO 6 SERVINGS

- 3 **tablespoons unsalted butter**
- 1½ **cups white or yellow cornmeal**
- ½ **cup all-purpose flour**
- 2 **teaspoons baking powder**
- 1 **teaspoon baking soda**
- 1 **teaspoon salt**
- 1 **to 2 tablespoons sugar, to taste**
- 1½ **cups buttermilk (or a mixture of ¾ cup plain yogurt and ¾ cup cold water)**
- 2 **large eggs**

**1.** Preheat the oven to 425°F. Heat a 9-inch **cast-iron skillet** over low heat. If you don't have a cast-iron skillet, place a heavy 9-inch round cake pan with the butter in the oven as it preheats.

**2.** Sift all of the dry ingredients together into a large bowl. Measure the buttermilk in a 2-cup glass measure. Add the eggs and blend well with a wire whisk or fork, stirring vigorously. Melt the butter in the skillet; add it to the milk-egg mixture, beating vigorously (or if you've used the cake pan in step 1, carefully—the pan is hot—pour it from the cake pan into the egg-milk mixture). Quickly mix this wet mixture into the dry ingredients with a few decisive strokes of a wooden spoon or large rubber spatula. Pour the batter into the hot skillet or cake pan.

**3.** Carefully pop the pan into the preheated oven and bake for 25 to 30 minutes, or until the top is light golden brown. Serve warm, directly from the skillet or pan, with butter.

Keep your pot holders handy for this one—lots of handling of hot stuff.

Using a cast-iron skillet for baking the cornbread makes for even heat all around, coloring the bread an appetizing golden brown. Plus, the cornbread can be served directly from the skillet.

If berries aren't easy to find, try these with **diced ripe pears or apples.**

**What's a standard-size muffin pan?** The muffin cup itself is usually about 2½ inches in diameter at the top. Sizes can range from 1½-inch gems to large inch miniature or gem pans. And then there's muffin-top pans—the muffin top without the bottom.

While I'm not a kitchen gadget fanatic, I find a **nonstick muffin tin** an excellent investment (no more muffins without bottoms because they're stubbornly stuck in the pan)—just as I do non-stick baking or cookie sheets. Avoid black metal pans, which can overbrown the muffins.

**Do I really need to sift the flour?** Sifting flour or other dry ingredients together incorporates air, resulting in baked goods with a lighter texture. It also incorporates several dry ingredients together more evenly.

# CORNMEAL-BERRY MUFFINS

These are tender, light muffins with just a slight crunch of cornmeal, which combines nicely with the berries.

MAKES 1 DOZEN

1½ cups sifted all purpose flour (sift before measuring)

½ cup yellow or white cornmeal

¼ cup sugar

1 tablespoon baking powder

1 teaspoon baking soda

¼ teaspoon salt

1 cup (generous) buttermilk (or substitute plain yogurt thinned with a little milk or cold water to equal 1 cup)

3 large eggs

4 tablespoons (½ stick) unsalted butter, melted

1½ cups blueberries or cranberries, picked over, rinsed quickly, and shaken dry (if using cranberries, you may want to toss them with a couple of spoonfuls of extra sugar, since they can be very tart)

**1.** Preheat the oven to 425°F.; position a rack at the center level. Generously butter a **standard-size** 12-cup muffin tin (even if you are using a **nonstick pan,** butter it lightly); set aside. (If you prefer, butter only the upper rims of the muffin cups and then line the cups with paper muffin liners.

**2. Resift** the flour along with the cornmeal, sugar, baking powder, baking soda, and salt into a large bowl. Stir once or twice with a fork to blend even more. Pour the buttermilk into a 4-cup glass measuring cup; add the eggs and melted butter and mix with a fork until smooth. Make a well in the dry ingredients; pour the liquid mixture into the well. With a large rubber spatula, gently but quickly mix the dry and moist ingredients together, folding in the berries just until the dry mixture is thoroughly and evenly moistened (no traces of flour)—the batter will still be lumpy; that's okay. **Do not overmix** or the muffins will be tough. Spoon the batter into the muffin cups, dividing evenly.

**3.** Place the pan in the oven; immediately lower the heat to 400°. Bake until the muffins are set and pale-medium gold and a wooden pick inserted in the center **comes out clean,** with no crumbs attached, 20 to 25 minutes (the timing can vary based on the depth of the muffin cups; do not overbake). Place the muffin pan on a wire rack for a minute or two. Gently turn the muffins out and serve warm, with sweet butter.

When mixing any muffin batter, it's important **not to overmix**—just a few broad strokes with a large rubber spatula should do it. Leave the batter a little lumpy and you'll end up with tender muffins. Overmixing activates the gluten in the flour, which leads to tough muffins.

**How do I tell a muffin is done?** As with other quick breads (which is really what a muffin is), stick a wooden pick in the top center of the muffin; when you pull it out, there should be no crumbs attached to the pick. If there are, pop the pan back into the oven briefly.

These muffins are delicious on their own with a pat of butter or drizzled with honey and as an accompaniment with ham, roast pork, or even stir-fries.

If using a four-sided hand grater to grate your zest, use the next to the smallest holes, not the smallest which are almost punched-out nail holes. If using a zester, chop the long strands once or twice, but don't overchop— you want some texture in the muffin.

**What's crystallized ginger?** A confection or sweet made from fresh ginger that has been coarsely chopped, cooked in a sugar syrup, and then coated in sugar. You should be able to find it in jars in the spice section of your supermarket.

**Nonstick cooking spray** is one of those modern inventions that work, especially if you're watching the fat in your diet. This turns practically any cooking utensil into a nonstick variety and makes a nonstick pan even more so.

# LEMON-GINGER MUFFINS

One morning while visiting Rhode Island, I tasted a delicious lemon-ginger muffin in a restaurant converted from an old barn. Here's my cakey version, partially based on a recipe from my friend, cookbook author Martha Rose Schulman, who knows plenty about baking muffins. The crystallized ginger gives these muffins a gentle bite.

MAKES 1 DOZEN (OR 15 TO 16, IF YOUR MUFFIN CUPS ARE SHALLOW)

> 4 tablespoons (½ stick) unsalted butter
> 1¾ cups all-purpose flour
> ½ cup sugar
> 1 teaspoon baking powder
> ½ teaspoon baking soda
>   Good pinch of salt
>   **Grated zest** of 3 large lemons (the outer yellow skin only, no bitter white pith)
> ¾ cup coarsely chopped **crystallized ginger** (about the size of peas)
> ¾ cup plain low-fat yogurt (or use lemon or vanilla yogurt)
> 2 large eggs, lightly beaten
> ¼ cup fresh lemon juice (about 2 lemons)

**1.** Preheat the oven to 400°F.; position a rack at the center level. Coat a standard-size (page 216) 12-cup muffin tin with **nonstick cooking spray** (or rub with soft butter); set the pan aside. (If you have one, a deep-cup muffin pan works best here. But don't use a black metal one; it will overbrown the muffins.) If you prefer, butter only the upper rims of the muffin cups and then line the cups with **paper muffin liners.** Melt the butter in a small skillet over low heat; set aside.

**2.** Meanwhile, sift together the flour, sugar, baking powder, baking soda, and salt into a large bowl. On a cutting board, use your fingers to toss together the lemon zest and chopped ginger. Set aside about ¼ cup of this mixture; stir the rest into the flour mixture.

**3.** Measure the yogurt into a 2-cup glass measuring cup; then add the eggs, melted butter, and lemon juice and stir with a fork until blended. Make a well in the center of the flour mixture, pour the yogurt mixture into the well. With a large rubber spatula, gently but quickly mix the dry and moist ingredients together just until the dry mixture is thoroughly and evenly moistened (no traces of flour)—the batter will still be lumpy; that's okay. Don't overmix or the muffins will come out tough.

**4.** Spoon the batter into the muffin tin, filling the cups about three-quarters full. (Depending on the depth of your tin, you may have some extra batter. If that's the case, coat a couple of ramekins or custard cups with nonstick cooking spray, fill with the extra batter, and bake them alongside; the baking time may vary slightly.) Scatter the reserved lemon-ginger mixture over the batter.

**5.** Bake for 20 to 25 minutes, or until the muffins are light golden brown and a wooden pick inserted in the center comes out with no crumbs attached. Place the pan on a wire rack and let cool for a few minutes. Turn the muffins out onto the rack. Serve lukewarm or split and toast.

Any muffin can be baked with **paper pan liners**. Butter only the upper rims of the muffin cups and then line with paper muffin liners.

**Muffin batters are basically the same as those for quick breads** (like banana bread or Cranberry-Orange Quick Bread with Nutmeg-Rum Glaze, page 220). You can make virtually any quick bread recipe as muffins, baking them at 400° or 425°F until set and golden. Conversely, you can take most muffin recipes and bake them in a loaf pan (most likely a 9 × 5 × 3-inch pan) at 350° until golden and a wooden pick inserted in the center comes out clean.

**Extra muffins?** They are easily frozen. Wrap first in plastic wrap, then overwrap with aluminum foil and freeze for up to 2 months. To use, let thaw completely at room temperature. To reheat, place on a baking sheet, lightly cover with foil, and slip into a 350°F. oven for 5 to 10 minutes, or until warmed through.

# CRANBERRY-ORANGE QUICK BREAD WITH NUTMEG-RUM GLAZE

This bread can be made in miniature loaves (great for gifts) or larger ones. It is based on a recipe that dates from the American Revolution, from Fraunces Tavern in New York City. Black pepper was frequently included in old recipes for spiced cakes and breads—and we thought bold, spicy flavors were a recent culinary development.

MAKES 6 SMALL LOAVES (OR 2 LARGE ONES)

- 4 cups all-purpose flour
- 1 cup granulated sugar
- 1 cup packed light brown sugar
- 2 teaspoons *each* baking soda and cream of tartar
- 1 teaspoon *each* ground cinnamon and ground allspice
- $1/2$ teaspoon *each* freshly grated nutmeg and salt
  Pinch of freshly ground black pepper
- 2 tablespoons grated orange zest (the outer orange skin only, no bitter white pith) (page 18)
- 4 cups (about 1 pound) fresh or frozen (unthawed) cranberries, picked over, rinsed, and drained
- 1 cup pecan or walnut pieces (about 4 ounces)
- $1/2$ cups fresh orange juice (from 3 large oranges), seeds removed but pulp left in
- 6 tablespoons (¾ stick) unsalted butter, melted
- 2 large eggs

**Nutmeg-Rum Glaze**

- 2 cups **sifted confectioners' sugar**
- 2 tablespoons milk
- 2 tablespoons dark rum, brandy, or apple cider, or more as needed
- $1/2$ teaspoon pure vanilla extract
- 1 teaspoon freshly grated nutmeg

**1.** Butter 6 small loaf pans, $5\frac{3}{4} \times 3\frac{1}{4} \times 2$ inches, or use two $9 \times 5 \times 3$-inch or three $8\frac{1}{2} \times 3\frac{5}{8} \times 2\frac{5}{8}$-inch loaf pans. Spoon a little flour into each pan and shake and tap the pans to evenly dust the sides and bottoms. Whack the bottoms a few times to loosen any excess flour and then tap out the excess; set the pans aside. Preheat the oven to 350°F.; position a rack in the center.

**2.** Sift together the flour, both sugars, the baking soda, cream of tartar, spices, and salt into a large bowl. Stir in the black pepper.

**3.** Place the orange zest, cranberries, and nuts in a food processor and pulse on and off just until the berries are coarsely chopped, no longer. In a 4-cup glass measuring cup, whisk together the orange juice, melted butter, and eggs until blended. Make a well in the dry ingredients; pour the liquid mixture into the well. Stir the dry ingredients and liquid together lightly with a large rubber spatula just until the dry ingredients are moistened but not thoroughly mixed. Add the cranberry mixture and fold in gently just until thoroughly mixed, no longer.

**4.** Spoon the batter into the prepared pans, filling each about two-thirds full. Tap each pan on a work surface to remove any air bubbles and gently smooth the tops with a rubber spatula. Place the filled pans on a baking sheet (you won't need the sheet if using larger loaf pans), spacing them slightly apart. Place on the center oven rack.

**5.** Bake for 50 to 60 minutes, or until the loaves are golden and a wooden pick inserted in the center emerges clean without any crumbs sticking. Set a large wire rack over a large sheet of wax paper. Remove the pans to the rack and let cool for about 5 minutes. Carefully invert the loaves onto the rack; carefully turn the loaves right side up and let cool until warm.

**6. Make the nutmeg-rum glaze:** In a medium bowl, stir together all of the glaze ingredients with a fork. You should be able to drizzle the glaze in thin lines from a teaspoon; if too thick, stir in a little more rum. If too thin, sift in a little more confectioners' sugar. With a teaspoon, drizzle the glaze over the loaves, forming thin lines back and forth across the narrow width of each loaf. Cool completely. Wrap each loaf in plastic wrap and return each to its foil pan.

Ten

# HOMEMADE DESSERTS

Brown Butter Pear Cake

**Techniques:** browning butter/sifting flour

Warm Apple Crumble Cake

**Techniques:** using pure vanilla/greasing and flouring baking
pan/sifting flour/not overmixing/doneness test

Individual Fruit Shortcakes

**Techniques:** using buttermilk/preparing dough with food
processor or by hand

Black and White Chocolate Chunk–Coconut
Cookies

**Technique:** creaming

Fudgy White Chocolate Chunk Brownies

**Techniques:** toasting nuts/moist crumb test

Grandma Gorman's Chocolate Cake

**Techniques:** greasing and flouring baking pans/melting butter
and chocolate/ribboning/frosting

Raisin Bread Pudding

**Techniques:** making a water bath/tempering/scalding

Double-Berry Sauce

Technique:

**This chapter is a repertoire, admittedly very selective, of homey dessert recipes easily mastered even by those who have never touched a baking pan.** As I've often mentioned in these pages, the best strategy is to keep things simple. But remember, in a perfectly planned meal (which is not to be read as elaborate), the impressions are as carefully paced as the movements of a symphony. And the dessert, often a climactic moment, should be as carefully thought out as the rest.

There's no reason to overwhelm your guests with a baroque finish. The ending should be satisfying, with a touch of sweetness, but it should not leave guests reeling. In fact, I often like to clear the table and have people return to the living room or outside, weather permitting, and then serve dessert and coffee a little later. Now that moods have been enhanced with good food and a glass or two of wine, let people continue their conversations. No need to rush things.

The desserts I offer here are simply prepared and are the kind of traditional, unpretentious comfort favorites that are always pleasing. Leftovers, if any, easily become a snack, the centerpiece of an afternoon break, or even, as outrageous as it may seem, breakfast—not to become a habit, however.

One more thought: Keep in mind that a homemade dessert is always a much-appreciated contribution to a dinner party. I've never known anyone not delighted to receive a homemade dessert from an arriving dinner guest. And for the beginning cook, this is the perfect venue for practicing dessert-making skills without the pressure of creating the whole meal.

# BROWN BUTTER PEAR CAKE

Sort of a "quick pie without the crust," this cake has become one of my all-time favorite, most-often-made recipes. It originally came from Karolyn Nelke in New York.

MAKES 8 SERVINGS

- 12 tablespoons (1½ sticks) unsalted butter
- 3 firm-ripe pears, such as Bosc, peeled, quartered, cored, and sliced
- 1 teaspoon fresh lemon juice
- 2 tablespoons plus ¾ cup sugar, plus more as needed
- 2 teaspoons ground **cinnamon**
- 2 large eggs, lightly beaten
- ½ teaspoon pure vanilla extract
- 1 cup **sifted** all-purpose flour
  Vanilla ice cream, for serving

**1.** Preheat the oven to 350°F. Generously butter a 9½- or 10-inch pie plate.

**2. To make browned butter:** Melt the butter in a small saucepan over medium heat; continue cooking until lightly golden, about 7 minutes. Watch carefully to avoid burning. Pour the butter into a medium bowl, leaving behind any sediment in the pan.

**3.** While the butter is browning, mound the pear slices in the pie plate and sprinkle with the lemon juice, 2 tablespoons of the sugar, and the cinnamon. Toss gently with your fingers to coat the pear slices, then spread the fruit in an even layer in the pie plate.

**4.** Stir ¾ cup of the sugar into the butter. Gently stir in the eggs and vanilla; stir in the flour just until blended; don't overmix. Spread this batter evenly over the pears. Sprinkle with 1 or 2 tablespoons more sugar.

**5.** Bake until lightly golden and crusty, about 45 minutes. Cool on a wire rack. Cut into wedges and serve warm or at room temperature, with vanilla ice cream.

**Serve this warm.** It wants vanilla ice cream.

Remember that **cinnamon and other spices** are not worth using unless they are fresh. If the ones on your shelf are more than a year old, replace them. If in doubt, take a sniff. If they're not fragrant, they won't contribute much to your baking.

Note that in this recipe I am first **sifting the flour** before measuring to get a lighter texture (see Measuring Basics, page 27).

This is barely a cake at all—just a custardy batter quickly poured over fruit in a Pyrex pie dish and baked to a crusty gold. **Browning the butter** slightly adds a mellow flavor but isn't necessary.

Cake flour is a fine-textured, soft wheat flour that makes for a particularly tender crumb. If you can't find cake flour, improvise by placing 2 tablespoons of cornstarch in a 1-cup ~~measure and then~~ ~~fill with all-purpose~~ ~~flour until you have 1~~ level cup. Substitute this for 1 cup cake flour.

I've tasted vanilla extracts from all over the world, and nothing comes close to the vanilla extract made by the Penzey family at Penzey's Spice House in Milwaukee, Wisconsin, a source of extraordinary herbs and spices. Over 250 chemical elements combine to create natural vanilla flavor—artificial vanilla contains only one, synthetic vanillin, made from by-products of paper manufacturing. Look for only pure vanilla extract. Penzey's Spice House, P.O. Box 1448, Waukesha, WI 53187; (414) 574-0277.

# WARM APPLE CRUMBLE CAKE

This is a tender butter cake topped with apples and then with a crumbled coconut streusel—almost a cake version of apple crisp.

MAKES  8  SERVINGS

Cake

1¼ cups plus 2 tablespoons cake flour (not self-rising), spooned lightly into the measuring cup

1 rounded teaspoon baking powder

¾ teaspoon baking soda

¼ teaspoon salt

12 tablespoons (1½ sticks) unsalted butter, softened

¾ cup granulated sugar

Grated zest of 1 lemon (page 18)

3 large eggs

2 teaspoons pure vanilla extract

¾ cup buttermilk

2 apples, peeled, quartered, cored, quarters halved crosswise, and then sliced

**Crumble Topping**

⅓ cup all-purpose flour, or more as needed

¼ cup walnut pieces

¼ cup granulated sugar

¼ cup packed light brown sugar

1 teaspoon ground cinnamon or pumpkin pie spice, or a mixture of ground cinnamon, ground allspice, ground nutmeg, and ground cloves

8 tablespoons (1 stick) unsalted butter, melted

⅔ cup shredded coconut (half of a 3½-ounce can)

Premium vanilla ice cream, for serving

1. Preheat the oven to 350°F. Butter or coat a 9-inch square baking pan with nonstick cooking spray. Sprinkle in a little **flour**; tap the side of the pan and rotate to coat the bottom and sides. Tap out the excess flour and set the pan aside.

2. **To make the cake:** Sift together the flour, baking powder, baking soda, and salt onto a sheet of wax paper; set aside. In an electric mixer, beat the butter briefly at medium-high speed. Add the sugar gradually along with the **lemon zest** and beat until very light and fluffy, about 5 minutes. Add the eggs, 1 at a time, and then the vanilla. Lower the speed slightly; add the sifted flour mixture and **buttermilk** alternately, beginning and ending with the flour mixture and mixing just until blended; do not overmix (page 217). Scrape the batter into the prepared pan, smoothing it with a large rubber spatula. Scatter the apple slices evenly over the batter.

3. **To make the crumble topping:** In a bowl, stir together the flour, walnuts, granulated and brown sugars, and spice(s). Add the melted butter, stirring with a spoon until the mixture comes together as a thick paste. If the paste is too moist and greasy, sprinkle on another tablespoon of flour. With your fingers, break this mixture into little clumps and scatter it evenly over the apples. Scatter the coconut over the top.

4. Bake the cake for 50 to 55 minutes, or until the top is golden and a wooden pick inserted in the center emerges clean.

5. Cool the cake in the pan on a wire rack until warm. Then cut into large squares and serve warm, with the ice cream.

Flouring the pan after greasing helps to firm up the edge of the cake and makes for a cleaner release from the pan.

To get the most out of the lemon zest, it's best to add it when you cream the butter and sugar together—the sugar acts as an abrasive, releasing the fragrant citrus oils from the zest.

Buttermilk adds a tang and extra richness to this cake. It's used in many low-fat baking recipes (don't worry, this recipe is certainly not low-fat) because it mimics the mouth feel of fat.

The standard doneness test for cakes is an emerging clean wooden pick after it's been inserted in the top center. If there are wet crumbs adhering to the pick, return the cake to the oven for another 5 minutes or so of baking. Then recheck. Remember that baking times can vary depending on your oven, the weather, and a whole host of other imponderables.

Try these **other fruit variations:** for summer, blueberries/blackberries, blackberries/nectarines/ plums, raspberries/ peaches/red currants, and both sweet and sour cherries/nectarines;

and pears/bananas/ mangos.

**Dry buttermilk powder** is a good product to know about, especially if you're not used to moving quarts of butter-milk through your household. Or the yogurt mixture is a good substitute.

# INDIVIDUAL FRUIT SHORTCAKES

Warm buttermilk biscuits are slathered with a delicious fruit mixture of nectarines, peaches, and berries.

MAKES 6 SERVINGS

Fruit

4 firm-ripe nectarines

3 firm-ripe peaches

Juice of 1 lemon

2 plums, halved, stoned, and sliced

1½ to 2 cups blueberries or a combination of blueberries and blackberries, picked over

½ teaspoon minced or grated fresh ginger

¼ cup packed light brown sugar

3 tablespoons granulated sugar

½ teaspoon ground cinnamon

**Light Biscuit Dough**

1½ cups all-purpose flour

⅓ cup granulated sugar

1 teaspoon baking powder

½ teaspoon baking soda

½ teaspoon salt

4 tablespoons (½ stick) cold unsalted butter, cut into pieces

½ teaspoon pure vanilla extract

⅔ cup **buttermilk,** or as needed (or substitute ⅓ cup plain yogurt mixed with ¼ cup skim milk or cold water)

Milk and sugar, for glaze

**1. Prepare the fruit:** Peel the nectarines and peaches by immersing them in a large pot of boiling water for about 30 seconds; then rinse them under cold water in a colander. The skins should slip off easily. Halve the fruit, remove the stones, and cut into thick wedges, letting them fall into a large bowl and tossing them with the lemon juice to prevent discoloration. Pour off any excess liquid, leaving the fruit somewhat moist. Add the plums, berries, and ginger; toss to combine.

**2.** In a small bowl, stir together both sugars and the cinnamon with a fork or small whisk until free of lumps. Sprinkle this mixture over the fruit and toss gently with your fingers or 2 large spoons until thoroughly mixed. Let sit at room temperature for about 2 hours.

**3. Make the biscuit dough:** In a food processor, combine the flour, sugar, baking powder, baking soda, and salt; pulse once or twice. Add the butter and process, pulsing on and off, until the mixture is crumbly. Add the vanilla and drizzle most but not all of the buttermilk over the dry mixture; pulse to combine. The dough should hold together and be moist but not sticky. If necessary, add more buttermilk. Gather the dough onto a floured sheet of plastic wrap or wax paper, pulling it together to form a cohesive disk. (The dough can be made several hours **in advance** up to this point, wrapped, and refrigerated until needed.)

**4.** Preheat the oven to 425°F. Butter a baking sheet and set aside.

**5.** Pat the dough out on a lightly floured sheet of wax paper to about ¾ inch thick. Cut with a biscuit cutter or glass dipped in flour. Gather the scraps together, pat out, and cut out more biscuits. Brush the tops with milk and arrange on the baking sheet, spacing apart. Sprinkle the tops with sugar.

**6.** Bake about 12 minutes, or until golden brown. Remove the biscuits to a wire rack to cool slightly. With a serrated knife, slice each biscuit horizontally in half. Place the bottom halves of the biscuits on dessert plates. Spoon some of the fruit mixture over and cover with a biscuit top. Spoon more fruit over all.

The **dough** can also be made by hand (this is how we did it before the food processor). Combine all of the dry ingredients in a bowl. Scatter the pieces of butter over the flour mixture, and with a pastry blender, 2 knives held scissors fashion, or with the tips of your fingers, cut in the butter until the mixture is crumbly. Drizzle in the liquids, tossing with a fork, until the dough comes together.

As with other similar baked goods, **don't overwork the dough** or you'll wind up with tough biscuits.

Use a **high-quality white chocolate** such as Tobler Narcisse or Lindt Blanc.

First **creaming or beating together the softened butter and sugar** insures that the sugar is well blended and avoids dry portions.

# BLACK AND WHITE CHOCOLATE CHUNK–COCONUT COOKIES

My mother remembers well cutting up a bar of chocolate to bake cookies when she was a teenager. Then, in the 1930s, the Nestlé Company (which had bought the rights to Ruth Wakefield's recipe for Toll House Cookies) began manufacturing a product measured to the crumbly bodies we pour, and the right name to Toll House Cookies.

The morsels were introduced in 1939, and the rest is history.

MAKES 2 1/2 DOZEN

    8 tablespoons (1 stick) unsalted butter, softened
    1/4 cup plus 2 tablespoons packed dark or light brown sugar
    1/4 cup plus 2 tablespoons granulated sugar
    1 large egg
    1/2 teaspoon pure vanilla extract
    1 cup plus 2 tablespoons sifted all-purpose flour
    1/2 teaspoon baking soda
    1/2 teaspoon salt
    3 ounces best-quality semisweet chocolate, cut into coarse chunks (you can also use 1/2 cup semisweet chocolate morsels)
    3 ounces best-quality **white chocolate,** cut into coarse chunks
 1 1/3 cups (one 3 1/2-ounce can) shredded coconut

**1.** Preheat the oven to 375° F. Lightly butter 2 baking sheets; set aside.

**2.** In an electric mixer, **cream,** or beat together, the butter with the brown and granulated sugars at medium speed until light, about 3 minutes. Add the egg and then the vanilla and 1/4 teaspoon water, mixing until blended.

**3.** Meanwhile, sift the flour with the baking soda and salt onto a sheet of wax paper. Lower the mixer speed and add the flour mixture to the butter mixture, mixing just until blended, no longer. Add both types of chocolate chunks and the coconut, mixing just until evenly distributed.

**4.** Drop well-rounded teaspoonfuls of the dough onto the prepared baking sheets, spacing them about 2 inches apart.

**5.** Bake the cookies for 10 to 12 minutes, or until lightly golden. Carefully transfer the cookies to a wire rack and let cool completely.

# FUDGY WHITE CHOCOLATE CHUNK BROWNIES

MAKES 32

1¼ cups (about 4½ ounces) coarsely chopped pecans or walnuts

2 ounces unsweetened chocolate, coarsely chopped

8 tablespoons (1 stick) unsalted butter, cut into pieces

2 large eggs

1 cup sugar

1 teaspoon pure vanilla extract

⅔ cup all-purpose flour

Pinch of salt

4 ounces best-quality white chocolate, cut into coarse chunks

**1.** Preheat the oven to 350°F. Lightly butter an 8-inch square baking pan; set aside. Place the chopped pecans on a baking sheet and **toast,** stirring occasionally, until fragrant and lightly colored, about 7 minutes. Set aside to cool slightly.

**2.** Meanwhile, place the unsweetened chocolate and butter in a heavy saucepan and **melt** over low heat, stirring occasionally. Set aside to cool slightly.

**3.** In an electric mixer with the whisk attachment, whisk the eggs at medium speed until light and frothy, about 3 minutes. Gradually add the sugar, beating constantly. When all of the sugar has been added, add the vanilla; remove the mixing bowl from the machine.

**4.** Meanwhile, sift the flour and salt together onto a sheet of wax paper; set aside.

**5.** When the egg-sugar mixture is ready, gently fold in the melted chocolate mixture with a large rubber spatula—don't incorporate it completely; there should still be a few streaks of chocolate visible. Now gently fold in the flour mixture. When that's not quite incorporated, fold in the toasted pecans and white chocolate chunks just until everything is well blended, no longer. Transfer the batter to the prepared pan, smoothing it gently to the edges of the pan with a rubber spatula.

**6.** Bake for 25 minutes; the top should be dry, but a wooden pick inserted in the center will emerge with some traces of melted chocolate (look for **"moist crumbs"**). Place the pan on a rack and cool completely. Don't try to cut the brownies when warm. When cool, cut into 32 bars, each 1 inch wide and 2 inches long.

There's still nothing like a fudgy brownie, dry and crackled on top, moist and dense within, with a glass of cold milk.

**Toasting** the nuts brings out their nuttiness and adds a rich flavor to the brownies.

To **melt the chocolate and butter** together in a **microwave oven,** combine in a small bowl and microwave at 100% power for about 2½ minutes.

Unlike the usual cake doneness test, here you want some **moist crumbs adhering** to the wooden pick since this brownie is moist and fudgy.

Brownies can usually be kept in the **refrigerator for up to 3 days,** if inquiring hands don't find them first.

**Gently melting** together the butter and chocolate over simmering water or gentle heat avoids separation, making for a smooth consistency.

# GRANDMA GORMAN'S CHOCOLATE CAKE

Who can say "no" to chocolate cake? This old-fashioned two-layer classic is the kind you only can find these days when you bake it at home. This particular recipe I've borrowed from my editor.

MAKES 10 TO 12 SERVINGS

Cake

| | |
|---|---|
| 8 | tablespoons (1 stick) unsalted butter, cut into pieces |
| 4 | ounces unsweetened chocolate, coarsely chopped |
| 2 | large eggs |
| 1⅔ | cups granulated sugar |
| 2 | cups all-purpose flour |
| | Pinch of salt |
| 1½ | teaspoons baking soda |
| 1⅔ | cups milk |
| 2 | teaspoons pure vanilla extract |

**Chocolate Frosting**

| | |
|---|---|
| 2½ | cups confectioners' sugar |
| ⅓ | cup best-quality unsweetened cocoa powder |
| | Pinch of salt |
| 8 | tablespoons (1 stick) unsalted butter, cut into pieces and at room temperature |
| ½ to ⅓ | cup heavy cream |
| 1 | teaspoon pure vanilla extract |

1. **Prepare the cakes:** Preheat the oven to 350°F. Butter two 9-inch-round cake pans. Dust the insides of the pans generously with unsweetened cocoa powder or all-purpose flour (tap out any excess).

2. **Melt** together the butter and chocolate in a small heatproof bowl placed over a small saucepan of simmering, not boiling, water.

**3.** Meanwhile, beat the eggs in a medium bowl with an electric mixer on medium speed. Gradually add the sugar and continue to beat until the mixture becomes very light and a **ribbon** forms when the mixer is turned off and the beaters are lifted.

**4.** Stir the chocolate mixture to blend. Add to the egg mixture and beat to combine well.

**5.** Stir together the flour and salt in a bowl. Stir together the baking soda and milk in a small bowl to dissolve the baking soda. Working in batches, stir with a wooden spoon the flour and milk mixtures into the chocolate mixture, beginning and ending with the flour. Stir in the vanilla. Don't worry if the batter seems thin—that's the way it should be.

**6.** Pour the batter into the prepared cake pans, dividing equally. Tap them gently on the counter to eliminate any air bubbles.

**7.** Place the pans on the center rack in the oven and bake until a cake tester or wooden pick inserted in the centers of the cakes comes out clean without any crumbs attached, 25 to 30 minutes. Transfer the pans to a wire rack to **cool for 5 minutes.** Then turn the cakes out onto the rack to cool completely.

**8. Prepare the frosting:** Sift together the confectioners' sugar, cocoa powder, and salt into the bowl of a standing electric mixer. Add the butter and beat on medium speed until the mixture is well blended and smooth; the mixture will be very stiff. Beat in enough of the cream to make a spreadable frosting. Beat in the vanilla.

**9.** Place one cake layer, bottom side up, on a cake platter. Brush off any crumbs. Spread the **frosting** with a metal spatula or rubber spatula over the top of the layer. Place the second cake layer on top, bottom side down. Spread the top and sides of the cake with frosting.

Beating a cake batter to the **ribbon stage** insures a light-textured cake with a delicious crumb.

**First cooling the cakes briefly in the pans** allows the cakes to shrink away from the sides of the pans, making for a cleaner release when unmolded.

To **neatly frost** a cake, slide strips of wax paper under the bottom of the cake layer all around the edge, covering the plate. Then go ahead and frost the cake. When finished, gently pull out the wax paper strips. A spotless plate!

This cake **keeps well** for a day or two, covered, in the refrigerator. Let it come to room temperature before serving. Remember, cold dampens flavor, and you certainly want to enjoy the full, rich chocolate taste of this cake.

A **water bath,** or *bain marie* as the French call it, is a technique for gently cooking delicate egg dishes such as custards. The container of food is placed in a larger pan of warm ~~water~~ ~~against direct~~ which can curdle the egg mixture and toughen the edges before the center has set. This can be done either on top of the stove or in the oven.

To **scald** a liquid is to heat it to a point **just below boiling**—little bubbles will appear around the edge of the pan. Scalding milk rather than boiling it prevents an unsightly skin from forming on top.

Adding a little hot liquid to an egg mixture before incorporating it into a custard or other egg-based mixture is a process called **tempering.** Gradually warming the eggs in this manner prevents curdling.

# RAISIN BREAD PUDDING

Not too long ago bread pudding was something passé, and then came the 1980s and the rediscovery of comfort food. What could be more comforting than bread pudding?

~~MAKES 8 SERVINGS~~

½ cup boiling water

½ cup dark seedless raisins

12 slices day-old French bread, diagonally cut into ¾-inch-thick slices

5 tablespoons unsalted butter, at room temperature

3 cups milk

6 large eggs

¾ cup sugar

¾ teaspoon pure vanilla extract

**1.** To make a **water bath,** place a large roasting pan on the center rack in the oven. Fill it one-third with water. Preheat the oven to 350°F.

**2.** Pour the boiling water over the raisins in a small heatproof bowl. Let stand for 5 minutes for the raisins to plump.

**3.** Spread both sides of the bread slices with the butter. Set aside.

**4.** Heat the milk in a small saucepan over medium-low heat until **just below boiling;** small bubbles will appear around the edge of the pan.

**5.** Meanwhile, whisk together the eggs, sugar, and vanilla in a medium bowl until smooth. Pour **a little of the hot milk** slowly into the egg mixture, whisking constantly until the mixture is smooth and the sugar is dissolved. Remove the milk from the heat. Stir the egg mixture into the remaining milk in the saucepan.

**6.** Arrange half the bread slices in an even layer over the bottom of an ungreased 8 × 8 × 2-inch baking dish. Drain the raisins, discarding any liquid. Scatter the raisins over the bread in the dish. Pour half of the egg or custard mixture over the bread. Top with the remaining bread and pour the remaining custard over the top. The bread will float a little. Let the pudding stand until the bread absorbs enough of the custard to sink a little, about 10 minutes. Cover the dish with aluminum foil. Place the baking dish in the roasting pan in the oven.

**7.** Bake the pudding for 45 minutes. Using pot holders, carefully remove the baking dish from the roasting pan. Remove the roasting pan from the oven. Return the pudding, still covered, to the oven and bake for another 30 minutes. **Remove the foil** and continue baking the pudding until it is set and firm around the edges but still a little jiggly in the center, about 15 minutes. Remove the baking dish to a wire rack. Cool to tepid or refrigerate to chill for serving.

**Baking the pudding uncovered** for the last 15 minutes allows the top to brown lightly.

# DOUBLE-BERRY SAUCE

Whole berries are bathed in a crimson puree.

MAKES 2 GENEROUS CUPS

- 1 pint ripe strawberries, hulled
- 2 half-pints ripe raspberries, picked over
  Superfine sugar, if needed
  Few drops of fresh lemon juice

**1.** Puree the strawberries and slightly less than half of the raspberries in a food processor until smooth. Set aside the whole raspberries. Strain the puree through a sieve to eliminate seeds, pushing the puree through with a rubber spatula or the back of a spoon.

**2.** Flavor the puree to taste with sugar, if needed, plus lemon juice. Stir in the reserved whole berries. Cover and chill the sauce.

## VARIATION: SPIKED DOUBLE-BERRY SAUCE

Stir in 1 to 2 tablespoons crème de cassis, framboise, or other berry eau-de-vie or liqueur.

**Serve** over ice cream, angel food or pound cake, or cake and ice cream.

**You can also make this** with 2 pints of raspberries or with blueberries and blackberries.

**This sauce keeps,** refrigerated, for 2 or 3 days.

# INDEX

American cooks use standard containers, the 8-ounce cup and a tablespoon that takes exactly 16 level fillings to fill that cup level. Measuring by cup makes it very difficult to give weight equivalents, as a cup of densely packed butter will weigh considerably more than a cup of flour. The easiest way therefore to deal with cup measurements in recipes is to take the amount by volume rather than by weight. Thus the equation reads:

1 cup = 240 ml = 8 fl. oz.        ½ cup = 120 ml = 4 fl. oz.

It is possible to buy a set of American cup measures in major stores around the world.

In the United States, butter is often measured in sticks. One stick is the equivalent of 8 tablespoons. One tablespoon of butter is therefore the equivalent to ½ ounce/15 grams.

## LIQUID MEASURES

| Fluid Ounces | U.S. | Imperial | Milliliters |
|---|---|---|---|
| | 1 teaspoon | 1 teaspoon | 5 |
| ¼ | 2 teaspoons | 1 dessert spoon | 7 |
| ½ | 1 tablespoon | 1 tablespoon | 15 |
| 1 | 2 tablespoons | 2 tablespoons | 28 |
| 2 | ¼ cup | 4 tablespoons | 56 |
| 4 | ½ cup or ¼ pint | | 110 |
| 5 | | ¼ pint or 1 gill | 140 |
| 6 | ¾ cup | | 170 |
| 8 | 1 cup or ½ pint | | 225 |
| 9 | | | 250, ¼ liter |
| 10 | 1¼ cups | ½ pint | 280 |
| 12 | 1½ cups or ¾ pint | | 340 |
| 15 | | ¾ pint | 420 |
| 16 | 2 cups or 1 pint | | 450 |
| 18 | 2¼ cups | | 500, ½ liter |
| 20 | 2½ cups | 1 pint | 560 |
| 24 | 3 cups or 1½ pints | | 675 |
| 25 | | 1¼ pints | 700 |
| 30 | 3¾ cups | 1½ pints | 840 |
| 32 | 4 cups | | 900 |
| 36 | 4½ cups | | 1000, 1 liter |
| 40 | 5 cups | 2 pints or 1 quart | 1120 |
| 48 | 6 cups or 3 pints | | 1350 |
| 50 | | 2½ pints | 1400 |

## SOLID MEASURES

| U.S. and Imperial Measures | | Metric Measures | |
|---|---|---|---|
| Ounces | Pounds | Grams | Kilos |
| 1 | | 28 | |
| 2 | | 56 | |
| 3½ | | 100 | |
| 4 | ¼ | 112 | |
| 5 | | 140 | |
| 6 | | 168 | |
| 8 | ½ | 225 | |
| 9 | | 250 | ¼ |
| 12 | ¾ | 340 | |
| 16 | 1 | 450 | |
| 18 | | 500 | ½ |
| 20 | 1¼ | 560 | |
| 24 | 1½ | 675 | |
| 27 | | 750 | ¾ |
| 32 | 2 | 900 | |
| 36 | 2¼ | 1000 | 1 |
| 40 | 2½ | 1100 | |
| 48 | 3 | 1350 | |
| 54 | | 1500 | 1½ |
| 64 | 4 | 1800 | |
| 72 | 4½ | 2000 | 2 |
| 80 | 5 | 2250 | 2¼ |
| 100 | 6 | 2800 | 2¾ |

## OVEN TEMPERATURE EQUIVALENTS

| Fahrenheit | Celsius | Gas Mark | Description |
|---|---|---|---|
| 225 | 110 | ¼ | Cool |
| 250 | 130 | ½ | |
| 275 | 140 | 1 | Very Slow |
| 300 | 150 | 2 | |
| 325 | 170 | 3 | Slow |
| 350 | 180 | 4 | Moderate |
| 375 | 190 | 5 | |
| 400 | 200 | 6 | Moderately Hot |
| 425 | 220 | 7 | Fairly Hot |
| 450 | 230 | 8 | Hot |
| 475 | 240 | 9 | Very Hot |
| 500 | 250 | 10 | Extremely Hot |

## EQUIVALENTS AND SUBSTITUTES FOR INGREDIENTS

all-purpose flour—plain flour
arugula—rocket
beet—beetroot
coarse salt—kitchen salt
confectioners' sugar—icing sugar
cornstarch—cornflour
eggplant—aubergine
fava beans—broad beans
granulated sugar—caster sugar

scallion—spring onion
shortening—white fat
snow pea—mangetout
sour cherry—morello cherry
squash—courgettes or marrow
unbleached flour—strong, white flour
vanilla bean—vanilla pod
zest—rind
zucchini—courgettes

light cream—single cream
heavy cream—double cream
half and half—12% fat milk
buttermilk—ordinary milk

baking sheet—oven tray
cheesecloth—muslin
parchment paper—greaseproof paper
plastic wrap—cling film